A Second Look in the Rearview Mirror

A SECOND LOOK
IN THE
REARVIEW MIRROR

FURTHER
AUTOBIOGRAPHICAL REFLECTIONS OF A
PHILOSOPHER AT LARGE

Mortimer J. Adler

MACMILLAN PUBLISHING COMPANY
New York

MAXWELL MACMILLAN CANADA
Toronto

MAXWELL MACMILLAN INTERNATIONAL
New York Oxford Singapore Sydney

Macmillan Publishing Company
866 Third Avenue
New York, NY 10022

Maxwell Macmillan Canada, Inc.
1200 Eglington Avenue East, Suite 200
Don Mills, Ontario M3C 3N1

Macmillan Publishing Company is part of the Maxwell Communication Group of Companies

Library of Congress Cataloging-in-Publication Data
Adler, Mortimer Jerome, 1902–
A second look in the rearview mirror: further autobiographical reflections of a Philosopher at large/Mortimer J. Adler.
p. cm.
Sequel to the author's autobiography: Philosopher at large, c1977.
Includes bibliographical references and index.
ISBN 0-02-500571-5
1. Adler, Mortimer Jerome, 1902– . 2. Philosophers—United States—Biography. I. Title.
B945.A286S43 1992
191—dc20
[B] 92-5062
CIP

Macmillan books are available at special discounts for bulk purchases for sales promotions, premiums, fund-raising, or educational use. For details, contact:

Special Sales Director
Macmillan Publishing Company
866 Third Avenue
New York, NY 10022

Designed by Michael Mendelsohn of M 'N O Production Services, Inc.

10 9 8 7 6 5 4 3 2 1

Printed in the United States of America

To My Wife
Caroline Pring Adler
with loving gratitude for the
last thirty years of my life

CONTENTS

PROLOGUE

Fifteen years ago, when I was only seventy-five years old, I wrote my autobiography prematurely. It was published in 1977 under the title *Philosopher at Large: An Intellectual Autobiography.*[1]

Much has happened in my life since then. In addition, now that I am approaching ninety, further retrospection has been illuminated by what I have learned and done in the intervening years. I am, therefore, impelled to take a second look in the rearview mirror, and hope that those who found the earlier volume engaging will be similarly entertained by this one.

In *Philosopher at Large*, I told all or most of the stories about episodes in my life that I could document by materials in my voluminous files. I could add to them, but that is not the purpose of this book. Like the earlier volume, it is mainly concerned with the use of my mind, but unlike the earlier autobiography, its structure is much less controlled by chronology.

Following Parts One and Two, which deal respectively with things that happened before 1976 and events that have occurred since then, the third and longest part of this book is a reflective appraisal of the main streams in my life as a whole—my involvement in teaching and learning, with philosophical thought and the pursuit of truth, and with religion and theology. In the Epilogue, I list the blessings of good fortune that have attended the course of my life.

1. It is now available in a paperback edition. I will refer to it from time to time.

Like *Philosopher at Large*, this, too, is largely an intellectual autobiography rather than a set of reminiscences that dwell on personal relationships or intimacies. For that reason, I have used Notes appended to some chapters to reproduce a number of items that consist of fugitive papers, unpublished materials, or materials no longer in print and therefore inaccessible—or difficult to obtain. I have placed these appended materials at the end of the chapters to which they are most relevant.[2]

With the publication of this book in the autumn of 1992, I will be in my ninetieth year. I can look back upon my life almost as if I were in the position of the person who is called upon to speak about me at my funeral or memorial service.

That is the vantage point from which I am writing this book. It is superior to the position I was in when, in 1974–1975, I wrote my earlier autobiographical memoir. Then I was just past seventy. Now I can see how the last fifteen years have realized what then seemed only promising—a vision of the last part of my life that began to dawn on me sometime after I had turned the corner at fifty.

Looking back at the whole, divided into decades or quarters, I am persuaded that life gets better as one gets older. I have written more books in the last stretch of years, some of them much more readable and even, perhaps, slightly wiser than anything I wrote earlier. I have learned more and profited more from what I have learned; and I have enjoyed the work I have done more fully.

If one lives long enough, one enjoys a pleasure that is totally absent from earlier stages of life—the pleasure of being publicly honored for one's accomplishments and of having more and more persons explicitly acknowledge the influence one has exerted on their lives and the debt they owe for it.

I should add that in the last period of my life, I have worked harder and to better effect than ever before. The only exception to this statement may be the time in the middle forties when I wrote the 102 essays on the great ideas in twenty-six months, with no time off at all, no vacations, and seven days a week. That probably

2. Instead of an Appendix placed at the end of the last chapter, I have placed Notes appended to certain chapters, because I would like the materials contained therein to be immediately accessible to readers after they have finished reading the chapter.

was the most sustained and exacting application of energy to a task that had to be performed on schedule.

Being genetically endowed with health and vigor, I have been more vigorous mentally, if not physically, than at earlier periods. The only sense in which I feel my ripening age is my diminished bodily mobility. I can no longer run or hop, skip, and jump, and I walk much more slowly than I did ten years ago. But in the use of my mind, I feel younger, not older, as the years go by.

All of this, it seems to me, is summed up in "Rabbi Ben Ezra," a poem by Robert Browning. The first stanza reads as follows:

> Grow old along with me!
> The best is yet to be,
> The last of life, for which the first was made:
> Our times are in His hand
> Who saith, "A whole I planned,
> Youth shows but half; trust God: see all nor be afraid!"

I read this poem in college, when I was very young and immature. In spite of that, I somehow felt good about what Browning said about taking an optimistic view of aging—of completing one's life by being able to do in the latter part of it what one could not do in the earlier portion. But only mature men and women can fully understand the fundamental truth expressed in Browning's poem, and by fully mature I mean after sixty.

ACKNOWLEDGMENTS

Five persons read the manuscript of this book after it was completed and have given me excellent suggestions for its revision. They were Jacques Barzun, Clifton Fadiman, Otto Bird, John Van Doren, and William Rosen, my editor at Macmillan. I am most grateful for their many improvements and interventions. When I had conflicting advice from the first four of them, I turned to my editor, Bill Rosen, for adjudication of the conflict.

I have in mind one particular conflict. The question was the propriety of including in the Notes to Chapter 8 the complimentary evaluation of me as a philosopher and of my philosophical work by Professor Ralph McInerny of the University of Notre Dame. Messrs. Fadiman and Van Doren thought it was self-serving and should be deleted—that it was not needed by those who agreed with it and that it would not alter the opinions of those who disagreed with it. Messrs. Barzun and Bird thought that it should be included as serving to balance the quite contrary views held by most professors of philosophy in our secular universities. To keep it in was Bill Rosen's decision.

I would also like to take this opportunity to comment on one serious criticism that Mr. Fadiman made of the book as a whole. He said that it was a departure from the accepted style of autobiographical writing, while being offered as an autobiography. It included, both in the chapters and in the appendices to them, materials not written by me and even materials written by me but not, when written, intended to be autobiographical—not an account of my life written in the first person, however relevant I may think these materials are to the account of my life.

I think Mr. Fadiman is correct in saying that this is not a conventional autobiography. It is not written as a strictly chronological narrative. I have already confessed in this Prologue that it includes much that is not, in the strict sense, autobiographical writing, even though some of it was written by me in earlier periods of my life.

In my judgment, what Mr. Fadiman regards as nonautobiographical writing (both in the chapters themselves as well as in the Notes to them) serves to document, enrich, and explain the account I have here given of my life and my work. I have thought it useful to preserve in this book fugitive materials that are not otherwise accessible, especially when they have so obvious a bearing on the story I am trying to tell.

To three persons I wish to express grateful acknowledgment for reading the manuscript while it was being written and helping to improve it: to General Robert Taylor, who read chapters as I wrote some of them in Aspen during the summer of 1991; to my secretary and editorial assistant, Marlys Allen; and to my wife Caroline, to whom this book is affectionately dedicated as being, in the last thirty years of my life, my best friend and severest critic.

PART ONE

The Years Before 1976

CHAPTER 1

RETROSPECTION

1

I was recently asked by the editor of Encyclopaedia Britannica's *Medical and Health Annual* to write an article on growing old with pleasure and profit.[1] What follows is an adaptation of that piece.

I began by reflecting on the point that is made in the first book of Aristotle's *Nicomachean Ethics*. Aristotle said that it was ill-advised to give lectures on ethics to the young. Their immaturity, which means their lack of experience and their emotional instability, prevents them from understanding with their hearts as well as their minds what might be done to lead a good human life.

The more I have thought about this, the more I have come to appreciate the difference between youth and age with regard to making prudent choices about the means to be employed in the pursuit of happiness, which means the effort to make a good life for oneself.

Socrates said the unexamined life is not worth living. Aristotle added that the unplanned life is not worth examining. But the one thing that the young can never think about or plan for is life as a whole. I would almost define youth or immaturity as that state of the human being in which it is impossible to think at all about the long future of one's life as a whole.

Paradoxically, that is the very time when one has a long future

1. Adler, "On Growing Old with Pleasure and Profit," *1989 Medical and Health Annual*, Chicago, Encyclopaedia Britannica, Inc., 1989, pp. 6–12. Reprinted by permission.

ahead to think about. As we grow much older and have less and less of a future to hope for and look forward to, only then are we more and more able to think about our whole life and plan for what future is left to us.

That is the reason why Aristotle thought it impossible to teach ethics to the young, by which he did not mean giving them lectures on moral philosophy that they could memorize and pass back verbally on examination papers. He meant that the young are simply unable to do the kind of practical thinking that is requisite for pursuing happiness properly.

In addition, they cannot restrain their desires for the sake of deferred gratification. They want what they want in a hurry—next week, next month, or at the most next year. Only as we grow older and habitually acquiesce in deferred gratification can we make choices in favor of remote goods instead of immediate pleasures, and we are inclined to suffer pains for the sake of achieving those goods instead of trying to avoid hardships here and now.

George Santayana expressed this insight very eloquently. In *My Host the World*, he wrote:

> . . . Old persons . . . have an intrinsic vitality of which youth is incapable; precisely the balance and wisdom that comes from long perspectives and broad foundations.

The only sound moral judgment are long-term judgments. Almost all short-term judgments are likely to be unsound and to end in the frustration or defeat of the goals we ought to seek. But youth is the time when we are incapable of making long-term judgments. We can only do that when we have become genuinely mature.

If practical wisdom consists in aiming at the right long-term objectives in life and in making the right choices for achieving the distant and remote goals we ought to seek, then a wise young person is, like a round square, a contradiction in terms. To be both young and wise is a sheer impossibility.

It is also impossible to be both young and educated. I cannot find this said anywhere in the great books, but it is the first principle of my own educational philosophy.

No one can become a generally educated person in school, college, or university. Persons can be trained there in some technical or professional expertise or specialization, but that is quite different from their becoming generally educated persons. If schools and colleges were at their best, which they never are, then the young might get from school and college the preparation they need for the continued learning they must engage in for all the years of their life in order to become generally educated in the final years after the age of fifty or sixty. I think I am now at last a generally educated person, but that did not begin to happen until after I turned sixty.

The reason why general education can be begun in school and college but can never be completed there is the same reason as the one that explains all the other deficiencies of youth. Immaturity is the insuperable obstacle to completing one's general education in school or college. To speak of a generally educated young person is as much a self-contradiction as to call young men and women wise.

In his treatise on *Old Age*, Cicero puts the following three passages into the mouth of the elder statesman Cato. In the first, Cato says:

> The great affairs of life are not performed by physical strength, or activity, or nimbleness of body, but by deliberation, character, expression of opinion. Of these old age is not only not deprived, but, as a rule, has them in a greater degree.

In the second, Cato continues:

> The course of life is fixed, and nature admits of its being run but in one way, and only once; and to each part of our life there is something specially seasonable; so that the feebleness of children, as well as the high spirit of youth, the soberness of maturer years, and the ripe wisdom of old age—all have a certain natural advantage which should be secured in its proper season.

And in the third, we have this from Cato:

> The fact is that old age is respectable just as long as it asserts itself, maintains its proper rights, and is not enslaved to any one. For as I admire a young man who has something of the old man in him, so do I an old one who has something of a young man. The man

who aims at this may possibly become old in body—in mind he never will.

The great Roman Stoic Seneca expressed sentiments similar to those of Cicero. In *Letters to Lucilius* he wrote:

We should cherish old age and enjoy it. It is full of pleasure if you know how to use it. Fruit tastes most delicious just when its season is ending. The charms of youth are at their greatest at the time of its passing. It is the final glass which pleases the inveterate drinker, the one that sets the crowning touch on his intoxication and sends him off into oblivion. Every pleasure defers till its greatest delights. The time of life which offers the greatest delight is the age that sees the downward movement—not the steep decline—already begun; and in my opinion even the age that stands on the brink has pleasures of its own—or else the very fact of not experiencing the want of any pleasures takes their place. How nice it is to have outworn one's desires and left them behind!

In Chaucer's *Canterbury Tales*, in "The Knight's Tale," we find the following lines:

For true it is, age has great advantage;
Experience and wisdom come with age;
Men may the old out-run, but not out-wit.

Finally, we have the following marvelous witticism from Jonathan Swift in his *Thoughts on Various Subjects*:

No wise Man ever wished to be younger.

Now, of course, you would expect to find some negative voices among the authors of the great books. They are there, but they by no means counterbalance or outweigh the sober wisdom in favor of life's final years.

Martin Luther in this *Table Talk* tells us that

Young fellows are tempted by girls, men who are thirty years old are tempted by gold, when they are forty years old they are tempted by honor and glory, and those who are sixty years old say to themselves, "What a pious man I have become!"

Much more adverse to aging is the opinion expressed by Michel de Montaigne:

> Old age puts more wrinkles in our minds than on our faces; and we never, or rarely, see a soul that in growing old does not come to smell sour and musty. Man grows and dwindles in his entirety.

Finally, we come to the English poet Lord Byron, who, in a poem entitled "Childe Harold's Pilgrimage," calls our attention to one serious deprivation that cannot be avoided in old age and that we must admit is one of its chief disadvantages.

> What is the worst of woes that wait on age?
> What stamps the wrinkle deeper on the brow?
> To view each loved one blotted from life's page,
> And be alone on earth, as I am now.

To the cornucopia of wit and wisdom that one can find by plumbing the great books, I have only a few things to add of a serious nature.

One is the insight that I learned from a paper in a medical journal in which a physician argued persuasively against retirement, if that means the relinquishment of important work to do. He summed up his argument pithily by saying: we don't wear out; we rust out.

I would also add that, if we retain the unimpeded use of our intellectual faculties, even though our limbs may falter, our desires may diminish, and our senses may fail, then we become more educable, not less so.

The loss of sensory acuity, even the loss of sight or hearing, does not weaken our imaginative powers and, in my judgment, tends to increase our intellectual powers. As the body weakens in any or all of its corporeal organs, the intellect grows stronger. We can think better, more clearly, more soundly. The loss of immediate or short-term memories that inevitably accompanies advancing years is an annoying practical disability, but it in no way diminishes the power of creative, analytic, and reflective thought.

We do not think *with* our brains, though we cannot think *without* them. A healthy brain is, therefore, an indispensable condition for intellectual activity at any time of life. Given that condition, our power to think reflectively and analytically never diminishes and, on the contrary, appears to increase with age.

2

On the occasion of my eightieth birthday, my associates at Encyclopaedia Britannica threw a party for me, in a room made festive by balloons all over the place, on which were imprinted the words "How to Think About Mortimer." My friend and associate, then Editor-in-Chief of the *Encyclopaedia Britannica*, Tom Goetz, introduced me in a very witty speech, in the course of which he said:

> The years, 1902 to 1914, our hero is born and enjoys the only period of his life in which he and the academic community are in harmony. He attends Public School 186 in upper Manhattan and actually receives a diploma, an event not to occur for many, many years.

At the end of his remarks, he called upon me to speak. I began by stating the ten rules or recommendations I had tried to follow. They were:

1. With regard to health, vigor, and vitality: Never exercise. As for dieting, eat only the most delicious calories.
2. With regard to marriage: If at first you don't succeed, try again.
3. Never work more than seven days a week or twelve hours a day, and sometimes a little less. To grow younger with the years, work harder as you get older.
4. Never take money for work you would not do if you did not need the money.
5. If you have the inclination and ability, the best way to spend time is to write books: The next best is to edit them: And if you cannot do either, then sell them.
6. Never write more than one book a year, because it doesn't pay;

but edit as many as possible: and sell them by the hundred thousands.

7. Have a secretary who thinks she understands what you are up to as well as you understand yourself.
8. Surround yourself with friends and associates with whom you can be almost as honest as you are with yourself.
9. Get over the folly of thinking that there is any conflict between high living and high thinking: Asceticism is for the birds.
10. Never give up; never say die; always say "If I die," *NOT* "When I die."

One recommendation above, I now honor in the breach. The time remaining to me has dwindled to the point where I think it more desirable to write two books a year instead of just one. That violates Rule 6.

I close by adding one serious reflection on eighty years of life.

Eighty years can be neatly divided into four periods of twenty years each. It has been my good fortune to have the four quarters of my life arranged in an ascending order. The first twenty years, the hardest and the worst; the last twenty, the easiest and best. The period between twenty-one and forty was much better than the first twenty years—because they were the Hutchins and Chicago years. The second forty years (the last two quarters) were much better than the first forty years—because they were the Britannica years, the Institute years, and the Aspen years (much better than the years of being a professor in a university).

And of the second forty years, the last twenty were the best of all—because Caroline was foolish enough (at age twenty-six), courageous enough, and tolerant enough to marry me when I was sixty.

CHAPTER 2

ACADEMIC MISIMPRESSIONS

O would some power the giftie gie us," sang Robert Burns, "to see ourselves as others see us." Any writer of an autobiography should echo that wish, adding the reciprocal wish that others might see us as we see ourselves.

The variance between these two views—between how others regard us and how we regard ourselves—constitutes the misimpressions that my academic colleagues formed of me. Calling them "misimpressions" begs the question, of course. It amounts to claiming that my view of myself is more correct than their view of me. It might be more judicious on my part to try to explain the impressions they formed even though I still think that what they have said about me are more like caricatures than characterizations.

Before I give examples of the misimpressions that have only recently come to my attention, I should remind readers of the academic misbehavior that I mentioned in *Philosopher at Large* in the chapters dealing with my conduct at the University of Chicago in the thirties, especially the chapter entitled "The Young Rush In" (where angels fear to tread).

In that earlier autobiographical account, I confessed my emotional and intellectual immaturity. I thought that it, combined with my habitual unrestrained impatience, might explain conduct that was distasteful or annoying to others. I was more than chronologically very young when I entered Columbia University as a student in the college in 1920, and a few years later achieved my ambition on graduation in 1923 to become a teacher, an ambition that led me to go to college in the first place. But though I had that ambition very early in my life, I did not know or understand myself well enough to realize that, by temperament and disposition, I was destined to become a misfit in academic life.

Those academically inappropriate tendencies in my nature revealed themselves, but not to me, when I was an undergraduate and then a graduate student, as well as a member of the faculty at Columbia. There is no question that, as an undergraduate, I was a good student, so far as learning and passing courses with A's was concerned. But I was also a very troublesome one so far as my teachers were concerned.

I wrote adversely critical letters to John Dewey when I attended a course of lectures he gave after he returned from China. They were sufficiently annoying and frequent to cause Professor Dewey to have his assistant ask me to refrain from continuing my letter writing.

I would get so vehemently excited by my disagreements with what another of my teachers had to say in class that the teacher, Professor Irwin Edman, met me at the door of his class one day and recommended that I not attend that session of his class because my argumentative excitement was too disruptive.

I took a course with Professor A. T. Poffenberger, Jr., in Experimental Psychology and before many sessions of that class I would seek him out in his office with a long list of questions that I wished him to answer about his last lecture and before he continued with the next one. Poff was long-suffering, but my doing this time and time again must have been an annoyance to him about which he, nevertheless, never complained. It never occurred to me that I was not behaving in the manner of most students, that my youthful zeal as a student was unusual and perhaps, reprehensible.

Ludwig Wittgenstein was an academic misfit in his first years at Cambridge. A recent biography of him by Ray Monk tells of his encounters with W. E. Johnson and Bertrand Russell. Professor Johnson was an eminent logician and Fellow of King's College. Russell advised Wittgenstein to study with him. Wittgenstein reported to F. R. Leavis that in his first hour Johnson had nothing to teach him; and Leavis was told by Johnson that "At our first meeting he was teaching me."

Wittgenstein came to Russell in great excitement when he learned that Johnson had said that "he wouldn't take him any more, practically saying he argued too much instead of learning his lesson like a good boy." Russell's own comment at this point was "he is terribly persistent, hardly lets one get a word in, and is generally considered a bore."

Too intense a passion to learn on the part of a student detracts from docility (teachableness), which is the virtue a student should have in relation to his teachers, the virtue of being neither submissive nor contentious. Wittgenstein certainly lacked docility. Clearly, I did, too. The comparison ends there. We were both academic misfits, each in his own way.[1]

2

After I joined the faculty in 1923 and became an assistant in the psychology laboratory as well as a teacher in the great books seminars that John Erskine had initiated at Columbia, I misbehaved as a member of the faculty. I have told the story of my unconventional behavior with regard to the final examination in a course on the psychology of aesthetics that I was teaching. I conspired with the students to give them their grades before they took the final examination in the gym a few weeks later on condition that, when they wrote answers to the questions I would prepare for them, they would do so in a playful and witty rather than in a serious manner.[2]

What occasioned this thoroughly unorthodox behavior on my part was my feeling of being completely fed up with the academic mentality as a result of a protracted and unsatisfactory argument I had had with one of my colleagues that day when lunching with

1. Bertrand Russell said of the young Wittgenstein that he had excellent manners, but "in argument he forgets about manners and says what he thinks." This difference between social politeness and intellectual impoliteness explains why those who, however good their social manners, are intellectually impolite, are academic misfits.

2. See Adler, *Philosopher at Large: An Intellectual Autobiography*, pp. 68–69.

him at the Faculty Club. This should have taught me I was out of place in the university, where I found myself so much at odds with its professorial types. I should have realized that I was temperamentally unsuited to behave the way that most professors are expected to behave and in fact do behave.

Professor Poffenberger, who in the late twenties had become head of the Psychology Department, insisted that I become a candidate for the Ph.D. He regarded my doing so as an indispensable condition of my tenure and promotion in the department. I was reluctant to take the time and to do the necessary work required. Since in Poff's eyes I was doing a satisfactory job as a teacher, I could see no value in the exercises involved in getting a Ph.D. I did not want the degree as a badge of academic merit.

The story of all the evasions I resorted to in the process of getting the Ph.D., which included not attending the graduate courses in which I was supposed to earn credit, getting others to do much of the spadework in gathering the data to be used in writing the dissertation, and the manner in which I conducted myself in my final oral examination, is not something I am proud of. During those years, I spent most of my time in philosophical inquiry and analysis and in teaching great books, things which greatly interested me, with little time left for the chores involved in getting a Ph.D., which did not interest me at all.

I should have learned from all this that I was an academic misfit. But at the time in 1930 that I left Columbia to go to the University of Chicago at the invitation of President Robert M. Hutchins to become a professor there at age twenty-seven, I was still too immature to realize that I would have difficulties with my colleagues by behaving in a thoroughly unprofessorial manner.

I got off to a bad start at the University of Chicago. My first official performance in September of 1930 was to give an address to the members of the local chapter of the Social Science Research Council, which I did in a manner unbecoming a professor. In the armed services, one gets cashiered for conduct unbecoming an officer and a gentleman. In academic circles, the reaction to conduct unbecoming a professor is less drastic, but no less negative.

In the summer before coming to Chicago, my friend Arthur Rubin had urged me to consider what he called the pretensions of the social sciences. I wrote a series of memoranda on the subject and finally an essay on the difference in the methods of inquiry in the exact natural science and in the much less exact disciplines that have come to be called social sciences.

I sent a copy of this essay to Robert Lynd, earlier the author of the best-seller *Middletown* and at that time Secretary of the National Social Science Research Council. He found it of sufficient interest to send a copy to my friend from Yale, Donald Slesinger, who was then Acting Dean of the Social Science division at the University of Chicago.

It was Slesinger, not I, who proposed to the local chapter of the Social Science Research Council that when they met that September, they invite me to read my paper, entitled "The Social Scientist's Misconception of Science."

I should have known better, and I should have decided to do so on the grounds of its impropriety, but I obviously had no inkling of what was proper or improper in academic behavior. Professors do not tell their peers in public meetings how incompetent they are. That, in effect, was the gist of my paper; certainly that was the way in which it was interpreted by my audience.

The session ended in an uproar. Charles E. Merriam, Senior Professor of Political Science, took me aside and, putting his hand on my shoulder in a fatherly manner, gently reprimanded me for my imprudence in stepping so heavily on the toes of colleagues. That simply was not done. I should have submitted questions for them to respond to, not post these in the defiant manner of a Martin Luther, arguing for their acceptance in a tone that suggested they were irrefutable.

I am sure that if I were to reread that paper now, I would find it juvenile—full of holes and errors. But the merits of my argument are not what concern me here. It is rather the impression of me that it engendered in my academic colleagues at Chicago. I repeat the story only because I recently read an account of this episode in a book about the Hutchins years at Chicago by Professor William McNeill, in which he calls me a "show-off" and attributes my behavior on that occasion to a desire to be in the limelight, to attract attention. That, as I remember the event, was no part of my motivation. I had been invited to present a critical essay that I then thought was sound and I could see no reason for not accepting, even if it involved my telling my colleagues in no uncertain terms that their work was seriously blemished.

Though Professor McNeill changed the title of his book in order to present it as a personal memoir rather than as an official history of the Hutchins years at the University, some of the things said about me were not his own firsthand impressions, but rather were hearsay reports of gossip that circulated on the campus.

It is true that, in lectures that I gave at the University in those early years and in conversations that I had with my colleagues, I appeared to be an exponent of philosophical principles and conclusions derived from my study of Aristotle and Thomas Aquinas. But in the great books seminar that I conducted with President Robert Hutchins, we read selections from Aristotle and Aquinas in at most two or three out of more than fifty sessions.

More important than that is the fact that I was not in those early years a Thomist if that designation applies to persons whose published books are offered as scholarly contributions to the philosophy of Aquinas. The period in which I wrote such books occurred much later—1938 to 1943.

Most important of all is the fact that, in that later period, the books or papers I then wrote—about democracy, about the problem of species, and about the demonstration of God's existence—were rejected by the orthodox Thomists in the American Catholic Philosophical Association as unwarranted attempts by me to be a revisionist in the sphere of Thomistic thought. The adverse reaction to my Thomistic writings was more vehement than the adverse reaction of my professorial colleagues to my holding Aristotle up as a source of great philosophical wisdom.

In sending me the manuscript of his book on the Hutchins' university, Professor McNeill wrote me a letter in which he said, "I imagine that some of my remarks may displease you a bit, but tell me anyway; and I can perhaps be persuaded to change my opinion." I read the manuscript with increasing shock as I discovered that his version of what had happened in my first three years at the University of Chicago differed strikingly from my account of the same years in *Philosopher at Large*, a copy of which I had loaned Professor McNeill when, before writing his book, he spent hours in my office interviewing me about various matters and asked to borrow my autobiography.[3]

I wrote him three very long letters in which I called attention to discrepancies between his account and mine. Professor McNeill was not at the University in those early years. When he became a student at the college some years later, he had picked up the prevailing view and had adopted it without question.

After the interchange of many letters, he reworked his manuscript and finally wrote me a letter in which he said, "I am genuinely grateful to you for the corrections and remonstrances you made about my ms. I have now completed revision; and hope the end result will not offend you as much as the first draft did. I hope my portrait of your activity on campus is not too much of a caricature."

3

Reviewing in retrospect the things that happened in those early years, at such great distance from the time of their occurrence, I am impelled to register the following judgments.

(1) In my genuine and abiding concern with getting at the truth about any question at issue, I was relentless in argument; and whenever a difference of opinion became manifest, I always resorted to argument as the only means for trying to resolve the dispute. In proceeding argumentatively, I did not take into account the seniority of the persons I might be talking with, their superior academic status, or their greater scholarly eminence. Such differences between them and me seemed to me totally irrelevant, because my arguments were directed solely against opinions I thought incorrect. They were not in any way *ad personam.* I was not restrained by any deferential considerations concerning the age, the rank, or the reputation of my opponents. I argued with them as if they were simply other persons, undistinguished from me in any respect except the only one I would have acknowledged to be relevant, namely, that their arguments were better than mine.

3. See *Philosopher at Large*, Chapters 7, 8, and 9.

(2) That, however, was not the way in which many of my colleagues viewed my argumentative style. They thought that I was attacking them personally, not the opinions they espoused. They thought that I was challenging their authority and prestige, not their doctrines. In short, they thought I was being impolite—an unforgivable sin in academic interchanges.

(3) This did happen in the case of all the persons with whom I was associated at the University of Chicago. In conducting great books seminars, my method of questioning was persistently argumentative. It may have intimidated a few of my students, but most of them found that being required to follow the course of the argument that I engaged them in was a more instructive experience than what happened in their other classes.

Of course, they were my *students*, not my *colleagues*; but I was no less argumentative with my colleagues in the Law School without their becoming in any way disaffected. My argumentative style did not prevent them from becoming my friends, who joked with me about the give and take of controversy. Nor did it present an obstacle to the formation of a group of teachers and graduate students in the English Department who asked me to give them talks on the liberal arts of grammar, rhetoric, and logic. I met with them in many sessions in a most amicable atmosphere even though I was no less argumentative about disputable matters.

(4) The resentment I aroused in some of my colleagues, especially those in the social and natural sciences and in philosophy, is not adequately explained by the fact that, at the University of Chicago in the 1930s, anyone who proclaimed there was much to be learned from Greek and mediaeval philosophy, much that should be used to correct modern errors, was *ipso facto* out of touch with the cultural progress that has been made since the seventeenth century.

The reason why the charge that I was trying to revive mediaevalism is not an adequate explanation is that my friend Richard McKeon taught courses in which he expounded the philosophy of Aristotle and Aquinas, without generating the adverse reactions directed at me. Dick McKeon and I had become friends at Columbia University when we were both on the faculty there. I was instrumental in bringing him to the University of Chicago, where he became both a Professor of Philosophy and Dean of the Humanities Division.

As I explained in *Philosopher at Large*, "McKeon did not have to learn what not to do by observing the miscarriages that resulted from the tactics employed by Bob Hutchins and me. He was temperamentally addicted . . . to a different method of gaining his point." He was temperamentally inclined to behave as professors normally behave.

After his appointment as Dean of the Humanities in 1935, McKeon paid a visit to Scott Buchanan at the University of Virginia at a time when Scott was considering an invitation to come to Chicago to work with the Committee on the Liberal Arts that Hutchins was then in the process of establishing. McKeon tried to persuade Scott to accept the invitation and, in the course of doing so, told Scott about the mistakes I had made. According to McKeon, I had been "utterly blind to the possibilities of a more subtle approach and in consequence I had all but eliminated myself from the picture." He assured Buchanan that if I would behave myself, which meant behave as a professor should behave, "he would succeed in getting me established in the next five years."

Shortly afterward, McKeon and I had a conversation in which he repeated what he had told Buchanan, adding that if I would follow his prescriptions for polite and proper academic behavior, he would even succeed in getting me reinstated in the Philosophy Department. Knowing myself well enough by then to know that I could not, temperamentally or intellectually, behave in the prescribed professorial manner, I responded by telling McKeon not to trouble himself about my future. In addition, I had lost all interest in being a member of the Philosophy Department at the University of Chicago.

4

My reading in the summer of 1990 of Professor McNeill's manuscript was not the first contact with misimpressions of me written in recent years. In that same year, but before reading McNeill's manuscript, Professor Edward Shils wrote an article about Robert

Maynard Hutchins, published in *The American Scholar* (Spring 1990), in which he commented on my behavior in the early thirties. Shils is now a Professor of Sociology and Social Thought, but his recollections of Hutchins and me go back to the time when he first came to the University of Chicago in the early thirties. He was then a graduate student and research assistant.

To the best of my memory, I had no acquaintance with him, certainly no personal contact, never any conversation. As his published article makes clear, his direct acquaintance with me occurred on only two occasions, once when he audited a session of the great books seminar that Hutchins and I conducted, and once when he audited a session of the course in Systematic Social Science that Dean Beardsley Ruml had persuaded me to conduct with him. Nevertheless, Professor Shils repeats all the slanders and slurs about me that he picked up from his disaffected colleagues in the social sciences—such mistaken impressions as that I was a Thomist and that I wanted to return to the Middle Ages.

Let me concentrate and comment on the two occasions when Shils actually observed me in action as a teacher.

The course in Systematic Social Science was itself an academic fiasco. It was misconceived by Ruml. He dragooned me into my collaborating with him in the conduct of it. His avowed aim was to break down the barriers that separated the various disciplines that comprised the division of the University of which he was Dean: economics, anthropology, political science, sociology, etc. My part in it was misconceived by me. I gave lectures to the participants on formal logic, the theory of probability, and philosophical psychology.

Professor Shils was thoroughly justified in his negative reaction to the one session of the course he attended, but what he said about it shows little understanding of my behavior. The sessions were attended mainly by the senior professors in the Social Science Division. They were in attendance because the course was being given by the Dean of their division, not because I was assisting him. During the sessions, Ruml seldom said anything. I should have helped him to ask questions in pursuance of his aim. Instead I made the unforgivable mistake of taking almost the whole time of each two-hour session by giving formal lectures on subjects that were totally irrelevant to the scholarly concerns of my audience as well as not being germane to the purpose Ruml had in mind.

My offense was clear, but it was not as Professor Shils has described it. It was the offense of a very young member of the faculty presuming to instruct his elders about matters of which they were ignorant, but which were of little concern to them. Professor Shils is quite correct in saying that my lectures "had no connection with what was being done in the social sciences and what could reasonably be expected of them." But I did not claim that "social science could be practiced only on the foundation of a syllogistic system constituted by question-begging definitions and problematical derivatives pretending to be logical." Nor, to use his words, was there any "theological penumbra," which according to Shils, "obsessed Adler's detractors" and which "Adler did nothing to dispel." I may have compounded my error of giving lectures instead of asking questions in what Shils describes as "the domineering tone with which [Adler] spoke. . . . He looked very angry; he seemed to surge with impatience"; but my biggest mistake was in behaving in a thoroughly unacademic, unprofessorial manner.

With regard to the second of the two incidents in which Professor Shils witnessed my performance as a teacher, let me quote from the paragraph in which he describes his one-time visit to the great books seminar that Hutchins and I conducted. Shils writes:

> I occasionally met students who had attended this course. They were ecstatic about it. I once attended a class to see what it was like and was sorry to see as harsh a piece of academic browbeating of a student as I have ever witnessed, carried out by Mortimer Adler. Table slapping was as much a part of the technique of interpretation of texts as it had been part of the techniques of exposition of "systematic social science." . . . Adler's and Hutchins's procedures, different as they were from each other, made a remarkably effective combination. Those students who survived Adler's harsh schoolmasterly style looked back upon the "great books courses" as a glorious moment in the history of their education.[4]

4. Edward Shils, "Robert Maynard Hutchins," *The American Scholar*, Vol. 59, No. 2, Spring 1990, pp. 215, 217. Copyright © 1990 by the author.

From the many students of mine whom I have met in recent years, I can amply confirm the last sentence quoted above. In my youthful intensity about following the argument to get at the truth, I may have thumped the seminar table and gesticulated in other ways. But what Shils calls browbeating was not a manifestation of pedagogical sadism on my part; it was rather a manifestation of my impatience with answers that were irrelevant, inadequate, or simply wrong.

5

Professor Sidney Hook, shortly before he died, published an autobiographical book entitled *Out of Step*. In it there is a chapter entitled "God and the Professors," which was the title of my address at the First Conference on Science, Philosophy and Religion, held in New York in September of 1940.

Professor Hook devotes a good part of his chapter to an attack on my address at that conference, as well as to invidious comments on my stance as a philosopher—my so-called Thomism, my addiction to Aristotle, and so on—none of which he accurately delineates.

In this same chapter, he also treats the dispute that raged in the thirties between John Dewey and Robert Hutchins with regard to basic schooling and the undergraduate college. This I would like to reserve for later considerations when I discuss my activities as an educational reformer, especially *The Paideia Proposal* that was dedicated to both Dewey and Hutchins as the seminal sources of its central thesis. Nor is this the place to try to correct the many caricatures of my philosophical views that fill the pages of Professor Hook's chapter. That, too, will be dealt with later.

I had been invited by Rabbi Finkelstein to become a member of the committee to plan the First Conference on Science, Philosophy and Religion. After attending a number of the meetings of this committee, I told Rabbi Finkelstein that I was a minority of one about how the conference should be organized. He flew to Chicago to persuade me not to resign and he, together with my dear friend Jacques Maritain, also tried to persuade me to read a paper at the conference, which would present my minority view of how the conference should be conducted.

I was reluctant until the last moment because I could so easily predict how my remarks would be received and misinterpreted. The decade of my experiences at the University of Chicago had prepared me for that. Sidney Hook's chapter entitled "God and the Professors" confirms the correctness of my foresight.

Professor Hook was probably justified in his angry reaction to what he regarded as gall on my part to address the assembled professors in such a fashion. There were, however, some amusing incidents which occurred on the afternoon of the speech. But first let me report the events that led up to my writing and delivery of the speech. What follows is a long quotation from my account of this affair, as it appears in *Philosopher at Large*, pp. 186–190.

> The founding members included the most eminent names in American academic life, representing the entire range of disciplines relevant to the theme of the conference—"Science, Philosophy and Religion in Their Relation to the Democratic Way of Life." The much smaller steering committee, whose meetings I attended on several occasions, included Prof. William Albright of Johns Hopkins University, Prof. Lyman Bryson of Teachers College at Columbia, Prof. Harlow Shapley of Harvard University, Prof. I. I. Rabi of Columbia, and Prof. Harold Lasswell, who had been a colleague of mine at Chicago. My friend Jacques Maritain was also a member of the steering committee, but other obligations prevented him from attending its meetings.
>
> I went to these meetings with the hope that something might be done that would sharply distinguish this conference from the annual meetings of learned societies at which professors read papers at one another. No one feels compelled to listen, because the papers can be read in the published proceedings. I have always regarded such sessions as exercises in futility. What I hoped might be planned under Rabbi Finkelstein's auspices was a disciplined colloquy of scholars representing the three great areas of science, philosophy, and religion, in the course of which they might make a patient effort to understand one another's positions and gradually reach agreement on a small number of fundamental prop-

ositions about the relation of their disciplines; or, failing that, to acknowledge the roots of their disagreement. If that could be done, then this conference might make a genuine contribution to modern culture, in a manner comparable to the contribution made by the great disputations in mediaeval universities to the culture of their day.

My hope did not survive the month of May. What shattered my illusion was the reaction of my fellow members to my proposal for the conduct of the conference. No delivery of formal addresses; no polite discussions from the floor afterward; no publication of proceedings. Instead, I urged the steering committee to draw up an orderly list of questions about the relation of science to philosophy and about the relation of both to religion—questions of the sort that had been the focus of the disputes at Chicago—and to agree to try to answer them in the order in which they were placed. I proposed that we then carry on discussions aimed at formulating answers to which we could get substantial agreement from all parties to the conference. The least we should settle for was a frank acknowledgment of our inability to agree, and an appraisal of the causes and consequences of our disagreements—consequences not only for our universities but also for democracy.

Accustomed as I was to being rebuffed, the reaction to this proposal surprised and dismayed me. I was told that the very idea of laying down a set of questions to be answered by all conference participants in a certain order was fundamentally authoritarian and undemocratic. When I observed that all we had to agree upon initially was a set of questions and their orderly arrangement, and that I was neither dictating the questions nor the answers, I was told that that made no difference. Any attempt to prescribe the content of the conference that went beyond the statement of a theme which the scholars should have in mind when they prepared their papers departed from the democratic ideal of freedom of thought and discussion. . . .

When I realized that Rabbi Finkelstein's conference would be exactly like all other scholarly conventions, I decided to withdraw from the whole affair. At the end of May, I wrote Rabbi Finkelstein that though I was deeply devoted to the original project, I now thought that nothing of any distinctive value would or could come of it. "My reason," I wrote to him,

> is very simple: the professors you have gathered together for these discussions are not willing to make the effort to understand one another, and even less are they interested in trying to reach agreement about anything, or even to join issue clearly in agreement. . . . The best thing for me to do is to withdraw. I'm an impolite sort of fellow and I am likely to insult my colleagues if they talk the way they usually do. If no real good comes from the sessions, you would like them to be at least gentle and friendly, and I am likely to be a gadfly and a nuisance to you.

Many letters passed between Rabbi Finkelstein and me during the rest of June and July, in which he persisted in urging me not to withdraw. Finally, toward the end of July, I sent him a six-page memorandum in which I set forth my reasons for thinking that the conference could not achieve any objective that I thought worthwhile. I also sent my friend Jacques Maritain a copy and found that his attitude toward the conference resembled mine. Yet he, too, urged me not to withdraw.

When he received my letter, Rabbi Finkelstein suggested that I come to the conference and present a paper that incorporated the substance of my memorandum. I could not believe that he really meant me to deliver an address in which I expressed my dissatisfaction with the procedure of the conference and predicted that it would fail to accomplish any significant results. When he assured me that that was precisely what he wanted and that he was fully cognizant of both the content and the temper of my message, I yielded. That was a mistake on my part, as it was a mistake on his part not to accept my resignation.

The conference sessions took place in the inner courtyard of the Jewish Theological Seminary. I delivered my paper on a bright sunny afternoon in mid-September to an audience of about two hundred academicians. They were protected from the sunshine by canvas awnings stretched across the courtyard. It had rained the night before, and little pools of water had gathered in the corners of the awnings.

"God and the Professors" was the title of my paper, as I had warned Rabbi Finkelstein it would be. It plainly signalled the tenor of my remarks. If my aim had been to make friends and influence people, or to persuade any part of my audience, I could not have been more misguided or inept in the rhetoric I employed. But persuasion was no part of my intention, because I had no hope of succeeding. My sole intention was to tell the professors exactly what I thought of them in relation to the theme of the conference. That purpose my rhetoric served effectively. . . .

One event occurred that afternoon which caused my audience, otherwise stonily grim, to smile or even laugh out loud. After presenting the propositions which I thought ought to be affirmed if the conference were to become a significant enterprise, I read the passage in my paper which said:

> If a group of men do not come together because they have common problems, and ultimately seek to reach common problems, there is no more community among them than there is in a modern university, or in modern culture itself.

Then, in a tone of voice that I probably hoped would sound like an Old Testament prophet predicting impending doom, I declared: "The tower of Babel we are building invites another flood." At that very moment, the seams of some of the awnings opened up and the rainwater that had gathered there fell on the professors below.

I believe the content of my address at the First Conference on Science, Philosophy and Religion is so relevant to the main concerns of this chapter that I have put a large excerpt from the first half of it in the Note appended to this chapter. My reason for doing this is not that I endorse everything that I then wrote, word for word. I would now make many emendations and additions. But the main thrust of the argument helps to explain, more fully than I have done so far, my deep antipathy to the professorial mentality.

I would like to urge readers to examine carefully this appended material before continuing with the next chapter of this book.

NOTE TO CHAPTER 2

Excerpt from "God and the Professors"*
(Paper Presented at the First Conference on Science, Philosophy and Religion, New York City, September 10, 1940)

The Founding Members of this Conference are, for the most part, professors in American colleges and universities. They are eminent representatives of the various academic disciplines, among which are the three mentioned as most relevant to this Conference—science, philosophy and religion. The presence of historians and humanistic scholars is justified by the modern extension of science to include the so-called social sciences, with which all research about human affairs and culture can be affiliated. Most of these professors belong to one or more of the several learned societies which meet annually for the reading and discussion of papers that purport to make contributions to truth, or at least to what is academically recognized as learning.

Hence the reason for this Conference, for this additional meeting at which more papers are being read and discussed, must be some need for the professors to get together in a different way and for a different purpose. If the public wonders why we are gathering here this September, we must justify this Conference as trying to do something which is not, and perhaps cannot be, accomplished in the ordinary processes of our academic life—in classrooms, faculty meetings, or the sessions of learned societies.

Some explanations have already been given. We have come together because we all share, for different reasons and in varying degrees, an uneasiness about something we call the present situation. Whether or not we are ready to say that God's in his heaven, we cry with one voice that all's not right with the world. I wish I could credit my colleagues with one further agreement, namely, that the present crisis is only superficially a conflict between democracy and totalitarianism in the political arena, or between individualism and collectivism in the eco-

* Mortimer J. Adler, "God and the Professors," *Science, Philosophy and Religion: A Symposium* (Conference on Science, Philosophy and Religion in Their Relation to the Democratic Way of Life, Inc., September 9–11, 1940), New York, 1941, Chapter VII, pp. 120–30, 134–35.

nomic sphere. If that were the full nature of the crisis, why should we waste time talking about science, philosophy and religion?

The fact that we have chosen to consider three major components of human culture should indicate that we all have a vague sense of cultural disorder as the root of our troubles, as the source of a threatening doom. Far from being prime movers, Hitler and Mussolini, or, if you wish, the Stalins and Chamberlains, are but paranoiac puppets, dancing for a moment on the crest of the wave—the wave that is the historic motion of modern culture to its own destruction.

A culture is not killed by political conflicts, even when they attain the shattering violence of modern warfare; nor by economic revolutions, even when they involve the dislocations of modern mass uprisings. A culture dies of diseases which are themselves cultural. It may be born sick, as modern culture was, or it may decay through insufficient vitality to overcome the disruptive forces present in every culture; but, in any case, cultural disorder is a cause and not an effect of the political and economic disturbances which beset the world today.

The health of a culture, like the health of the body, consists in the harmonious functioning of its parts. Science, philosophy and religion are certainly major parts of European culture; their distinction from one another as quite separate parts is certainly the most characteristic cultural achievement of modern times. But if they have not been properly distinguished, they cannot be properly related; and unless they are properly related, properly ordered to one another, cultural disorder, such as that of modern times, inevitably results.

This Conference, one might suppose, has been called to consider the illness of our culture; more than that, to seek and effect remedies. One of the troubles is that scientists, philosophers, and theologians, or teachers of religion, have long failed to communicate with one another.

The structure of a modern university, with its departmental separations, and its total lack of order among specialized disciplines, represents perfectly the disunity and chaos of modern culture. Since nothing can be expected of the professors locked up in their departmental cells, since reforming our institutions of higher learning (to make them truly universities) seems to be impossible, since the ordinary processes of academic life manifest the very defects which must be remedied, the professors have been assembled under the special auspices of this Conference with the hope that lines of communication can be established. That done, one might even hope for communication to lead to mutual understanding, and thence to agreement about the truths which could unify our culture.

If what I have said is not the purpose of this Conference, I can see no justification for it whatsoever. The fact that all the professors gathered mention the Present Crisis, without trying to agree about its nature and causes; the fact that they manifest some concern about Democracy, without trying to define it and understand its roots; the fact that, in a baffling variety of senses, they refer to Science, Philosophy and Religion, without trying to solve the intricate problem of the relationship of these disciplines,—all this amounts to nothing.

An undertaking of this sort is not needed to make professors think or talk this way. Nor is it needed to give them an opportunity to write and read papers which do credit to their specialized scholarly achievements. Unless this be a Conference in more than name only, unless it be a concerted effort to reach a common understanding of our cultural failure and a common program for its reform, this gathering will be as vacuous and futile as many another solemn conclave of professors, advertised by high-sounding and promising titles.

But if I have stated the only purpose which might justify this Conference, then I must also say that it cannot possibly succeed. I do not bother to say that a conference, however good, cannot succeed in reforming modern culture, or even in correcting one of the main causes of its disorder, namely, modern education. That goes without saying. To expect such results would be to ask too much from even the best of all possible conferences. I mean, much more directly, that one cannot expect the professors to understand what is wrong with modern culture and modern education, for the simple reason that that would require them to understand what is wrong with their own mentality.

If such a miracle could be hoped for, I would not be without hope for a peaceful deliverance from our manifold confusions. Since professors come to a conference of this sort with the intention of speaking their minds but not of changing them, with a willingness to listen but not to learn, with the kind of tolerance which delights in a variety of opinions and abominates the unanimity of agreement, it is preposterous to suppose that this Conference can even begin to realize the only ends which justify the enterprise. . . .

We do not even have to wait until this Conference is over to discover its futility and the reasons therefor. The glorious, Quixotic failure of President Hutchins to accomplish any of the essential reforms which American education so badly needs, demonstrates the point for us. In fact, if he *could* have succeeded, this Conference would not be necessary now. The fact that he did not succeed may make this Conference necessary, in the sense that fundamental rectifications of modern culture are imperative; but if we understand why, in the nature of the situation, Hutchins could not succeed, we also see why a conference of professors about the defects of the modern mentality must be self-defeating.

What did Mr. Hutchins propose? He proposed, in the first place, that man is a rational animal, essentially distinct from the brutes, and hence, that education should cultivate the moral and the intellectual virtues. He proposed, in the second place, that science, philosophy and theology are distinct bodies of knowledge, radically different as to methods of knowing as well as with respect to objects known. But he went further. He said that theoretic philosophy delves more deeply into the nature of things than all the empirical sciences; that, as theoretic knowledge, philosophy is superior to the sciences by reason of the questions it can answer. He said that practical philosophy, dealing with ethical and political problems, is superior to applied science, because the latter at best gives us control over the physical means to be used, whereas practical philosophy determines the ends to be sought, and the ordering of all means thereto.

Hence the structure of a university should not be a miscellaneous collection of departments from astronomy to zoology, with all treated as equally important theoretically and practically, but a hierarchy of studies, ordered educationally according to their intrinsic merits. Because of the fact that our secular universities harbor a diversity of religious faiths, Mr. Hutchins placed metaphysics at the summit instead of theology. For man the highest knowledge, and the most indispensable to his well-being, is the knowledge of God; and since the ultimate conclusions of metaphysics comprise a natural theology, metaphysics is the supreme subject-matter in the domain of natural knowledge.

But Mr. Hutchins would have to admit (and he indicated his willingness to do so) that if there is a better knowledge of God, and man's relation to God, than metaphysics offers, then such knowledge is superior to philosophy, both theoretically and practically, just as philosophy is superior to science. Traditional Judaism and Christianity do, of course, claim that there is such knowledge, the sacred theology that rests on faith in God's revelation of Himself. It is properly distinguished from both science and philosophy as a supernatural knowledge, which man cannot have without God's direct aid.

Why did Mr. Hutchins fail? Anyone who has ever attended a faculty meeting knows the answer. It can be discovered by anyone who will read the reviews of *The Higher Learning in America*, written by the professors, or what is worse, the professional educators. He failed not because his analysis was patently *demonstrated* to be in error; not because someone *proved* that philosophy does not exist or is inferior to science; or that religion is superstition, and sacred theology a rationalization of some make-believe. He failed because he was asking the professors to change their minds and to agree about something. He failed as much with the professors of philosophy as with the professors of science; he failed even more with those teachers of religion who regard themselves as liberal.

What Hutchins proposed ran counter to every prejudice that constitutes the modern frame of mind, and its temper. The professors being in the vast majority, and ultimately controlling, *as they should,* educational policy, it was naïve of Mr. Hutchins to suppose that he could reform education by appealing to truths the professors ignored or denied. Worse than naïve, he had the effrontery to assume that if the professors were ignorant of certain truths or had neglected the implications of others, they would submit themselves to teaching on these points. Since the professors cannot conceive themselves as being taught, certainly not by anyone without a Ph.D. in their field, the man who tries to argue with the plain intention of winning agreement must really be trying to impose his doctrine. The simplest way to deal with a fellow like Hutchins is to call him a fascist.

Now I want to make one thing absolutely clear. I am not begging the question in this issue between Mr. Hutchins and his opponents, by proceeding as if I have proved the former right and the latter wrong. I know I have not proved the truth of any of the theses mentioned, nor have I proved the falsity of their contraries. With the time at my disposal that would be impossible to do under any circumstances; and even with much more time I would not try with this audience.

With a few notable exceptions, the members of this Conference represent the American academic mind. It is that fact itself which makes it unnecessary, as well as unwise, for me to make any effort in the way of reasoning. I know too well, from much experience, the opinions of this audience, and of all the professors they represent—about the nature and relationship of science, philosophy and religion.

I also know, because I have tried so many times to present an analysis with the fullest of supporting arguments, precisely what reactions such procedure calls forth. Fortunately, there is no need to verify this once again, because on this occasion I am concerned only to show the futility of a conference of professors about science, philosophy and religion.

That can be shown very simply. Either the prevailing opinions of the professors are right or they are wrong. Let us suppose, for the moment, that they are right, that what is now generally taught in American schools about the relation of science, philosophy and religion, is the true account. If it is true, there is nothing wrong with modern culture, for modern culture, in all its practices and institutions, embodies these opinions. On this alternative, therefore, it is difficult to see why there should be any conference about science, philosophy and religion.

If, however, on the other alternative, the prevailing professorial opinions on these matters are wrong, and if, in addition, modern culture suffers grave disorders precisely because it embodies these opinions, then there is some point to a conference which would seek to correct the prevalent errors. But then it is pointless to ask the professors to consider the problem. They have already considered it and told us their answers in all their teaching and all their educational decisions. The same majority point of view will dominate this Conference, as in the Hutchins controversy.

Of course, the minority view will get a hearing, with all that indifference about the truth which hides behind the mask of tolerance, but it is a foregone conclusion that nobody's mind will be changed; in fact, everyone knows that is not the aim of a conference, anyway. Hence, when all is said and done, the relative weights of majority and minority opinion will be registered once more. The Conference will have exhibited the characteristic mentality of our culture, and those who are deeply concerned about changing that mentality will be confirmed in their pessimism that nothing, simply nothing, can be done to reform our education or to reorient our culture.

Now I am well aware that my colleagues do not think there is any such clear-cut division between a majority and a minority view of science, philosophy and religion. For one thing, they do not like to acknowledge the existence of clear-cut issues, with truth on one side, and error on the other; if there were such issues, then anyone who undertook to think about them might be obliged to risk his academic reputation by coming to a definite conclusion.

For another thing, the professors do not like to feel that they share even a common majority opinion with each other. The sacred individuality of each professor can be preserved only by differing. When one is in substantial sympathy with what a colleague has to say, he still safeguards his freedom of opinion by saying the same thing some other way. Most professors seem to feel that agreement, even if freely reached, violates their personal integrity.

Nevertheless, I charge the professors—and here I am speaking of the vast majority—with being in substantial agreement on one side of the crucial issues this Conference faces. I say that most of them are positivists. I know that there are enough varieties of positivism to permit the professors to retain their individuality, but I insist that behind the multiplicity of technical jargons there is a single doctrine. The essential point of that doctrine is simply the affirmation of science, and the denial of philosophy and religion.

Again I am aware that the professors will smile at my simplicity. Whoever heard anyone, except a few violent extremists, flatly denying philosophy and religion; as a matter of fact, such dogmatic denials are made only by a small circle of "philosophers" who blantantly advertise themselves as positists. . . .

Within brief scope, the easiest way to force the professors into the open is by making the issues sharp and clear. Let me do this first with respect to philosophy, and then with respect to religion.

With respect to philosophy, the following propositions must be affirmed. He who denies any one of them denies philosophy.

(1) Philosophy is public knowledge, not private opinion, in the same sense that science is knowledge, not opinion.

(2) Philosophical knowledge answers questions which science cannot answer, now or ever, because its method is not adapted to answering such questions.

(3) Because their methods are thus distinct, each being adapted to a different object of inquiry, philosophical and scientific knowledge are logically independent of one another, which means that the truth and falsity of philosophical principles or conclusions does not depend upon the changing content of scientific knowledge.

(4) Philosophy is superior to science, both theoretically and practically: theoretically, because it is knowledge of the being of things whereas science studies only their phenomenal manifestations; practically, because philosophy establishes moral conclusions, whereas scientific knowledge yields only technological applications; this last point means that science can give us only a control over operable means, but it cannot make a single judgment about good and bad, right and wrong, in terms of the ends of human life.

(5) There can be no conflict between scientific and philosophic truths, although philosophers may correct the errors of scientists who try to answer questions beyond their professional competence, just as scientists can correct the errors of philosophers guilty of a similar transgression.

(6) There are no systems of philosophy, each of which may be considered true in its own way by criteria of internal consistency, each differing from the others, as so many systems of geometry, in terms of different origins in diverse, but equally arbitrary, postulates or definitions.

(7) The first principles of all philosophical knowledge are metaphysical, and metaphysics is valid knowledge of both sensible and supra-sensible being.

(8) Metaphysics is able to demonstrate the existence of supra-sensible being, for it can demonstrate the existence of God, by appealing to the evidence of the senses and the principles of reason, and without any reliance upon articles of religious faith.

These eight propositions are not offered as an exhaustive account of the nature of philosophy, its distinction from, and relation to, science. I have chosen them simply because they will serve like intellectual litmus paper to bring out the acid of positivism.

Let the professors who claim to respect philosophy—and this goes as much for the professors of philosophy as for the others—decide whether they affirm every one of these propositions. Those who say that philosophy is just another kind of knowledge but not superior to science might just as well call philosophy opinion and deny its existence. Those who suppose that philosophical principles or conclusions are dependent on the findings of science; those who suppose that real technical competence is necessary in order to solve scientific problems, whereas none is needed for philosophical problems; those who think that philosophy comprises a variety of logically constructed systems, among which you can take your choice according to your preference among postulates; those who say philosophy is all right, but metaphysics is nonsense, and there is no rational knowledge of God—all these deny philosophy. They are positivists.

If the professors were clear of mind and forthright of speech, they would come right out and say that they regard philosophy as opinion, not knowledge. But professors are unaccustomed to simple affirmations and denials. They give true-false tests, but never take them. They will, therefore, avoid the test I have presented by saying that it is all a matter of how you use words, or that it all depends on your point of view, or something equally evasive. Yet, by their evasions shall you know them, for those who affirm philosophy to be knowledge neither hesitate nor quibble on any of these points. . . .

To which, let me add, a few more paragraphs from the second half of my address.

The various propositions I have enumerated are either true or false. Each, therefore, can be regarded as constituting a problem, a two-sided issue at least. Should it not be the business of this Conference to take up such problems in a definite order, and to direct all its intellectual energies to their solution? If a group of men do not come together because they have common problems, and ultimately seek to reach common answers, there is no more community among them than there is in a modern university, or in modern culture itself.

As I have already said, the failure of this Conference to do the only work which justifies its existence, perfectly symbolizes the absence of cultural community in the modern world; worse than that, it justifies the most extreme pessimism about an impending catastrophe, for until the professors and their culture are liquidated, the resolution of modern problems—a resolution which history demands shall be made—will not even begin. The tower of Babel we are building invites another flood.

The failure of this Conference is due not only to the fact that the professors are, for the most part, positivists; but even more so to their avoidance of what is demanded for fruitful intellectual procedure. Unlike the mediaeval man of learning, the modern professor will not subject himself to the rigors of public disputation. He emasculates discussion by treating it as an exchange of opinions, in which no one gains or loses because everyone keeps his own. He is indocile in the sense that, beyond the field of science, he cannot be instructed, because he acknowledges no ignorance.

Hence anyone who would try to instruct him about philosophical or religious truths would be regarded as authoritarian, as trying to impose a doctrine. He is scandalized by the very notion of a commonly shared truth for all men. Even though such truth can be attained only by the free activity of each mind, the fact that no mind is free to reject the truth seems like an infringement upon his sacred liberties. What he means by truth in science and by agreement among scientists permits him to talk as if he were a truth-seeker and willing to agree; but that is because the contingent and tentative character of scientific knowledge so perfectly fits the egoism, the individualism, the libertinism, of the modern mind. . . .

Hence he would not participate in a conference which required everyone to agree upon the fundamental questions to be answered, and measured its success by the degree to which such answers were commonly achieved as a result of the most patient discussion.

CHAPTER 3

DEPARTURE FROM ACADEMIC LIFE

1

I formally resigned my professorship at the University of Chicago in May of 1952, and moved to San Francisco to establish the Institute for Philosophical Research, with which I have been associated ever since. It has served for most of the last forty years as the ivory tower in which I have been able to do philosophical work free from the burdens and distractions of dealing with people.

I departed from academic life, but I did not depart from a life of teaching and learning, from my concern with educational reforms, from my activities in connection with the Aspen Institute, from my editorial work for Encyclopaedia Britannica, Inc., and from my giving lectures and writing books that represented my lifetime preoccupation with philosophy and with the pursuit of philosophical truth.

All of these interests of mine were major aspects of my life in the period between 1945 and 1977, but they were now carried on without being affected or diverted by the complications and intrigues of academic life. I define the period I am referring to by the dates 1945 and 1977. In 1945, I took a leave of absence from my teaching post at the University in order to devote all my time to the construction of the *Syntopicon* and to assisting Bob Hutchins in the preparation for publication of *Great Books of the Western World* in 1952.

That work had begun in 1943, but not until 1945 did I realize that it could not be completed on schedule unless I ceased to be an active member of the faculty. The other date defining this period,

1977, is the year *Philosopher at Large* was published. I mentioned this in order to tell readers that much that happened in this period is covered in that book, much but not all. Hence, there are things of interest to be covered in this *Second Look in the Rearview Mirror.*

The relation between these two autobiographical memoirs is like the relation between old business and new business in the minutes of a meeting. Part One of this book is a return to old business; Parts Two and Three are entirely new business—things not covered at all in the earlier books.

My taking a leave of absence in 1945 was really not the beginning of my departure from academic life. As I look back at the bibliography of my books and articles in *Philosopher at Large*, I perceive that 1938 begins the period of my life in which I spent most of my time writing, both about education and about philosophy, with very little time devoted to teaching other than in the great books seminars with Bob Hutchins, and no time at all engaged in disputes with my colleagues about educational reforms at the University.

I would characterize these years, especially those between 1938 and 1945 as my "Thomistic Period"—years in which I delivered speeches at annual meetings of the American Catholic Philosophical Association and in which the books and articles I wrote about the theory of democracy, the problem of species, and the demonstration of God's existence (all deviating from what was then expounded as orthodox Thomist doctrine) plunged me into heated controversy with the proponents of the so-called perennial philosophy of St. Thomas Aquinas, perennial and unrevised.

Throughout this period I remained actively engaged in teaching the great books and lecturing about the great ideas, but mainly in what was called the downtown college, the adult education agency of the University. It was in this period that Hutchins and I established the Great Books Foundation for carrying on this work, not only in the city of Chicago but across the country; and in this period also, at the instigation of Cyril Houle, who was then Dean of the downtown college, I set up the Program of General Education for Adults, which was a four-year program modeled on the new curriculum at St. John's College in Annapolis, which came into existence in 1937.

From the beginning of the New Program at St. John's, I was involved in it as a visiting lecturer and spent time at the college in Annapolis, collaborating with Stringfellow Barr and Scott Buchanan and helping them to realize the ideals they had in mind for their radical innovation in collegiate education. This, in turn, lead to my helping St. Mary's College in Moraga, California, and the University of Notre Dame in Indiana, to set up collegiate programs that, like the Program of General Education for Adults in the downtown college of the University of Chicago, adopted the principles and procedures of Buchanan's new plan for St. John's College in Annapolis.[1]

As I said earlier, my departure from academic life at the University of Chicago was not a cessation of my interest or activity in educational matters. But the display of that interest and the performance of that activity in what I did for St. John's College and in connection with all its by-products (in Chicago's downtown college, at St. Mary's College, and at Notre Dame) were totally devoid of the difficulties I had had throughout most of the thirties with my colleagues at the University of Chicago because of my temperamental disinclination to behave in a properly professorial manner.

In the chapters of Part Two to follow, I will deal consecutively, in the period after 1977, with the Paideia proposal for the radical reform of elementary and secondary public schooling in the United States; with editing the second edition of *Great Books of the Western World* and, in that connection, with the revision of the *Syn-*

1. There is one more offshoot of the New Program at St. John's College at Annapolis,Thomas Aquinas College in Santa Paula, California. It was established as recently as 1971. It is itself an offshoot of St. Mary's College in Moraga, California, where Ronald P. McArthur, its instigator, was a student at the time I helped to set up the educational program modeled on the New Program at St. John's. He retired as its president in 1991. A letter from him on that occasion said that, from the time of being a student at St. Mary's, "I believed from then on that you and Hutchins . . . were right about education. . . . Everything I have done as a teacher has been with the Great Books exclusively, and all I believed has been borne out in practice. As a Catholic I have for years bemoaned our slavish imitation of, in your terms, 'the worst features of secular education,' and knew that the only real reform was along the lines of St. John's. Hence Thomas Aquinas College."

topicon; and with my involvement at the Aspen Institute, culminating recently in the celebration of its fortieth anniversary in the summer of 1990. That is all new business. What, then, remains of old business, to be retrospectively examined in this chapter?

I have gone back to my voluminous files in order to discover what was not treated in *Philosopher at Large*. I have pulled out of it documents, not previously recorded, that I think deserve attention in this *Second Look*. Some of these were written by me; some, by others. One consists of two addresses I delivered about Robert Hutchins; another consists of my own reminiscences about teaching in the Law School at the University of Chicago, which I found so pleasant, together with a letter to me from one of my students there; and the third consists of excerpts from two speeches by Clifton Fadiman, my oldest living friend and the wittiest man I know, about the great books and the great ideas.

Ample excerpts from these materials will be found in the sections to follow or in the Notes to this chapter.

2

Because Bob Hutchins played such a large part in my life and influenced me so pervasively in what I did at the University of Chicago and in our editorial work together at Encyclopaedia Britannica, Inc., *Philosopher at Large* is filled with stories about our collaboration and with excerpts from our correspondence. But nothing will be found there that is an appraisal, accurate as well as adulatory, of the man himself and of what it was like to be so closely associated with him.[2]

Here, it seems to me, I can remedy that defect by presenting my assessment of Bob Hutchins on two memorable occasions—the first in 1965 at a dinner party in New York, organized to honor his

2. I should, perhaps, add the following comment. The fact that I was known by the faculty to be a close personal friend of the University's president and the fact that we were associated in teaching students in the college (university presidents rarely teach undergraduates), was probably one of the reasons why the faculty was so sensitive to every utterance of mine—as if it were also coming from him. This worked as a disadvantage to him as well as to me. He had certain mannerisms that also tended to work to his disadvantage with the faculty, especially his air of condescension which, in fact, covered his shyness and aloofness.

leadership of the Center for the Study of Democratic Institutions; and the second, at a memorial tribute to him in the Rockefeller Chapel at the University of Chicago in 1977, shortly after his death.

On the first occasion, I began by saying these speeches are limited to five minutes not because you (in the audience) are impatient, or because brevity is the soul of wit, but because, for Bob Hutchins, brevity is the essence of intelligent communication. The higher the intelligence, the fewer the words—the less the mind needs or can tolerate having things spelled out, explained, or repeated. Since the intelligence of Bob Hutchins outranks, outspeeds, and outruns all the minds with which he has any dealings—I mean *all without exception*—poor Bob has had to put up with an almost unbearable amount of prolixity on the part of his friends and associates.

Bob's innate politeness, fortified by his mother's injunction never to be rude, prevents him from showing his impatience in most cases; but even he could not always contain himself in the face of needless recitations of facts or reasons. In his office at the University of Chicago he had a sign in his desk drawer which, from time to time, he would take out and put on the front of his desk. It read: "Please do not tell the President things he already knows."

Having thus set the stage, I went on as follows.

In the tradition of the great books from Homer to Hutchins, there are no other great authors half as brief as he is, not even Aristotle who, for most of us, tends to let matters stand insufficiently explained. The nearest runner up to the rarity of the Hutchins intelligence is Isaac Newton. When Newton first read Euclid's *Elements* at Cambridge University, he complained to his tutor that the lengthy demonstrations were a waste of his time: all the theorems of Book I seemed to him just as self-evident as the axioms and didn't need proof.

Bob is that kind of reader. I remember his first reading of the difficult proofs for the existence of God in the *Summa Theologica* of St. Thomas Aquinas. He understood the argument so well on the first reading that he could boil it down to a few paragraphs and improve on it in the process. Some of his letters seldom run beyond a single sentence . . . ; and his books say so much in so few words that only an intelligence equal to his can understand them as he would like to have them understood.

At that point in my address, I tried to summarize the whole of Bob's teaching with maximum brevity. I said that he has taught us that Western civiliztaion, in its highest reaches, is the civilization of the dialogue and that the essential progress mankind . . . has made and must still make consists in the fullest realization of that civilization's ideals.

He has taught us that the civilization of the dialogue rests on the exercise of our highest faculties; that it grows with the application of our intellectual powers to every human concern; and that we participate in it to the extent that reason and reasonableness pervade our private conduct and our public actions.

He has taught us that the civilization of the dialogue is dedicated to the search for truth, to the advancement of learning, and to the dissemination of knowledge through the free interplay of minds engaged cooperatively in these pursuits; that it conceives education and politics as connected enterprises having the moral and the intellectual virtues as their common goal and rational discussion as their common means; that it conceives the state as a community of free men deliberating and acting for the common good; that it conceives government as the work of law, law as the work of reason, and reason as the source of the supremacy of right over might.

He has taught us that the civilization of the dialogue will expand with peace, and that peace will enable mankind to move toward the fullest realization of the potentialities of the human mind, but only if it is imbued with an evangelical universalism that seeks to unite all men as equals in dignity and as kinsmen in the life of reason.

I concluded by saying that Robert Maynard Hutchins had devoted his whole life and all his works to the civilization of the dialogue. He is for us its clearest symbol and its surest hope. We see in him its living essence—civility in all things. In mind and character, in thought and action, he is its paragon—the civilized man.

Being one of the speakers in the Rockefeller Chapel on the second occasion, I was fully aware of the solemnity of that ceremony. I followed James H. Douglas, one of Bob's best friends on the University's Board of Trustees, and preceded Edward Levi, then President of the University. Solemn though the occasion was, I thought it appropriate to introduce some levity into my remarks. I began as follows.

The friends and family of Robert Hutchins who are gathered here today do not need the utterance of a eulogy. The loss they feel and the memories they cherish bear silent testimony to the influence he exerted upon their lives and the affection he aroused in all who had the good fortune to be touched intimately by the elegance of his style; by the integrity of his character; by the beauty and grace of his person; by the keenness and wit of his mind; and by his gentleness, kindness, and compassion.

May I speak for them in trying to explain to others less closely associated with him and to those who knew him only by hearsay why we feel that the measured judgment which will be formed retrospectively, with the passage of time, cannot exaggerate his contribution to the improvement of this University and of education generally, here and abroad; to the realization of the highest ideals of a democratic society; to world peace and the establishment of a world community, founded, with justice, on liberty and equality for all the peoples of the earth; to the furtherance of the moral, intellectual, and spiritual revolution that was always the controlling objective of his thought and action; and last, but not least, to the advancement of knowledge itself, knowledge illuminated by the light that is cast upon what we know by the understanding of basic ideas, and is directed toward the wisdom derived from a consideration of first principles and final ends.

I then went on in a lighter vein.

Those who loved Bob Hutchins dearly must be excused for the excesses to which their admiration for him sometimes impelled them. Many years ago, in the summer just before Bob came to the University of Chicago, his secretary at Yale Law School wrote me a letter about the postponement of a meeting with Scott Buchanan that I had been trying to arrange. It would have to be put off until the fall, she wrote, adding, "until then, Mr. Buchanan will have to dream of Mr. Hutchins, and nothing he will dream will compare with the actuality."

And after Bob departed from these precincts to join Paul Hoffman at the Ford Foundation, a friend, whose admiration for him may seem overzealous, referred to Bob as "the president of the ex-University of Chicago." We should be able to smile with tolerance at such hyperboles, recognizing the truth they contain and correcting their exaggerations.

Mr. Levi, I know, will do just that, for he will talk of realities, not dreams, and he will describe and justly appraise the heritage that Bob Hutchins left this University, a heritage that continues to inform its life and spirit to this day.

Resolutely concerned, as Bob Hutchins was, with bringing about a moral, intellectual, and spiritual revolution, he never tired of preaching the gospel of the moral and intellectual virtues, of teaching the doctrine which underlies that preachment, and of assiduously cultivating these virtues in his own life.

The example he himself set was the most effective way to guide others to their acquirement, especially the students he taught and the colleagues he admonished. His moral virtues are, perhaps, best exemplified by his courage in undertaking the Manhattan Project that three great Eastern universities had turned down because they feared the risk of failure in the enterprise; and by his actions to preserve academic freedom on this campus, and freedom of speech in this country during the dark days of McCarthy.

His intellectual virtues are best exemplified by his scholarship in the field of law and jurisprudence; by his understanding of the great ideas in the tradition of Western thought through the study of its great books; and by the philosophical cast of his mind that made him pursue wisdom by grappling with fundamental issues in every sphere of thought, always patiently submitting his mind to the controversies they engendered.

He was always patient with and tolerant of those who disagreed with him in a rational manner, but his profound distaste for the irrational made him impatient with those whose disagreement bespoke emotional prejudices; and the acuity, as well as the rapidity, of his intelligence made him impatient with those who spoke at length but said little.

The sharpness and speed of his wit often embarrassed or angered those who suffered from its lightning flashes. When, as Dean of the Yale Law School, he attended a reception for the justices of the Supreme Court, one of the old conservatives then on the bench said to him: "Mr. Dean, I understand that you are teaching the young men at New Haven what is wrong with our decisions." "Oh no," said Mr. Hutchins, "we let them find that out for themselves."

When, in his second year as President of the University, he began reading the great books with a group of freshman, Professor Paul Shorey, the eminent Greek scholar, questioned him about the advisability of discussing *The Divine Comedy* after only one week's study of it. "In my day at Harvard under Professor Grandgent," Shorey said, "we spent a whole year on Dante's poem. How can you expect your students . . . ?" Shorey started to ask, only to be interrupted by Bob's quick rejoinder: "The difference, you see, is that our students are very bright."

In fifty years of close association with Bob Hutchins—at the Yale Law School, at The University of Chicago, at Encyclopaedia Britannica, and at the Center for the Study of Democratic Institutions—I never ceased to be astonished by the extraordinary power of his intelligence in dealing with difficult books that he was reading for the first time; in dealing with the practical problems of an administrator; in dealing with the arguments involved in the dispute of theoretical issues. . . .

I concluded with reminiscences about Bob Hutchins as a teacher, as Chairman of the Board of Editors of the *Encyclopaedia Britannica*, and as President of the University of Chicago.

If anyone needs an explanation of the intellectual vitality and the excitement about ideas that, during the Hutchins' administration, distinguished this University from all others, before and after, he will find it in Bob's predilection and propensity for sustained discussion of fundamental issues.

That same predilection and propensity characterized his service to Encyclopaedia Britannica as a member of its Board of Directors from 1943, and as Chairman of its Board of Editors from 1949, until his retirement from both posts. During all those years, he was not only the moral conscience of the publishing company, but its persistent mentor as well. His leadership provided the guidance and the inspiration that led in 1952 to the publication of *Great Books of the Western World*, and to the production in 1974 of the radically reconstructed and greatly improved fifteenth edition of the encyclopaedia.

What may be, but should not be, forgotten is that, for fifteen of the twenty years that Robert Hutchins headed this University, he was also a teaching member of its faculty, actively engaged in teaching students in the University, in the University high school, and in the Law School. As is the case with every good teacher, his impulse to teach sprang from his desire to learn. He was a splendid teacher, one of the best I have ever known, because of his own avidity for learning, accompanied by an acute sense of the difficulties of learning, which made him sympathetic to the pains of others engaged in that process.

Though seldom free from preoccupation with the problems of money raising and of dealing with trustees and faculty, Bob Hutchins never lost sight of his chief problem as a University President—the future of its students.

To convey to you the character of that abiding concern, permit me, in closing, to quote from his "Address to the Graduating Class," in this chapel on Commencement Day, 1935.

> It is now almost fifteen years since I was in the position you occupy. I can therefore advise you about the dangers and difficulties you will encounter. . . .
>
> . . . My experience and observation lead me to warn you that the greatest, the most insidious . . . , the most paralyzing danger you will face is the danger of corruption. Time will corrupt you. Your friends, your wives or husbands, your business or professional associates will corrupt you; your social, political, and financial ambitions will corrupt you. The worst thing about life is that it is demoralizing. . . .
>
> . . . Believe me, you are closer to the truth now than you will ever be again. Do not let "practical" men tell you that you should surrender your ideals because they are impractical. Do not be reconciled to dishonesty, indecency, and brutality because gentlemanly ways have been discovered of being dishonest, indecent, and brutal. . . . Take your stand now before time has corrupted you. Before you know it, it will be too late. Courage, temperance, honor, liberality, justice, wisdom, reason, and understanding, these are still

the virtues. In the intellectual virtues, this University has tried to train you. The life you have lived here should have helped you toward the rest. If come what may you hold them fast, you will do honor to yourselves and to the University, and you will serve your country.

3

In 1932, I taught for the first time a course in the philosophy of law. In 1977, law students who graduated in 1932 organized a forty-fifth anniversary celebration. As one of their instructors in 1932, I was asked to speak at their dinner. Because it is of such biographical interest, I quote long excerpts from it here. But, first, I want to quote excerpts from a letter I received on that occasion from Frank Greenberg, one of the students in the Law School class of 1932.

> Your reminiscence about the Law School is charming and it has given me great pleasure. While I suppose I have a particular interest, at least as a passive observer if not a participant, in some of the events you recall, I hope that all the alumni will share my appreciation.
>
> I cannot resist the temptation to put my own gloss on several of your "confessions."
>
> I have a dim recollection of having sat in on the seminar on the law of evidence for one or two sessions, although I may not have been a senior at the time. . . . I do recall that the translation of judicial proof into a formal structure of symbolic logic was altogether beyond me. As I suspect it was beyond Judge Hinton. But while my recollection of the seminar on evidence is dim, I have a very lively and vivid recollection of the seminar on the philosophy of law which may, without exaggeration, have been the single most exciting experience in my education. . . .
>
> . . . You were, of course, an inveterate doodler on the blackboard and I recall that George James and I were always in such a state of excitement that we were occasionally rude enough to grab the chalk out of your hand and attempt to correct whatever those lines were that you were drawing. It must, Lord knows, have been a very

unorthodox seminar but as I say, I think the most exciting and enjoyable single experience I had at the University. . . .

Somebody (it may have been William James) defined education as that which is left over after you have forgotten everything that you set out to learn. It is that indefinable residue of what I learned from you and others in the Law School that I cherish and that I think has greatly influenced my life. For that, among other things, I am greatly indebted to you. . . .[3]

4

Finally, I come to a document in my file that represents a precious monument in my memory of Clifton Fadiman's contribution to my lifelong love affair with the great books.

Kip, as all his friends called him, was too busy with being the host of the famous radio program known as "Information Please" to participate in the editorial work that prepared the first edition of *Great Books of the Western World* for publication in 1952. But he was not too busy to accept Senator William Benton's invitation to be one of the speakers at the banquet given at the Waldorf-Astoria Hotel to celebrate its publication.

Lawrence Kimpton, then President of the University of Chicago, was in the chair. Benton, Bob Hutchins, Jacques Maritain, and I were other speakers on that occasion. I will have reason later to quote from what Jacques Maritain and Bob Hutchins had to say about the *Syntopicon*, which I had invented, edited, and for which I wrote 102 essays on the great ideas.

Kip Fadiman's speech on that occasion was a masterpiece of witty pertinence and impertinence. It was addressed to an audience that included, among other dignitaries, those who had, by their purchase of a special printing of the set called the Patrons Edition, enabled Encyclopaedia Britannica, Inc., to go to press at a time when the company had spent all it could afford on preparatory editorial work.

Chairman Kimpton, after telling the audience that illness had

3. Frank Greenberg to Mortimer Adler, April 14, 1977. I have placed as Item A in the Notes appended to this chapter excerpts from the speech I gave at the forty-fifth anniversary dinner of the Law School, Class of 1932.

prevented the Director of the Institute for Advanced Study at Princeton, New Jersey, Dr. Robert Oppenheimer, from being with us, introduced Clifton Fadiman with these words:

> Mr. Clifton Fadiman has an extensive experience with modern publishing and contemporary writing. He has been an editor of Simon and Schuster, literary critic of *The New Yorker* and is a member of the Book-of-the-Month Club Board and literary editor of *Holiday.*

I have placed Mr. Fadiman's speech as Item B in the Notes appended to this chapter. Let me add here one other memory. Kip was invited to address Britannica's sales managers assembled in Phoenix, Arizona, in 1965. On that occasion, he delivered one of his wittiest orations, in the course of which he told the managers that they earned much more on their commissions from selling the great books than their authors earned by writing them. I have placed a short excerpt from this speech as Item C in the Notes to this chapter.

NOTES TO CHAPTER 3

Item A

Excerpts of Speech Given at the Forty-fifth Anniversary Dinner, Class of 1932—The University of Chicago Law School, 1977*

... I forget which quarter of the academic year, 1930–1931, I came to bat at the Law School, but I cannot forget the auspices under which I first became engaged in its curriculum. Sometime that year Judge [Edward] Hinton and I offered a seminar for seniors on the law of evidence. Dear old Judge Hinton, who was from Missouri in more ways than one, did not know what he was getting into when he

*Adler, "Reflections on the Law School in the '30's," *The Law Alumni Journal*, The University of Chicago Law School, Fall 1977, pp. 37–40. Reprinted by permission.

accepted that assignment. Professor [Jerome] Michael and I were just in the process of completing a large treatise on *The Nature of Judicial Proof*, a book that employed the kind of symbolization then stylish in logic to formulate the distinctions and inferences involved in the trial of an issue of fact. During the seminar, I would go to the blackboard and cover it with the hieroglyphics of my trade as a logician, while Judge Hinton would sit back smiling his approval of generalizations to which he would never have given his consent if he had fully understood the significance of the symbols on the board. From time to time, he would interrupt my flight into the blue-sky of abstractions by bringing the seminar back to earth with an earthy story of a case he had tried when he was on the bench in Missouri.

During my first year at Chicago, I did not have a seat on the Law Faculty. My acquiring one resulted from the blowup in the philosophy department, with university-wide repercussions, which had been precipitated by the unorthodox initiative of Bob Hutchins, prompted by me, to alter the character of the philosophy department by new appointments. To quiet things down, Hutchins was compelled to acquiesce in my withdrawal from the philosophy department and to abstain from further appointments to it. A waif on a storm-tossed academic sea, I was rescued from drowning by Dean [Harry] Bigelow and his colleagues on the Law Faculty, who offered me their hospitality. It was thus that I became Associate Professor of the Philosophy of Law, a post that had not previously existed in the Law School and that was created to provide respectable academic status for me.

During the academic year, 1931–1932, I continued to teach a great books seminar in the college with Bob Hutchins and a seminar on the law of evidence with Judge Hinton, but, in view of my newly acquired title, I thought it was incumbent upon me to give a lecture course on the philosophy of law, open to seniors who had completed enough bread-and-butter courses to have some free time for inessentials. The course was scheduled for the winter quarter. I had never taught the philosophy of law before. In fact, at the time I put the course in the catalogue, I was as ignorant of the subject as the students who registered to take it in January, 1932. So far as I can remember, I had never even read a single treatise on jurisprudence or a book on the philosophy of law.

Compiling a bibliography of the subject, I quickly collected the books on the shelf of my study and, somewhat more slowly, started to plough through them. They were, for the most part, works written in the 19th and 20th centuries, mainly Anglo-American, with some smattering of continental writers. The more I read, the more bewildered I became. I stumbled over a terrain the topography of which remained hidden from my eyes. Wandering in a fog, I made little progress toward an outline of the course of lectures I would have to begin giving right after the end of the Christmas recess.

Throughout December, my failure to come to grips with the subject left me in a state of panic. I kept on reading and making voluminous notes; I even assembled the notes in neat piles on my desk; but the few ideas I then had in my head about the philosophy of law were in chaotic disarray. I remember vividly awakening one night in a cold sweat from a nightmare in which I had opened the window of my study on the fourteenth floor of 5400 Harper Avenue, had thrown the piles of notes on my desk out the window, and had then dived suicidally through them to the street below.

The members of the class of 1932, now celebrating the forty-fifth anniversary of their graduation from the Law School, will, I hope, remember that I survived that nightmare to give a course on the philosophy of law which I found as instructive as they did, for we were exploring that subject together for the first time. They will also remember the pivotal role played by Thomas Aquinas in the organization and illumination of the subject matter being considered. At the eleventh hour, when I was just about ready to give up in despair and petition the Dean to cancel my course, my prayers for help were answered by my pulling volumes of the *Summa Theologica* from the shelf and discovering that Aquinas had written a treatise on law which put the whole subject in clear perspective for me, raised most of the significant questions that a philosopher of law should think about, and provided most of the answers, as well as dealt with many persuasive objections to each of the answers that Aquinas himself espoused.†

The number of students enrolled in the course were few enough to allow for extended discussion of points raised in the lectures. The

† A little less than ten years later, I wrote and published an essay which raised challenging questions about Aquinas' *Treatise on Law*. I was now a much more critical reader of Aquinas and was unhesitant in calling attention to his equivocal use of the word "law," for human, natural, and divine law. See "A Question About Law," in *Essays in Thomism* (1941).

seniors in that class were not only extremely bright but very argumentative. Some of them aided my own learning of the subject, in gratitude for which I rewarded them with grades on their final examinations that shocked the Law School faculty and almost led to my being court-martialled for conduct unbecoming a law teacher. No one had told me that 80 or 85 was the highest grade conceivable on a final examination, and so I handed out a number of grades over 90 and two, I recall, in the neighborhood of 100. . . .

In the discussions of the curriculum which occurred during meetings of the Law Faculty, my voice expressed a point of view that Hutchins and I shared, and that point of view elicited sympathetic responses from such younger members of the faculty as Sheldon Tefft, Wilber Katz, Charles Gregory, and Malcolm Sharp. Their elders, Dean Bigelow and Professors Bogart and Ernst Freund were a little more skeptical or, shall I say, hesitant about drastic departures from the traditional content of a law curriculum, but they never allowed their doubts to shut the discussion down. It broadened to consider the kind of courses that should occupy students in the year just before entering the Law School—the so-called pre-law options in the third year of the College. I proposed that the Law School itself should develop its own pre-law course for students in the college, that it should be taught by members of the Law Faculty, that it should concentrate on the liberal disciplines of reading and writing, speaking and listening (the traditional liberal arts of the Trivium—grammar, logic, and rhetoric), and that full credit for one whole year should be attached to the taking of this single course.

I cannot remember how long it took to get the Law Faculty to approve this proposal or how the approval was finally won. All I remember is that Malcolm Sharp agreed to conduct the "Trivium course" with me, that we engaged two young men, William Gorman and James Martin, to assist us as tutors, and that the four of us constituted the teaching staff that took on about twenty students who were intending to enter the Law School. This was the only course they registered for that year. Malcolm Sharp and I conducted seminars for eight hours each week—four hours, morning and afternoon, on Tuesday, and four again on Wednesday; and the students met individually with their tutors at other hours on Thursday or Friday to discuss papers they had been assigned to write.

. . . I think I learned more about how to read a book in the three years of teaching the Trivium course than from any other experience in my life. Most of the rules of reading that I later set forth and explained in *How to Read a Book* emerged from the sessions of the Trivium course.

An educational success in almost every other way, not only for the students but for Malcolm Sharp, me, and our two tutors, the Trivium course failed in one signal respect. It had been intended to prepare students for the Law School; but more than half of the students had become so excited about the study of ideas or the reading of books, and the liberal disciplines involved in these activities, that they decided not to go to the Law School after they finished the Trivium, and chose instead to go on into the graduate school for further work in literature, philosophy, history, or the social sciences. However, those who did enter the Law School distinguished themselves there as students, and some of them later became members of the faculty. . . .

Item B

Excerpts from Speech by Clifton Fadiman in Celebration of Publication of the First Edition of *Great Books of the Western World*, Waldorf-Astoria Hotel, New York, 1952[‡]

Perhaps some of you, reasonably enough, are baffled by my appearance in this company. I find it bewildering myself. May I hasten to say that I am not a Founder. As an old book reviewer, it has never occurred to me to pay anything, much less $500, for a new publication. Furthermore, not only am I not a Founder, but I am a radio and television performer, and you may well ask, therefore, how I happen to be sitting in the same galley with great scholars such as Professor Maritain, with distinguished public servants such as Senator Benton. It is a bit like presenting on the same stage a Sir Laurence Olivier and a dancing bear. For sometime the gentlemen who are running this dinner have been importuning me to speak to you. I think what they had in mind, inasmuch as dignity and scholarship had already been arranged for, was to balance the program. At any rate, the dancing bear appears before you in two other guises tonight. First, as an ex-publisher, and second, as a useful museum exhibit.

‡ Reprinted by permission of the author.

As an ex-publisher, I must be careful about what I say, because I believe my old boss, Founder M. Lincoln Schuster, is in the audience. He is one of the few publishers who can afford to buy books these days as well as sell them.

As an ex-publisher, I should like to pay tribute, if I may use the language of the circus, to one of the most monumental publishing achievements of this or any age. The issuance of a set of Great Books, with its appended *Syntopicon*, is a landmark in the history of publishing. In historical importance, it is comparable perhaps with the first English printings of William Caxton in the 15th century, or with the completion in 1765 of the French Encyclopédie of Diderot and his associates.

While I have the greatest respect for the high office held by the junior Senator from Connecticut, I will lay odds that in 500 years (Great Books readers do not care to deal in periods of time smaller than that) the Senator will be remembered less for his political career, however eminent, than as the man whose courage and vision made possible what is symbolized by this evening. Some day, there will be told the whole story of the truly epic struggle to publish the Great Books.

Nine years passed, you remember, before the walls of Troy fell to the hands of the Greeks. And nine years passed in battle and turmoil before these fifty-four volumes could be delivered into your hands. During the darkest days of those nine years (around 1947, I think it was), some of the more cautious of Senator Benton's business associates wearied of the strife, and understandably so. They paled with a pallor quite properly known as editorial pallor at the vast expenses that were piling up. They paled and they quailed at the seeming impossibility of ever selling these books, even if they should get published. During those days it was Bill Benton who said, "Damn the budget; full speed ahead."

Well, to date, something like 2 million dollars—if there is anything like 2 million dollars—has been laid out on this daring investment in the future. In that future Senator Benton had faith, and as a minor exfunctionary of the trade I salute in our host a great publisher.

But I am here tonight not merely as a liberated galley slave, but, as already mentioned, a useful museum exhibit, or perhaps salesman's sample. Between you and me, your other speakers are not really in a good position to endorse the Great Books. Why not? Well, because they don't really need them. Dr. Hutchins and Dr. Adler were born in a state of advanced education, and I feel sure the same is true of the other gentlemen at this table. The point is not what the Great Books can do for them, but what they can do for people like me—that is, for those millions of Americans who have triumphantly escaped illiteracy without ever achieving true mental cultivation.

In so far as the Great Books have helped me to reduce the yawning gap stretching between the analphabetic and the educated man, I stand here as a kind of walking testimonial. I stand here to endorse that patent medicine compounded by seventy-one pharmacists, from Homer to Freud. I hereby state that this medicine, while no panacea, has made me feel like a new man. My mental backaches are much relieved, I no longer suffer from pains in the dialectic, and when I get up at night it is only for the purpose of consulting the *Syntopicon*. My acquaintance with the Great Books began thirty years ago. I was introduced to them at Columbia College, soon perhaps to be known as the Mother of Presidents. I was introduced to them by that noble educator, the late John Erskine, the only begetter of all the Great Books courses. At least two of my dearly beloved teachers are here tonight—Mark Van Doren, in the audience, and at this table the inventor of that marvelous intellectual instrument, the *Syntopicon,* Dr. Mortimer J. Adler.

Please do not imagine—I doubt that this has occurred to you—that I have read all of these 443 books. However, I have read some of them, and in the course of the three decades since my inoculation I have read some of them many times. For example, after a steady book reviewer's diet of the mediocre, I have often found Dante useful as a purge.

What have the Great Books and their champions, particularly Robert Hutchins and Mortimer Adler, done for a willing but not exceptional mind, to wit, my own? I shall mention only two things, but they are, I believe, the most important.

First, they have lifted from my imagination the curse of the contemporary. I am persuaded by these Great Books that we were not given our lives that we might be citizens only of that narrowly bounded country called today, situated, of course, in the topical zone.

A man and his newspaper are not soon parted. There lies one of the weaknesses of our times. Janus, you remember, the old Roman doorway god, owned two faces, one swiveled to the past, and the other fronting the future. We too are often Januses, one face turned to yesterday's headlines, the other to tomorrow's. Our brains have been hand-turned to house vast millennial phantasies, but how many of us have allowed them to be hammered thin on the flatbed of the newspaper printing press? So, no matter how rude may be my understanding of them, the Great Books have enlarged my living-space.

As the shell lifted to the ear seems to carry in its curves the rumor of the seas of the whole world, so this brief shelf of books, placed against the mind, makes audible to me the living voices of 3000 years of my civilization. He who has once heard these voices is forever freed from the thralldom of the current, and breathes to his last breath a purer and a larger air. Not that he becomes a passive dweller in the past; not so, for these books do not close doors but open them. They do not so much compel us to look back, though that is not a bad thing to do, as to look up, to look up and see where once we saw a ceiling the vast sky of possible ideas.

All great writers are contemporaries. The point is not that they have receded into their common past, but that we have not yet advanced into their common future. The Great Books, then, are a magic wand whose touch has broken for me that trance of the transient in which so many of us are frozen.

But they are also a magic wand to bear me away from the doldrums of despair. Today there are those who, like the Communists, are resolved to jettison the entire Western and Christian tradition because it makes nonsense of their vision of a closed history and a static state. And there are those, like Professor Maritain's eminent countryman, Jean-Paul Sartre, who believes, in his own phrase, that "man's long dialogue is coming to an end."

I think we will not vanquish either the iron faith of the Communists or the leaden faith of the defeatists unless we deploy in the struggle the armament of a profoundly felt and superior creed of our own. And I cannot see on what that creed can ultimately found itself unless it be the whole Scriptures, sacred and profane, of our Western world, that long dialogue, which, I trust, will never come to an end. For me, therefore, these books, often apparently so dry or so difficult, become, when studied to the point and very edge of love, a mighty fortress against the invasion of the barbarians.

This is my personal testimony, and yet I cannot help thinking that it is an echo, however faint and unclear, of your testimony. You who have bought the Great Books, you who have sought the Great Books, and you who have taught the Great Books, are taking upon yourselves part of the magnificent burden, the burden of preserving, as did the monks of early Christendom, through another darkening age, the visions, the laughter, the ideas, the deep cries of anguish, the great eurekas of revelation that make up our patent to the title of civilized man.

Item C

Excerpts from Speech by Clifton Fadiman Before the Division and District Managers of Encyclopaedia Britannica for the Publication of the First Edition of *Great Books of the Western World*, Phoenix, Arizona, 1965[§]

. . . Way back in 1923 when I was a Columbia undergraduate, Dr. Adler was a young instructor who had not yet learned that the road to success lay in *selling* books, not reading them. By the way, Dr. Adler is the only professor in recorded history who got his Ph.D. without ever getting his B.A. He never got a B.A. because he couldn't pass his swimming test, which was a requirement in those days. Every time they threw him in the pool he sank like a stone. He kept this up for four years, never varying his performance. Since those days he's improved. He's become less boyish but more buoyant. Anybody who can keep afloat for twenty-five years working for Encyclopaedia Britannica Incorporated has learned the art of self-preservation. If you want to stay above water at 425 North Michigan, you've got to be made out of cork.

By the way, just as Mortimer never got his B.A., I never got my M.A. I attended classes but never wrote my thesis. I remember my mother, who had only a vague idea of how the American educational system worked, reproaching me for my negligence: "You should get your degree," she said, "Why should you let Columbia keep it?"

Well, back in Columbia forty-two years ago I was a student in what was called the Honors Course. This was the *first* of all the Great

[§] Reprinted by permission of the author.

Books classes; and to that class you guys owe a great debt, because this very evening is a logical sequence of that Great Books class of almost half a century ago. For two years, once a week, we met and read and discussed Homer to Freud under the guidance of two instructors. Dr. Adler was one of these instructors. It was his first responsible teaching job, and his career partly depended on it. Well, for a young fellow he was brilliant.

Naturally that irritated me. I was only two years his junior, I felt sure I knew more than he did, and besides I could swim. I saw no reason why *he* should be teaching *me* rather than the other way around. My duty was clear: to make his life intolerable. Like Socrates I became a gadfly to Dr. Adler. So I did my homework with great care. I got so I could skim the cream off Aristotle while I was scraping plates in the cafeteria.

Whenever the class met I came loaded with questions that would have driven Plato crazy, and in those days Dr. Adler was no Plato. I cited references Adler had never heard of. I invented authorities *no one* had ever heard of. Well, after three weeks of this I had reduced Adler to a quivering jelly. I had him at my mercy. *He* had to be dignified, and I didn't. The poor fellow didn't dare open his mouth without first throwing an imploring look at me. You can imagine what being afraid to open his mouth would do to a man like Dr. Adler.

At the end of the fourth class it was too much for him. He took me aside, told me I was ruining his life by revealing his ignorance, and proposed a deal. Well, after all, he was young, and he appealed to my better nature, of which I had a token quantity. Finally I agreed to consult with him in advance before each class and during the session ask only questions to which he already knew the answers. He agreed to do the same for me. This worked out very well, and we have been close friends ever since, pretty much on the same basis.

This was one of the first evidences of Dr. Adler's extraordinary organizing ability. I could give you other illustrations. For example, it is obvious that Dr. Adler—just take a look at his beautiful wife—is extremely attractive to women. Back in our college days he was just as attractive. . . . He had a great many girls who were crazy about high I.Q.'s. They would do practically anything for Mortimer if he would only talk to them. Well, his involvements got so complicated that he was forced to use the organizing ability to which I have referred. He would parcel out the girls among his friends, of whom I was one. Each of us had the duty of seeing these girls regularly, spending many hours with them and talking to them about Mortimer, describing his charms, abilities, and future prospects as persuasively as we could. . . .

Well, let's get back to the story of the Great Books. A couple of years after I was graduated—I think it was in 1927—a group of Columbia instructors and graduates began to teach the Great Books to adults throughout the city. . . . There were just twelve of us teachers, twelve poor but earnest disciples. Like nuns, or Harlem cops, we worked in pairs. You may be interested to know that at one time Dr. Adler's colleague was the Communist courier, Whittaker Chambers. Adler and Chambers, though they read and taught the same books, drew different conclusions from them. Chambers decided to destroy the capitalist system. Adler made the system his junior partner. . . .

Well, for a couple of years Mortimer and I lived on the Great Books, getting $15 a week. It had not as yet occurred to anybody that you could make *more* than $15 a week out of them. Some years later, however, Senator Benton, Dr. Hutchins, and Dr. Adler got the ingenious idea of putting the great writers of the Western world between a set of covers and persuading the American family that there could be no true happiness until these fifty-four volumes were on the library shelf, perhaps even partially paid for. . . .

I used to visit Dr. Adler frequently during those agonizing years when he and his staff were preparing the *Syntopicon*. . . . To get the *Syntopicon* together, however, required live bodies who had to be fed. Every six months or so Dr. Adler would approach Senator Benton and explain that he'd run out of money. The Senator, who likes to see things through, would reach down into his right-hand pants pocket where he keeps his loose change, and hand Adler another $100,000. Adler would hire a few more starving academics and keep the pot boiling. When the money was exhausted, he would approach the Senator again, always with the same plea: "Bill, you can't let Aristotle down. You can't welch on Sigmund Freud. You can't be a piker with Dante looking you straight in the eye." . . .

Great Books of the Western World, mainly because of the *Syntopicon*, is absolutely unique in its field. As W. C. Fields once said about sex, "There may be some things that are better and some that are worse, but there's nothing exactly like it." There's nothing exactly like the *Syntopicon* either. . . .

PART TWO

The Years After 1976

CHAPTER 4

EDUCATIONAL REFORM: THE PAIDEIA PROJECT

1

I have spent a good part of my life in educational reform, either as a beneficiary of such reforms, as at Columbia University when I was a student there, or as a planner and promoter of them at the University of Chicago when I was on the faculty, or since then as part of the work of the Institute for Philosophical Research; and in the latter connection especially the Paideia Project, in which the Institute took the lead.

All these various activities in the sphere of educational reform can be divided in a number of ways. Some concentrated on the improvement of collegiate education or on the restoration of general, liberal education in our undergraduate colleges, most of which have become places of highly specialized training with an eye on its usefulness in the occupations or professions into which their graduates might go. Some focused on basic schooling from kindergarten through the twelfth grade, mainly in the public school system of this country.

They can also be divided by reference to the character of the activity in which I was engaged. Except for a relatively short time at the University of Chicago, much of my activity consisted in writing essays that called for the reform of schools and colleges.[1]

1. The titles of these essays will be found in the bibliography, appended to this book, for the years 1939–1976. Many of these are reproduced in *Reforming Education*, edited by Geraldine Van Doren, and published 1988 (see especially Chapters 1–17).

In contrast to writing about reforms to be undertaken, my activity at the University of Chicago and in the promotion of the New Program at St. John's College (Annapolis, Maryland), as well as in its offshoots at St. Mary's College (Moraga, California), and at the University of Notre Dame (Notre Dame, Indiana), involved dealing with institutions, teachers, and educational administrators, and suffering all the hurly-burly of practical life. One can stay in one's ivory tower while writing about educational reform; not so in doing something to bring about the desired improvements.

When I left the University of Chicago in 1952 to establish the Institute for Philosophical Research, my resolution was to devote a major portion of my energies to writing philosophical books, along with the work on the great books and the great ideas that I was doing for Britannica. It was not until the 1980s that I came down from the ivory tower onto the streets to confront educational institutions and their personnel in order to promote the Paideia Project for a radical reform of basic schooling in the United States.

In an earlier book I have written at length about the origin of the New Program at St. John's College. Its seeds were sown in the meetings of the Committee on the Liberal Arts at the University of Chicago in 1936–1937.[2] Here I would like to pay tribute to the extraordinary innovations made by Scott Buchanan in the construction of the New Program at St. John's, which began in the autumn of 1937; and I would also like to underline the connection between the New Program at St. John's College and the development of the Paideia Project in the 1980s.

2

In one sense, John Erskine is the grandfather of the New Program at St. John's. He was greatly influenced by Professor George Edward Woodberry, his own teacher, but it was he who originated the great books seminars at Columbia in 1921. It was he who first constructed a list of the great works in Western literature from Homer to Freud. But that, in my view, was not his chief contribution. It was the "invention" of the undergraduate seminar.

2. See *Philosopher at Large*, Chapter 10, especially pp. 208–209.

I have put the word "invention" in quotes to stress the fact that seminars pre-existed the great books seminars conducted by Professor Erskine at Columbia in the twenties. They occurred in the German universities of the nineteenth century, but the students who participated in them were there to do research on portions of the professor's current work; they were being trained as apprentices. In their attempt to model themselves after the German universities, the institutions of higher learning in the United States also established seminars for their Ph.D. candidates, in which the professors guided students in their own research for the Ph.D. But the use of the word "seminar" for a round-table discussion of a book that the undergraduate students had all read was truly an invention on Erskine's part; and with it the introduction of the Socratic method of teaching—by questioning rather than by lecturing.

After the New Program was established at St. John's College, the many articles about it in the public prints referred to it as "the great books college," for two great books seminars a week for four years were central in the New Program. Scott Buchanan cannot be credited with that curricular innovation. Scott became acquainted with great books seminars when he and I first became friends at Columbia University in the late twenties. He joined me in proposing the idea of great books seminars for adults to Everett Dean Martin, then Director of the People's Institute in New York, for the establishment of which Martin succeeded in getting a grant from the Carnegie Corporation. He as well as I took on the task of moderating one of these adult seminars in 1927–1929. When Scott Buchanan and Stringfellow Barr came from the University of Virginia to the Committee on the Liberal Arts in Chicago, they already were well informed about great books seminars. They acknowledged the primacy of such seminars in the reform of collegiate education.

The main contribution made by Buchanan to the great books seminars in the New Program at St. John's was the expansion of the reading list to include the great books of mathematics and the natural sciences along with those of imaginative literature, and works in history, philosophy, and theology. But that was by no means his chief contribution. It was rather his insistence that all members of the faculty become generalists, themselves becoming competent as liberal artists, regardless of what their previous academic specialty had been and regardless of what had been the subject of their Ph.D.

To achieve this end, he abolished all departments and professorial titles at St. John's College. Every member of the faculty was simply called a Fellow and Tutor of the College. Every member of the faculty was obliged to teach the whole program. The whole program was required for all students as the indispensable means to their general, liberal education; hence, it should be required for all teachers as a means to the same end.

The whole program consisted of three kinds of teaching and learning experiences: (1) the Socratically conducted great books seminars; (2) three tutorials, in which students were coached in mathematics; in the procedures of laboratory science; and in the acquisition of foreign languages; and (3) one lecture a week for the entire college, after which the students engage the lecturer in discussion of its themes or theses for an hour or two.

As the New Program developed, other elements were introduced, such as senior essays, oral examinations, don rags, and preceptorials, in which extremely difficult books were studied more intensively than their consideration in a two-hour seminar permitted. But after more than fifty years, the tripartite structure of the curriculum indicated above remains intact.

Anyone even slightly acquainted with the colleges in this country, presented with this picture of the New Program at St. John's College, will realize at once how difficult—in fact, how impossible—it was to try to persuade their presidents and their professors to adopt or imitate the St. John's model. The imitation of St. John's at St. Mary's College and at Notre Dame was limited to a small, select group of students and faculty—a college within a college. The only exception was Thomas Aquinas College where, as at St. John's, Buchanan's radical innovations were adopted, with some modifications, for the whole student body and the whole faculty.

The baleful influence of the Ph.D. degree as a certificate needed for appointment to a college faculty is the reason why almost all American colleges are thoroughly inhospitable to even a small sampling of the New Program at St. John's. From the forties through the seventies, I was invited by curriculum committees of undergraduate colleges to meet with them to discuss the reinstatement of some trace of general education into their catalogues of courses.

I would start off by saying that I did not expect them to abolish all their majors and minors, their areas of concentration, and their elective system. I would then add the proposal that they require one course for all students, to run for four years, meeting once a week for two hours, in which the students would read great or good books in all fields of subject matter and discuss them with their teachers in Socratically conducted seminars.

After presenting this proposal, the first question I would be asked was: what books do you have in mind for all members of the faculty to teach? I would answer by enumerating ten or twenty great books authors and the titles of their books, being sure that they represented a fair sampling of different chronological epochs and different academic subject matters.

When I had done this, the outcry from the professors present was always the same. "You cannot expect us to do that," they would say. "Why?" I would ask. Their reply was: "Because most of those books are not in my field—the narrow field in which I took my Ph.D., which prepared me to give didactic instruction in the specialized courses I was hired by this college to teach."

They had no interest in becoming generally educated themselves, nor any inclination to abandon their specialties for even a small portion of their time in order to take part in the general education of the students in their college. I should add that they also had no interest in any method of teaching other than the one to which they were accustomed—using their notes to give lectures. Their own education had not given them any preparation for Socratic as opposed to didactic teaching.

3

Readers will soon perceive how the New Program at St. John's College underlies the principles and the motivation of the Paideia Project for the reform of basic schooling in the United States. Two things in particular are responsible for my own part in the generation of the Paideia Project.

One was my experience of so many failures in trying to persuade colleges to introduce great books seminars and Socratic teaching, in order to reinstate a little bit of general education into their curriculums. I saw no possibility in the foreseeable future of getting the colleges to become the agencies of general, liberal education. If future citizens were to be given that kind of education, which I thought prerequisite for the intelligent discharge of their civic duties, then that would have to be done before they went to college, or after they graduated from college, or better, at both times in their lives.

The other way in which the New Program at St. John's College inspired the Paideia Project was its tripartite structure: great books seminars, coaching tutorials, and lectures—in descending order of importance. Here were the three kinds of teaching that became central in the Paideia proposal.

As I now look back at the essays I wrote in the four decades after the New Program was established at St. John's College, I can discern how deep in my own past thinking were the roots of the Paideia Project when it first emerged in the late seventies. I wish to call attention here especially to a lecture that I gave in 1941, entitled "The Order of Learning," reproduced in a book of mine already referred to, *Reforming Education*. That lecture looks backward and forward—backward to the basic ideas underlying the New Program at St. John's and forward to the basic ideas formulated in *The Paideia Proposal*, written and published in 1982. However, other factors were at work in the formation of the group of teachers and educators that I assembled in 1978 to think about what must be done to reform the public schools of the United States.

4

In the twenty-six years between 1952 and 1978, I gave not a moment's thought to the deplorable state of the nation's schools. During that time, all my energies were consumed by other things: in the fifties by the first stage of work at the Institute for Philosophical Research—the staffing of the Institute and the researches of that staff, eventuating in the Institute's first major production, the two-volume treatise on *The Idea of Freedom*, and its subsequent production of four more dialectical studies on the ideas of progress, love, justice, and happiness.

In the sixties, after my return to Chicago from San Francisco, I added to the philosophical work of the Institute, the enormous task of planning and helping to execute the enterprise of producing a fifteenth edition of the *Encyclopaedia Britannica*, then called Britannica 3 because of its tripartite structure involving a *Propaedia*, a *Micropaedia*, and a *Macropaedia*. In that enterprise, the planning and execution of the *Propaedia*'s outline of knowledge was as massive an undertaking as, in earlier years, had been the task of producing the *Syntopicon* of the great ideas to accompany the *Great Books of the Western World*.

In the middle seventies, I was asked by the Aspen Institute whether I would be willing to conduct a week-long seminar for young people, with some of the readings used in the Aspen Executive Seminar, which I will describe later in Chapter 6. I agreed to do so. Ruth B. Love, who was then Superintendent of Schools in Oakland, California, happened to be in Aspen at the time. She audited that seminar and was so impressed by what she observed that she invited me to come to Oakland to conduct a similar seminar for seniors at the Skyline High School there.

That seminar was not only a memorable experience for me but, so far as I can remember, it was my first experience of teaching in the public schools. I did not realize then what that experience foreboded for my becoming involved with educational reform at the level of basic schooling. But I was soon to find out.

In 1977, I had lunch with Jacques Barzun, who had been a student of mine in the college at Columbia University and had become a lifelong friend. *A Nation at Risk* had just been published by the U.S. Department of Education. Jacques and I discussed that report. We agreed with its indictment of the failure of the schools and with its appraisal of the seriousness of the plight the United States faced in the future, if that failure were not remedied. But we dismissed as inadequate the measures proposed for correcting the situation.

The gloom we obviously shared led me to ask Jacques whether we should not try to do something about it. What can we do? he queried. My reply was: let us form a small group of teachers and educators whom we know to be sufficiently like-minded about the need for drastic educational reform, and have them meet for the purpose of coming up with a better solution of the problem than the one outlined in *A Nation at Risk*.

To do this required some financing to pay the expenses of such meetings. The John D. and Catherine T. MacArthur Foundation had just come into existence. Their son, Roderick, was quarreling with its first Board of Trustees about his idea for MacArthur Fellowships. Rod, who had been a student of mine at the University of Chicago, asked me to help him persuade his colleagues on the Board to adopt his plan. I agreed to do so, and in return asked him to try to get the foundation to finance the meetings of the little group that Jacques Barzun and I had in mind. Rod attended all the meetings of the original Paideia Group, though he contributed little to the formulation of the plan. The prime contributors were Jacques Barzun, Clifton Fadiman, Richard Hunt, Theodore Sizer, Dennis Gray, and Alonzo Crim.

With two successive grants, amounting to a total of $150,000, we had the funds needed to invite persons to join the group and hold conferences at the Institute in Chicago, beginning in 1978 and continuing in the three years to follow. I cannot remember how the word "paideia" came to be used as the name for the group and its project of educational reform. One of the meanings of that Greek word is the general learning that everyone should have. Without being aware of that significance, many persons have had contact with the word, for it is to be found as one of the two roots in the English word "encyclo-pedia." The two roots together signify the comprehensive circle of general learning.

The Paideia Group, as it came to be called, had the following membership in the years between 1979 and 1981.[3]

3. The members of this group met frequently in the years 1979–1982. They wrote position papers and supplied ancillary ideas and formulations. In particular, I owe a special debt to Jacques Barzun for the work he did in editing my first draft of *The Paideia Proposal* (1982). As edited by Jacques Barzun, the other members of the group were willing to have their names attached to it, acknowledging that it was written on their behalf.

Mortimer J. Adler *Chairman*
Director, Institute for Philosophical Research; Chairman, Board of Editors, Encyclopaedia Britannica

Jacques Barzun, former Provost, Columbia University; Literary Adviser, Charles Scribner's Sons

Otto Bird, former head, General Program of Liberal Studies, University of Notre Dame

Leon Botstein, President Bard College; President, Simon's Rock of Bard College

Ernest L. Boyer, President, The Carnegie Foundation for the Advancement of Teaching, Washington, D.C.

Nicholas L. Caputi, Principal, Skyline High School, Oakland, California

Douglass Cater, Senior Fellow, Aspen Institute for Humanistic Studies

Donald Cowan, former President, University of Dallas; Fellow, Dallas Institute of Humanities and Cultures

Alonzo A. Crim, Superintendent, Atlanta Public Schools, Atlanta, Georgia

Clifton Fadiman, Author and critic

Dennis Gray, Deputy Director, Council for Basic Education, Washington, D.C.

Richard Hunt, Senior Lecturer and Director of the Andrew W. Mellon Faculty Fellowships Program, Harvard University

Ruth B. Love, General Superintendent of Schools, Chicago Board of Education

James Nelson, Director, Wye Institute, Inc., Queenstown, Maryland

James O'Toole, Professor of Management, Graduate School of Business Administration, University of Southern California

Theodore T. Puck, President and Director, Eleanor Roosevelt Institute for Cancer Research, Inc., Denver; Professor of Biochemistry, Biophysics, and Genetics, University of Colorado

Adolph W. Schmidt, former Chairman, Board of Visitors and Governors of St. John's College, Annapolis and Santa Fe

Adele Simmons, President, Hampshire College

Theodore R. Sizer, Chairman, A Study of High Schools; former Headmaster, Phillips Academy—Andover

Charles Van Doren, Associate Director, Institute for Philosophical Research; Vice President/Editorial, Encyclopaedia Britannica, Inc.

Geraldine Van Doren, Senior Fellow, Institute for Philosophical Research; Secretary, Paideia Project

John Van Doren, Senior Fellow, Institute for Philosophical Research; Executive Editor, *The Great Ideas Today*

We met two or three times a year with occasional visits by persons who were not members of the group. In the course of those conferences, each lasting a day or two, three points became dominant in our thought about school reform. One was a commitment to democratizing the public schools of this country. This involved a genuine understanding of equal educational opportunity, to which everyone paid lip service but which called for the same quality, not just the same quantity, of schooling for all the children in attendance at our schools. This meant a completely required program of studies, with no electives in our secondary schools.

A second controlling point in our discussions was our recognition of the three kinds of learning that should occur in the twelve years of compulsory schooling: (1) the acquisition of organized knowledge in a number of basic subjects, (2) the development of intellectual skills, all of them skills involved in the process of learning, and (3) the enlargement of the understanding of fundamental ideas and issues.

The third point grew out of the second and merged with it; namely, the three kinds of teaching required for aiding and abetting the three kinds of learning: (1) didactic instruction or teaching by telling, (2) coaching or teaching by prescribing activities to be performed and practiced, and (3) the Socratic conduct of seminars, or teaching by questioning and by discussion.

A chart gradually took shape in which these two related triads of learning and teaching became visible to us on a blackboard in our conference room. There was little or no disagreement in the group about that diagram of the structure of sound schooling, so different from what actually goes on in the schools of this country. But agreement about these fundamental points left many other problems to be solved. About these, the members of the group did not see eye to eye. They were sufficiently like-minded about the general outline of what had to be done, but far from it about filling in the details.

In 1981, I arranged for an eight-day conference of the group, to be held in Aspen in September. On Saturday, the sixth day of the conference, having listened to all the pros and cons on the moot points of detail that had been vigorously discussed in the preceding five days, I drew up a list of all the matters at issue and distributed it to those present, with the request that over the weekend each person should indicate the points with which he or she agreed and the points with which they disagreed.

I asked to have these lists returned to me on Monday and told them that if sufficient agreement existed in the group, I would take the points agreed upon as the basis for writing a report to which they could all willingly be signatories. The upshot of this procedure turned out to be a large enough measure of agreement for the purpose stated. I was, therefore, left with the task of writing a short book of seventy-nine pages, entitled *The Paideia Proposal: An Educational Manifesto*. After several revisions, it was published in September of 1982.

I persuaded my associates in the Paideia Group to dedicate *The Paideia Proposal* to Horace Mann, John Dewey, and Robert M. Hutchins. In the middle of the last century Horace Mann had successfully fought for providing all the children of Massachusetts with at least six years of public schooling, and argued for this then radical step on the grounds that education was the indispensable factor in the movement toward establishing equality in this country and toward the realization of the democratic ideal in the postbellum years. Hutchins had pithily expressed one of the principles of Paideia in his statement that "the best education for the best is the best education for all."

But why John Dewey, they asked, knowing that in the thirties Hutchins and I had been articulate opponents of the progressive education that Teachers College at Columbia was promoting nationwide in the name of John Dewey.

My answer at the time was that Dewey's *Democracy and Education*, published in 1916, was the first clear clarion call for a democratic school system. It did not then exist in this country and, as a matter of fact, still does not. I added that since our controversy with Dewey in the thirties, and particularly after Dewey's little book entitled *Experience and Education*, in which he severely slapped the wrists of his followers at Teachers College for not properly understanding his views, I had come to appraise John Dewey's contribution as incompatible with the tenets of progressive education attributed to him.[4]

The members of the Paideia Group reluctantly approved the dedication of *The Paideia Proposal* to Dewey, along with Mann and Hutchins. Since 1982, when that book was published, written by me "on behalf of the members of the Paideia Group," I learned how right I was. My enlightenment came from a statement by Dewey in 1900, which Diane Ravitch of Teachers College brought to my attention in an article she had written for *The American Scholar* (Autumn 1984). In that article, she quoted the opening lines of a book written by Dewey in 1900, entitled *School and Society*, at a time when he had established the Laboratory School at the University of Chicago.[5]

At the beginning of *School and Society*, John Dewey wrote the following two sentences which, in my judgment, epitomize Paideia.

> What the best and wisest parent wants for his own child, that must the community want for all of its children. Any other ideal for our schools is narrow and unlovely; acted upon, it destroys our democracy.

Following this quotation from Dewey, Professor Ravitch went on to spell out the content of the schooling that the best and wisest parents would want for their own children and that a democratic community should want for all its children.

> The best and wisest parents . . . want their child to read and write fluently; to speak articulately; to listen carefully; to learn to par-

4. In his chapter on "God and the Professors," in which he was so adversely critical of my educational philosophy, Sidney Hook made exactly the same point about the difference between Dewey and his disciples at Teachers College, without acknowledging that in later years I had come around to the same view; nor does he seem to have had any awareness of the Paideia Project, its fundamental commitment to democracy, and its controlling principles that are thoroughly in harmony with Dewey's own educational precepts.

5. We should remember that, in 1900, most of the children in this country left school after six years, obtained working papers, and turned from learning to earning. In 1900, less than 10 percent of those eligible by age for high school went to high school.

> ticipate in the give-and-take of group discussion; to learn self-discipline and to develop the capacity for deferred gratification; to read and appreciate good literature; to have a strong knowledge of history, both of our own nation and of others; to appreciate the values of a free, democratic society; to understand science, mathematics, technology, and the natural world; to become engaged in the arts, both as a participant and as one capable of appreciating aesthetic excellence. . . . Such parents would also want a good program of physical education and [also] even competence in a foreign language. Presumably, these mythical best and wisest parents want their child to have some sense of possible occupation or profession, but it [is highly doubtful] that they would want their child to use school time for vocational training . . . in the pre-collegiate years.[6]

That explication of Dewey by Professor Ravitch provides a good summary of what children would learn in a Paideia school, even though it does not touch on the two triads of learning and teaching that lie at the center of *The Paideia Proposal* and that are graphically presented in the diagram in the notes at the end of this chapter.[7]

Underlying the differentiation of the three kinds of teaching and learning is a basic insight that ties them together. What is common to all three is their embodiment of the principle that all genuine learning involves mental activity on the part of the learner. Memorization of what teachers tell their students in classroom lectures is not genuine learning at all, precisely because it does not engage the mind in mental activity. When the learning is active, not passive, the primary cause is the activity of the learner's mind. Hence the teacher is at best a secondary and instrumental cause of the learning that takes place, working cooperatively with mental activity on the part of the learners.

6. Diane Ravitch, "A Good School," *The American Scholar*, Vol. 53, No. 4, Autumn 1984, p. 489. Copyright © 1984 by the author.

7. This diagram first appeared in Chapter 4 of *The Paideia Proposal* (p. 23). I reproduce it as Item A in the Notes appended to this chapter, where I also present the revision of it that the Paideia Council approved in 1990 at the time that the National Center for the Paideia Program was established at the University of North Carolina at Chapel Hill. At the same time, the members of the Paideia Council signed their names to a *Declaration of Paideia Principles*, to guide the future work of the National Center. That is also reproduced in the same Item A.

I have summarized this basic point by saying that no one ever learns anything *from* teachers, but only by mental activity *with* or *without* the help of teachers. I repeat that here in order to point out one other aspect in which John Dewey is a forerunner of Paideia. He said, over and over again, that all genuine learning is by doing, not by memorizing. This was misunderstood by his followers at Teachers College. In their formulation of what came to be called "the project method" in progressive schools, they misinterpreted Dewey's stress on *doing* by narrowly conceiving it as practical activity of some kind. In my judgment, what Dewey meant by *doing* includes every form of mental activity, whether or not it also involves action of some practical sort. What Dewey meant is that there is no genuine learning that does not actively engage the learner's mind in thinking.

5

Three things in *The Paideia Proposal* I would like to reproduce here because they convey the atmosphere that surrounded the publication of that book in 1982.

The first is the note "To Our Readers." It follows.

To Our Readers

THE PAIDEIA PROPOSAL is addressed to those Americans most concerned with the future of our public schools:

To Parents who believe that the decline in the quality of public schooling is damaging the futures of their children.

To Teachers troubled that the increasing time spent in keeping basic order in the classroom undermines the real business of schooling: to teach and to learn.

To School Boards frightened by the flight of middle-class children and youth to private and parochial schools.

To College Educators burdened by the increasing need to provide remedial education which detracts from their ability to offer a meaningful higher education.

To Elected Public Officials searching for ways to improve the quality of education without increasing the cost to taxpayers.

To Employers concerned about the effects on productivity of a work force lacking skills in reading, writing, speaking, listening, observing, measuring, and computing.

To Minority Groups angered by widening gulfs between the better educated and the poorly educated, and between the employed and the unemployed.

To Labor Leaders attempting to deal with workers who lack the skills to find jobs in the new high-technology industries.

To Military Leaders needing brainpower among the troops capable of coping with sophisticated weaponry.

To American Citizens alarmed by the prospects of a democracy in which a declining proportion of the people vote or endeavor to understand the great issues of our time.

Such deep and legitimate concerns are addressed by our proposal for the reform of public schooling in America. The reform we seek is designed to improve the opportunities of our youth, the prospects of our economy, and the viability of our democratic institutions. It must be achieved at the community level without resorting to a monolithic, national educational system. It must be, in Lincoln's words, of the people, by the people, and for the people.

The second is in a note addressed "To School Boards and School Administrators."

To School Boards and School Administrators:

YOU ASK: What should we do next Monday morning to get started on the Paideia reform of basic schooling?

WE ANSWER:

1. Be sure that in every school—from grade one to grade twelve—there are the three kinds of learning and the three kinds of teaching represented by the Three Columns and see that they interact with one another.
2. In all Three Columns—the acquirement of organized knowledge, the development of intellectual skills (skills of learning), and the

enlargement of the understanding of basic ideas and values—set standards of accomplishment that challenge both students and teachers to fulfill the high expectations you have for them.

3. Eliminate all the nonessentials from the school day, or, if retained, make them extracurricular activities.
4. Eliminate from the curriculum all training for specific jobs.
5. Introduce the study of a second language for a sufficient period of time to assure competence in its use.
6. Eliminate all electives from the course of study except the choice of the second language to be studied.
7. Use as much as possible of the school day's time for learning and teaching.
8. Restore homework, and home projects in the arts and sciences, in increasing amounts from grade one to grade twelve.
9. Devise, in your community, appropriate ways of ensuring adequate preschool preparation for those who need it.
10. Institute remedial instruction (in the Paideia sense of that term) for those who need it, either individually or in very small groups.

Do these ten things in a manner that suits the population of your school, both teachers and students; do these things by making your own choice of the materials to be used and your own organization of the course of study from grade to grade; do them with the three fundamental objectives of basic schooling always in mind, and you will have started on its way the reform of basic schooling upon which the prosperity of this country and the happiness of its citizens depends.

The third is the "Epilogue by a School Administrator," written by Ruth B. Love, a member of the Paideia Group who was at that time General Superintendent of Schools, Chicago Board of Education.

> THE PAIDEIA PROPOSAL is truly an educational manifesto. It is both philosophical and practical, at once sound in theory and workable in fact.
>
> This proposal could well be entitled "The Reform of Our Public Schools," for it addresses all the critical areas of concern about our school system.
>
> —Teaching children to think, and to use their minds in all forms of learning, is the pervasive concept.
>
> —Underscoring the belief that all children are educable, it affirms the right of all children in a democracy to equal educational opportunity—the opportunity to become educated human beings.
>
> —Recognizing the importance of the preschool years, it stresses the necessity of early tutelage to provide the nurturing so essential as preparation for formal schooling.
>
> —Differentiating between three basic kinds of learning and of instruction, it draws our attention to the need for a clearly defined and carefully structured curriculum. All educators can benefit from the reminder that the mind can be improved by
>
> acquisition of information and knowledge
> development of intellectual skills
> increase of understanding and insight.
>
> —The role of the teacher is the key to the entire reform, and an acknowledgment of the necessary development and continuous education of the teacher reflects the prominence of the teacher in the learning process.
>
> —Principals with power and knowledge corroborate other research that places the responsibility for good schools in the hands of good educational leaders.
>
> Without a doubt, the recommendations presented in this book give hope and guidance for all educators interested in progress. Follow-

ing this road map, so aptly designed, will help them to cure the many maladies of our beleaguered public schools.

It is often true that "there is nothing more difficult to carry out, more perilous to conduct, or more uncertain of success than to initiate a new order of things." A new order is what is called for. The *Paideia Proposal* provides public education in this country with both a challenge and an opportunity!

6

The Paideia Proposal was followed, in 1983, by a second book entitled *Paideia Problems and Possibilities*, subtitled "A Consideration of Questions Raised by *The Paideia Proposal.*" The members of the Paideia Group affixed their names to this book, though it was written by me. It was provoked initially by a symposium published in the *Harvard Educational Review*, in which educators from various universities registered their misunderstanding of and their objections to the educational reform that had been proposed. It contained a number of appendices. The first presented a list of reviews and critical notices that *The Paideia Proposal* had elicited, unfavorable as well as favorable, followed by a list of educational conferences and meetings at which Paideia had been presented and discussed, both prior to and after the publication of the first book; and a list of interviews about Paideia on television and radio.

The second appendix contained a statement by Ruth Love about how Paideia was being implemented in the Chicago schools, and a similar statement by Alonzo Crim, then Superintendent of the Atlanta Public Schools, also about the implementation of Paideia there.

The third appendix—the longest of the three—was written by Theodore Sizer, who had been Headmaster of the Phillips Academy—Andover, and was then carrying on a study of the American high school. Professor Sizer had not yet become a Professor of Education at Brown University, whence he organized his Coalition of Essential Schools, an educational reform movement at the secondary level only, one that Professor Sizer acknowledged embodies Paideia principles at its core. For that reason I have placed it in its entirety as Item B in the Notes to this chapter.

In the Preface to *Paideia Problems and Possibilities*, I announced the publication in 1984 of the third book to be entitled *The Paideia Program*, a collection of essays by members of the Paideia Group, which might serve as guidelines for developing the reforms proposed and outlined in the first two books. Below is the Table of Contents of that third book.

THE PAIDEIA PROGRAM

Before I leave this trilogy of books published in 1982, 1983, and 1984, I cannot refrain from quoting a statement of John Amos Comenius, the Bohemian philosopher and educator, who wrote *The Great Didactic* in 1657, more than three hundred years ago. It is an extraordinary anticipation of Paideia's commitment to a thoroughly democratic school system. Comenius belongs with Horace Mann, John Dewey, and Robert Hutchins as one of Paideia's leaders. That statement is all the more remarkable because his ideal, stated more than three hundred years ago, is still not realized anywhere in the world today. Comenius wrote:

> The education that I propose includes all that is proper for a man and it is one in which all men who are born into this world should share. . . . Our first wish is that all men be educated fully to full humanity, not any one individual, not a few, nor even many, but all men together and singly, young and old, rich and poor, of high and lowly birth, men and women—in a word all whose fate it is to be born human beings, so that at last the whole of the human race become educated, men of all ages, all conditions, both sexes, and all nations.

7

I said earlier that on the Saturday of the eight-day conference of the Paideia Group in Aspen in September of 1981, I submitted to my associates an inventory of points that should or should not be included in the reform proposal that I was supposed to write at the end of the conference. I also said that, with the exception of two items in the list, I received unanimous assent. The extent of disagreement about the exceptional two persuaded me that they should not be included.

Readers may wonder what those two items were. One was concerned with early learning and with the advancement of kindergarten to age three, with the completion of the twelve years of basic schooling at age sixteen, not eighteen. In connection with this point, I even went so far as to suggest that the B.A. degree be given on graduation from high school, signifying the completion of the first stage of general education, and that undergraduate colleges become three-year institutions, giving the M.A., or some similar degree, for the completion of the specialized course of study, with a little general education retained as a carry-over from high school.

The second point depended on the first for its execution. If high school were completed at age sixteen instead of eighteen, then I proposed that, in the next two years, there should be compulsory nonschooling. Those who were college-bound in high school would not go directly to college, but would grow up as a result of two years of work experience, either in the private or the public sector of the economy. As a result, they would be better students in college, because they would be more mature; and they would have a better sense of what they wanted to do with their lives. Not all high school graduates should go to college, but only those who qualified by passing very discriminating tests.

My associates opposed these two recommendations, not because they disagreed with the underlying reasons for advancing them, but because they thought it would be imprudent to take on opposition from so many quarters. They thought that opposition would arise from the labor unions and from the colleges of the country, as well as from many parents who thought it more desirable to keep their offspring in the home environment until ages five and six.

8

The years between 1984 and 1988 were filled for me with a variety of Paideia activities—with lectures before educational associations and large public audiences; with consultations with teachers and school administrators; with the demonstration of the techniques for conducting seminars, sometimes with students in the elementary school and sometimes in high school; and with the work of training school principals and teachers, in order to prepare them to implement the Paideia recommendations in their schools.

These activities were more intense and time-consuming in Chicago than elsewhere in the country, though I should mention

Chapel Hill in North Carolina and Cincinnati in Ohio as places where I was also greatly involved in the effort to produce Paideia schools.

The reason for the concentration of effort in Chicago was partly that, at the very beginning, Ruth Love had set up a Paideia Coordinator to guide the reforms being instituted in the Chicago schools. That alone would not have done it. The other factor of great importance was the willingness of the American National Bank's charitable trust to fund sustained work in two minority schools—the Goldblatt Elementary School, an all-black school, with a record of gang wars, drug abuse, and other forms of delinquency, and the New Sabin Magnet School, a largely Hispanic school, with an equally unsavory record.

These ventures in Chicago, with substantial aid from the American National Bank and Trust Company of Chicago, came about as a result of the fact that the Chairman of its Board, Michael Tobin, had been in an Executive Seminar of mine at Aspen. In those years, I always held a special afternoon session in which I would talk about the seriousness of our national problem arising from the dismal failure of our schools, always, of course, presenting the Paideia solution of this problem.

Mr. Tobin was persuaded by my arguments. He came to me that autumn and asked whether, if adequate funding were provided, I and my colleagues at the Institute would try to develop Goldblatt and New Sabin as Paideia schools.

The work started in 1984 and now, more than six years later, the evidence of its success is massive and clear. On days when great books seminars are scheduled, there is almost no absenteeism. Both students and teachers are enthusiastic about all the changes we have helped them make in their schools. Perhaps, the best evidence of the effect of the changes introduced is something that happened two years ago.

That June saw the first graduating class of students who had Paideia in the years before the twelfth grade. Mr. Tobin was aware that these graduating students would go to high schools all over the city in which they would have no further contact with great books seminars. Dismayed by this, he proposed that we offer to conduct special Saturday morning seminars for them if they would volunteer to participate and their parents would support their willingness to attend them. As inducements to coming back to school on their day off, we offered the students busing from their homes to school, a box lunch at the end of the seminar, a set of books which would contain the readings to be discussed, and a week's outing in the country the following summer.

The American National Bank called this its "Scholars Program." The voluntary enlistment in it by Goldblatt and New Sabin students exceeded half of the graduating class, and the program itself has been an astonishing success, which the bank has supported financially. It also has recruited some of its employees to come on Saturday mornings to help coach the students in writing after the seminars have been concluded.

9

As I mentioned at the beginning of the preceding section, I barnstormed the country during the years 1984–1988 trying to promote the Paideia reforms by giving lectures to educational associations and assemblies of teachers. I began by telling them that all the basic points in my message to them ran counter to what they had been taught in schools of education and counter to what they were required to do by state and local mandates about what should be done in our schools and how the results should be measured.

The heart of the matter, I said, was Paideia's driving commitment to a democratic system of schooling in a country that has at last, within very recent years, become a political democracy. It must now begin to discharge its obligation to give all the children in our schools equal educational opportunity. It has never done this in the past. It is not doing this now.

These remarks were so contrary to the generally accepted assumption of our being a democracy from the beginning of our history and to the generally mouthed proclamation of equal educational opportunity that they required explanation.

When democracy is understood as constitutional government

with truly universal suffrage, its existence in the United States is as recent as this century, with the Nineteenth Amendment enfranchising the female half of the population (in 1920) and the Twenty-fourth Amendment abolishing the poll tax and enfranchising the poor in every state of the union, the last as recent as 1964. When the recency of a democratic constitution is acknowledged, it is not surprising that we have not yet democratized our school system and that the motivation for doing so is not engendered by a widespread public sentiment in favor of democratic principles.

Equal educational opportunity is the democratic principle that is still generally misunderstood even though the words are on most educators' lips. But that is merely lip service when those who use the words think of it merely in quantitative terms—the same number of days, months, and years of compulsory schooling for all children (with no thought about the many who drop out before twelve years of schooling are completed).

Properly understood, educational opportunity should be equal in quality as well as in quantity—the same quality of schooling for all the children; or as John Dewey pointed out in 1900, the quality of schooling that the best and wisest parents would want for their own children should be the quality that the community should strive to give all its children.

This will still be misunderstood if we do not immediately add that, with children initially unequal in their aptitude for learning, giving them truly equal educational opportunity will result in what appears to be an inequality of results. On the same track and from the same starting line with no handicaps, those who are initially unequal as runners will not go as far or as fast.

But this inequality of results disappears when we measure the results proportionately by reference to differential capacity. Consider three sponges, one small, one large, and one intermediate in size. Immerse all three in containers in which the purity of the liquid is the same in all three, representing the same high quality of schooling for all. Each sponge will absorb as much of that liquid as it is capable of absorbing. The amounts will be arithmetically unequal, but the three sponges will be equally full. Each full to its capacity is equally full.

If we use rich cream to symbolize the high quality of schooling that all children deserve, the small sponge should be, proportionately, *not* arithmetically, as full of cream as the large sponge. Our present system of schooling gives the small sponges dirty water, the intermediate sponges skimmed milk, and only the large sponges rich cream.

The most serious obstacle to the adoption of the Paideia reform is the way in which children have been and are still being graded in school, which is in terms of an arithmetic inequality of results. Unless we substitute a different method of grading, one that measures each child's achievement by reference to that child's capacity and not by reference to the achievement of other children, we cannot establish equal educational opportunity, so that all the sponges fill themselves to the brim with different amounts of rich cream.

I shall have more to say later about the radical changes in methods of testing and grading that must be made in order to discharge Paideia's commitment to equal educational opportunity. But I cannot refrain from adding here a comment about the astonishing fact that Paideia, when it was first discussed by professors of education, was charged with being elitist. How could it be elitist and at the same time so completely committed to equal educational opportunity?

The solution of that riddle, I finally figured out, was that the professors of education thought we were deceiving ourselves and everyone else when we proposed to give all the children the same quality of schooling in view of the fact that, if they were measured by the prevailing methods of testing and grading, half of them, or even more, would end up failing.

It never occurred to the professors that we were interested in seeing the smallest sponges absorb their full measure of rich cream even if that amount was very much less than the amount absorbed by the largest sponges. Paideia was thought elitist because, though it said it sought equal educational opportunity, in their view it really was concerned with a quality of schooling appropriate *only* for large sponges in the school population.

Elitism—the foe of democracy—has prevailed in American education from its beginning. In 1817, Thomas Jefferson proposed to the legislature of Virginia that it take the first small step toward public schooling in this country. He proposed that Virginia give all children three years of common schooling at the public expense. After three years, he added, let us divide the children into those destined for labor and those destined for leisure and learning. Let us send those destined for labor into the shops as apprentices or onto the fields as hired hands. Those destined for leisure and learning, let us send to college, which they could finish by the age of twelve.

The legislature rejected Jefferson's proposal on the grounds that those destined for labor did not need three years of schooling to prepare them for work. They would learn what had to be done on the job itself. They were not going to be enfranchised citizens in any case, and so did not need the bare minimum of literacy required for that political status.

More than a hundred and fifty years later, what we are doing is still elitist in the same way as Jefferson's proposal. We do not talk about those destined for labor and those destined for leisure and learning. Instead, we divide them into the college-bound and those not planning to go to college, and after the first six or eight years of public schooling, we send some to vocational high schools and some to secondary schools supposed to be devoted to the liberal arts. I need not add that these so-called liberal arts high schools fall far short of the quality of secondary schooling at which Paideia aims. Even if they were very much better than they are, elitism still would prevail in our system of public schooling.

Elitism will not be finally and fully expunged until the general public as well as the professional educators understand and affirm without reservation that all the children (all not institutionalized), all not just some, are educable, and educable in exactly the same sense of the term.

This does not mean that children can ever be fully educated in the course of schooling, even if that were at its very best. The insuperable obstacle to becoming a generally educated human being during one's school years is youth or immaturity. At its best, schooling should be preparation for becoming a generally educated human being in the course of adult learning after all schooling is left behind, a goal to be achieved sometime after one has reached fifty or more.

One can be prepared by school to earn a living or to become a technically trained specialist, but neither of these two kinds of preparation is the primary or sole aim of basic schooling. Preparation for the tasks involved in earning a living and preparation for further education in colleges and graduate schools in which one becomes a technically specialized professional are among the aims of the twelve years of basic schooling, but the prime objective that should be aimed at in those years is preparation for living a decent human life and making the most of one's native abilities. This, for all, not just for those who go to college, requires preparation for continuing to learn throughout one's adult life.

10

In his book *A Place Called School*, John Goodlad, after a lengthy survey of this country's schools, reported that 85 percent of all classroom time in the United States is spent by teachers talking at students, with students listening or not, taking notes or not; and less than 15 percent of the time is spent in teachers talking with students, in which they actively respond to questions and engage in discussion. If these figures could be reversed, the main pedagogical aim of Paideia would be achieved.

It is the current woeful misunderstanding of teaching and learning that prevents this from happening. There is not a teachers college in the United States in which the preparation of teachers is controlled by the understanding that teaching, like farming and healing, is a cooperative art, not a productive art like carpentry and cooking. In the three cooperative arts, the artist merely helps the natural powers and resources of the field, the body, and the mind to produce the fruits and grains of the field, the health of the body, and the improvement of the mind.

The cooperative artist works with nature. Teaching is totally misconceived when the teacher is thought of as the primary or principal cause of the learning that occurs in students. The primary cause is the activity of the learner's own mind. We learn much without teachers. When teachers, who are often dispensable, enter the picture, they should do so merely as aids in the learning process.

Socrates knew this twenty-five centuries ago. When asked how he conceived himself as a teacher, he likened himself to a midwife, who helps the mother through the pains of labor in the production of offspring. That is why Socratic questioning is called maieutic teaching—midwifery. It is the person questioned who labors to achieve knowledge, skill, and understanding. The questioning merely helps to stimulate and guide that activity on the learner's part.

In my addresses to educators and teachers, I told them that this is the background for Paideia's insistence that the curricular framework it recommends must involve three different kinds of teaching and learning, in all of which students are active as learners and teachers function as aids to this activity.

These three kinds of learning and teaching are represented in the three-column diagram that summarizes the Paideia program (see pp. 109–110, *infra*). I had various ways of explaining and commenting on the differentiation of the three columns. One was to point out that they differ in the way that three of the four grammatical modes of speech differ. In didactic teaching, declarative speech by the teacher predominates. In coaching, imperative speech; and in Socratic teaching, the interrogative. Memorization is a minor aspect in all three columns.

Coaching, for example, helps to develop habits of skill, which are totally different from recollectable memories. The coach prescribes how students should perform in order to acquire these habits, tells them what to do and what not to do, supervises their practice of the prescribed activity, and corrects errors in it. The habits thus formed are much more durable than verbal memories, which are highly volatile. Habits of skilled performance atrophy only if not exercised. That is why they are not as durable as understanding, which, once acquired, is never lost.

How does didactic teaching fit into this picture of teaching as a cooperative art and of learning as active. It does not at all if the entire fifty minutes of the didactic classroom sessions are entirely consumed by declarative speech on the part of the teacher and note-taking for the sake of memorization on the part of the students. It is only information about facts that can be thus acquired, not organized knowledge, which always involves an understanding of the facts about which the mind is informed.

To correct this, I used to tell my audiences that the fifty-minute didactic class in Column One must be divided into a first and second period—a first period of thirty minutes in which the teacher recites and a second period of twenty in which discussion occurs, involving questioning students and answering teachers. The very best questions are those the teacher cannot readily answer; good teachers should welcome such questions and make them the basis of further discussion.

Otherwise, didactic teaching is not teaching at all, but indoctrination. The learning that occurs is not genuine learning, but memorization for the sake of passing tests of the recollected information students have boned up to regurgitate.

All this is summarized in an essay of mine on teaching, learning, and their counterfeits. It will be found in *Reforming Education: The Opening of the American Mind* (1988).

11

In the early stages of my promotion of the Paideia reforms, I did not have an answer to the question that school systems, principals, and teachers always asked: how should they begin to bring about the changes recommended. It was obvious that many changes had to be made. Which should come first? Considering all the obstacles that had to be overcome to realize the aims of Paideia, it was obvious that all its objectives would take many years to achieve—probably not until well into the next century. That being so, what could be done tomorrow, or in the years immediately ahead?

I did not have an answer to these questions until 1987. In 1986 with financial help from the University of North Carolina at Chapel Hill and from Encyclopaedia Britannica, Inc., the University's Center for Public Television in Chapel Hill undertook to videotape five demonstration seminars. The students who were to participate in these seminars were drawn from the senior class in Millbrook High School, in Raleigh, where the principal, Vann Langston, was most cooperative. A small set of chosen teachers from Millbrook High School and from high schools in Chapel Hill and its vicinity were observers of the seminars and discussed them with me after the seminars were concluded. Patricia Weiss, who was then on the staff of the Frank Porter Graham Child Development Center at the University of North Carolina at Chapel Hill, assisted me in the selection of about twenty students, out of more than fifty candidates chosen from the senior class by its principal; she also did a remarkably fine job of editing the videotapes and the writing of the Program Guide, tasks that took more than a year.

What I learned from this whole enterprise gave me the answer I needed and led to my proposal of what I called the Wednesday Revolution. If a maximal achievement of the Paideia reforms would take well into the next century, the Wednesday Revolution was the answer to the question: What can we do right now in a minimal effort?

In the many speeches I delivered about the Wednesday Revolution, I always started by asking my audience what anyone would do under the following circumstances. Given a desirable goal of travel to a destination a hundred miles away, together with the circumstance that there was no means of getting there except by walking, what would anyone determined to get there do when faced with this prospect? The only pragmatic answer, I said, was to start walking now in the right direction. How should one do that in the case of Paideia? The Wednesday Revolution, which I was about to propose, was the answer—the opening wedge for changing schools in the direction of the complete, but distant, Paideia goals.

Before explaining the Wednesday Revolution as the minimal Paideia effort, I told my audiences how my experience with the videotaped seminars in Chapel Hill gave me the idea for it. The texts discussed in the five sessions from Monday to Friday were Plato's *Apology*, in which Socrates defended himself at his trial in Athens, the first eight chapters of Book I of Aristotle's *Politics* together with the first book of Rousseau's *The Social Contract*,

Machiavelli's *The Prince*, the Declaration of Independence, and Sophocles' *Antigone*.

The seniors from Millbrook High School had never read any of these texts before and had never before been in seminars in which texts they had read were discussed. Everyone agreed, both the students who participated in the seminars and the teachers who observed them, that the progress made in the course of just five days was remarkable—a progress that is visible to anyone who watches the five videotapes in succession.[8]

Given this visible evidence of extraordinary progress in the growth of understanding, I asked my audiences to imagine what the results might be if, instead of just five days in their senior year of high school, these same students had had seminars once a week throughout all four years of high school; or, going further, I asked them if they could imagine that these same students had had seminars once a week from the third grade on to the twelfth. I told them they would fail because, I said, that result would be unimaginable. It would be beyond their fondest dreams.

One other insight emerged from the Millbrook seminars. The seminars did more for the students than increase their understanding of basic ideas and issues. They clearly improved the students' skills in reading, speaking, and listening. Most of all, they had an extraordinary effect on their ability to think critically, a skill that cannot be taught in itself or in a vacuum, but only in the context of discussions that involved reading, speaking, and listening.

Vann Langston, the principal of Millbrook High School, accompanied his students on the bus in their hour's ride from Raleigh to Chapel Hill and back. I repeated something that he told me at the end of the week. He had been acquainted with these students for four years and, in his experience with them, they had never been found discussing anything but games, frivolities, making money, recreations of all sorts. But in the bus returning to Raleigh from Chapel Hill each afternoon after the seminar was over, they engaged in agitated discussion of ideas and issues with which they had been confronted in the seminars.

8. The videotapes entitled *Great Ideas: A Seminar Approach to Teaching and Learning* and accompanying Program Guide are available for purchase from Encyclopaedia Britannica Educational Corporation in Chicago.

With this as background, I then proposed my plan for the Wednesday Revolution. There are thirty hours in the school week. Let twenty-seven of these hours be used for doing what the state legislature or community school boards mandate should be done in its schools. Take just three hours each week out of that schedule and devote those three hours on Wednesday (it could be any other day of the week) to a seminar for an hour and a half, using the second half of the three hours for a coaching session based on a two- or three-page essay written by the students, answering the same question each time. How did your understanding of the text you read before the seminar change as a result of the seminar discussion? Did you understand the text better or differently? In what respects did your understanding of it change?

If all the students in a school, from the third grade on, were to have this experience once a week, all the teachers in the school could be assigned to participate in it also, four or five teachers or more for each three-hour session, since at least two teachers should be involved in the conduct of the seminar, and more than two for the coaching process after the written exercise was completed.

Since the certified teachers in our schools have, in their own education, no experience of seminars, certainly not in conducting them Socratically, and since most of them have little or no training in the process of coaching, the Wednesday Revolution cannot be instituted in schools until poorly educated and poorly trained teachers have been prepared to put it into effect. The education and training of the teachers, for one year or two, must come first, before any school has teachers able to put the Wednesday Revolution into effect. How can this be accomplished?

Paideia proposed the following steps in the retraining of teachers. The principal of the school, together with its teachers, should be involved in seminars—in observing them and in conducting them, either seminars in which students are participants or seminars in which the teachers are themselves participants. In the course of this extended process, they must learn how to ask the second and third question and so on, questions they cannot prepare in advance because they are questions about the answer to the first question. Their advance preparation must consist of a very small number of leading questions, leaving to the seminar itself the asking of the follow-up questions based on the answers elicited to these leading questions.

The three Paideia books, especially the third, as well as issues of the *Paideia Bulletin*, contain detailed recommendations about seminar and coaching techniques as well as advice about what must be done to acquire them and exercise them well. Here I need only add that the proposal of the Wednesday Revolution has been enthusiastically adopted and successfully effected by more than 100 schools all across the country—in Chicago, in Denver, in Los Angeles, in Cincinnati, in Chattanooga, in Moraga County, California, in Amherst, Massachusetts, and in many schools in North Carolina. That, of course, is only a drop in the bucket when we consider the more than 8,000 school districts in this country. This raises the question to be considered next—the obstacles that stand in the way of much greater success than anything we have been able to accomplish so far.

12

The Paideia proposal never promised that it would be a quick-fix to the problem the United States faces with regard to the dismal failure of its schools to provide the kind of basic, compulsory education that its future citizens deserve. This fact by itself—that the Paideia reforms cannot be accomplished nationwide in the immediate future of the next few years—constitutes one of the major obstacles to its being widely accepted. Impatient, disinclined to defer gratification of their desires, Americans want a quick-fix to the problems confronting them, even though anything that promised to be a quick fix would be necessarily inadequate and superficial. That certainly is the case with regard to the educational problem the country faces.

In early 1988, I distributed to my Paideia colleagues and associates a paper I had written for them to consider, entitled "A Pessimistic View of Paideia's Progress." The paper tried to explain two things: (1) why the Paideia reform cannot be accomplished in the remaining years of this century; and (2) why Paideia is a much more radical reform than is realized even by its most ardent adherents and practitioners in the Paideia schools across the country. What follows is a summary of that paper.

Two interdependent factors play a crucial role in any adequate reform of basic schooling in the United States. They are: (1) better trained and better educated teachers than 90 percent of the instructional personnel now certified by the states; and (2) a much sounder program of education than any that now exists in the schools of the United States.

The interdependence of these two factors means that each is a necessary condition of reform but neither by itself is sufficient. Better teachers cannot operate effectively in schools as school curriculums are now constituted. A better program of education in the schools cannot be accomplished without much better teachers than we now have.

It is axiomatic that the way in which students are tested and graded determines what teachers teach and how they teach, what students study and how they study. Unless the present system of testing and grading is radically altered or totally abandoned, none of the desired objectives of sound educational reform can be accomplished.

The present system puts a premium on the least effective kind of teaching, if it is teaching at all rather than indoctrination. It also lays excessive stress on what is not genuine learning at all, but only memorized information in certain fields of subject matter. It makes Column One in the Paideia diagram dominate and control what goes on in our schools, leaving at most one tenth of school time for Columns Two and Three (the Wednesday Revolution).

It promotes the pretension that Column One is concerned with the acquisition of organized knowledge, because it fails to distinguish between information memorized and facts understood. Only the latter is knowledge. Knowledge cannot be acquired through the kind of teacher-talk that now goes on in 85 percent of all classroom time in the United States. The poor training of future teachers in our schools and departments of education, their certification, and their evaluation are geared to the methods of testing and grading now dominant in the United States. In short, unless the existing methods of testing and grading are radically altered or abandoned, better preparation for teaching cannot and will not occur.

In addition, if grading solely on the bell-shaped curve is perpetuated, it will be thought imprudent to try to give *all* the children the same quality of schooling in kindergarten through twelfth grade; for all of us know in advance that, graded on the bell-shaped curve, a large number of students could not avoid failing, though, if properly graded, they might be expected to pass.

Finally, we know that any attempt to alter or abandon the present system of testing and grading would meet strong, if not intractable, opposition from professors of education, parents, personnel officers in corporations, and all those involved in administering the entrance requirements in our colleges. Overcoming this opposition will take well into the next century, if it can be done at all.

To get better teachers in our schools, basic reforms will have to take place in all the schools and departments of education in our colleges and universities. These reforms would have to involve a better understanding of the distinction between information and knowledge than now prevails. They would also have to involve a better understanding of the difference between the memorization of information for the purpose of passing the kind of tests now given, and the kind of understanding that is essential to acquiring knowledge, which cannot be acquired without discussion that involves thinking on the student's part.

The present methods of testing and grading measure only the ability of children to get through schools as schools are now constituted. They do not measure the growth of the mind in knowing, understanding, and skill.[9]

To get better educational programs in our schools, we must think in terms other than the present conception of a curriculum. That word stands for "subject-matter courses, didactically taught, with some courses required and some elective." All quick-fix ed-

9. See an essay by Daniel Koretz in *American Educator* (Summer, 1988), which explains how standardized tests exaggerate achievement and distort instruction.

ucational reforms are curricular reforms: they recommend that certain courses be required, and others dropped; or they propose a "core curriculum" of the most important courses to be taken—by some, seldom by all.

The basic terms of the Paideia reform are not curricular. Paideia is not concerned with courses at all, but with the three different kinds of teaching that must be present in every school and the three different kinds of learning that must go on there. The reforms with regard to Column One indicate that the kind of didactic instruction that now prevails in Column One must be altered to include the training of skills and the conduct of discussions.

After eight years of Paideia effort, there are no *completely* Paideia schools now in existence. The nearest approach to complete Paideia schools are in Cincinnati and Chattanooga. What we call "Paideia schools"—a hundred or a few more in the whole United States, a drop in the bucket—are like all the other bad schools in this country *with only one difference*: their deficiencies are slightly ameliorated by the fact that they devote one tenth of their time to some coaching and to one seminar a week for all the students. These are mainly elementary schools. There are fewer Paideia high schools, because at the secondary level there is much greater stress on courses, tests, and grades for the purpose of getting into college.

Since the great foundations and charitable trusts of this country are inclined to grant money for proposed educational reforms *only if the reforms promise a quick-fix* that can be accomplished in the years immediately ahead, the fiscal support goes in large quantities to reform proposals that can promise superficial quick-fixes but do not touch the heart of what is wrong with our educational system. Paideia proposals get little fiscal support because they do not promise any quick-fixes, but call for slow progress in the right direction with the hope that the present obstacles to genuine reform can be overcome in the next century.

13

When it is thoroughly understood that the present system of testing and grading, with which the federal and state governments, the educational establishment, and the public in general are obsessed, is an obstacle that must be surmounted, Paideia is called upon to propose a workable alternative.

That alternative is to be found in the proposition that a proportionate rather than an arithmetic equality of results must be our objective when we seek to give all the children equal educational opportunity, equal in quality, not just in quantity.

The existing methods of testing students are applicable only or mainly in the sphere of the first kind of teaching and learning—didactic instruction in the fields of subject-matter. Even there, they largely test memory for information and bits of knowledge rather than the mind's grasp of organized knowledge and its significance. They are inadequate for testing the development of intellectual skills, and totally worthless for testing the growth of understanding that occurs through the Socratic conduct of seminars. For the latter, only oral interrogation can appraise the development of the student's mind.

The Paideia reform, being dedicated to a one-track curriculum for all students, recognizes that giving all equal educational opportunity, equal in quality as well as in quantity, does not mean equality of results. Given the same opportunities for learning, students of unequal ability will be unequal in their accomplishments. But if each does *as well* as his or her capacity allows, each has acquitted himself or herself *perfectly.*

This being the case, they should not be graded along the curve, with some students failing because they have not made a fixed passing mark. Each student should be graded by an assessment of his or her accomplishment relative only to his or her initial capacity for learning, never by reference to what others of greater capacity can be expected to accomplish.

Using letters or numbers to keep educational scores as we now do, with certain letters or numbers signifying success and others failure, is therefore totally inappropriate as a way of evaluating the accomplishment of Paideia students. What should take its place? The answer is a narrative grade: *a written statement by teachers concerning each individual child's development as a learner.* This should be done from first grade on, either once or twice a year; and it should be done in greater detail at the end of four years, eight years, and twelve years.

The narrative grade given a student reports whether a particular student had done as well as that individual can be expected to do and, in addition, it should appraise the level of that accomplishment with reference to further learning by that individual and his or her competence for the performance of tasks in the world beyond school. If the narrative grade is negative in its appraisal, that should indicate a problem to be solved by the student's teachers and parents. The reason for the failure is never that the student negatively appraised *cannot* do as well as the individual's capacity for learning allows. The cause must be discovered elsewhere and, being discovered, steps must be taken to remedy it.

One and the same required curriculum for all, from K through 12, cannot work to produce a schooling that is equal in quality for all unless the achievement of each child is graded by reference to that child's own capacity. When grading is thus proportionate to individual capacity, there will be only three significant grades: *fail*, which means the child has not done what he or she is able to do; *pass*, which means that the child has done what he or she is able to do; and *honors*, which means the child has exceeded reasonable expectations.

Since we have not yet developed the methods of testing and grading that are prerequisite to installing in our schools the Paideia framework for a curriculum that will give all the children the quality of schooling that all equally deserve, it is no wonder that the undemocratic—or, more precisely, antidemocratic—educational proposal of Thomas Jefferson in 1817 still dominates the educational scene in this country in 1991.

14

Even if proportionate grading were to replace the present system, there would still be about one third of the children in our schools, preeminently in large urban centers, who would have to be judged failures, *because* they did not do as well as they can reasonably be expected to do. This astonishing fact needs further explanation. Why should any child not learn as much as his or her native aptitude warrants? If this is not to be attributed to failure on the part of that child's teachers, what is the reason for the failure?

The answer, I suggest, lies in the distinction between the intrinsic and extrinsic obstacles to successful educational reform. The intrinsic obstacles we have already considered. What are the extrinsic obstacles?

When the words "for all" are taken seriously in the statement that the democracy demands equal educational opportunity *for all*, there are many extrinsic obstacles in the way of making all Paideia reforms profitable *for all* the children, especially the seriously deprived and disadvantaged minorities in our large urban communities. These would remain obstacles even if Paideia's pedagogical recommendations were to be adopted, because their existence would prevent schools from working effectively for deprived and disadvantaged children.

Consider persons who wish to play tennis. Here are some of the extrinsic obstacles to the gratification of that wish. They may have serious disabilities with their feet, such as painful bunions or a lack of physical coordination. Chiropody and physiotherapy may remove these obstacles, but it neither trains them to play tennis nor gives them the opportunity to practice the game. Other obstacles may prevent this, such as poverty that stands in the way of buying or even renting a good tennis racket and paying the fees for the use of a tennis court. Removing these obstacles does not coach them in the skills of tennis. With all these obstacles overcome, they may still not have a competent coach to train them.

Another example can be taken from the field of reading. Poor eyesight, dyslexia, defective eye movements are extrinsic obstacles to learning how to read. Not being able to decode letters and words in print is another extrinsic obstacle. But removing all these obstacles to learning how to read well does not produce any skill in reading. Reading is not just an ability to decode. Removing that kind of functional literacy is far from enough. Here the intrinsic obstacles are not understanding the rules that must be followed to become a good reader, and also the time and effort that must be devoted to practice in reading under the guidance of an expert coach.

Understanding the intrinsic obstacles explains why a genuine nationwide reform of schooling cannot be accomplished in a quick-fix or in a few years here and there. Understanding the extrinsic obstacles explains why, even if the improvement of our schools were to occur, that would leave unsolved the problems involved in making it truly democratic, by giving the same quality of schooling to *all* the children.

Recognizing the distinction between the intrinsic and the extrinsic obstacles should not result in regarding the extrinsic obstacles as of little importance. Removing them is as necessary for the underprivileged groups in our big cities as restructuring the schools is for giving all who attend them the kind of education they deserve.

The intrinsic obstacles stand in the way of essential improvements in the teaching and learning that go on. Most important of all, changes must be made in the methods of testing and grading. These stand in the way of giving an educational opportunity that is qualitatively the same for all, not just equal in quantity. In sharp contrast, the extrinsic obstacles are those that would prevent many children in our urban schools from being able to profit from genuine school reform even if it were accomplished. They also stand in the way of attracting more able persons into the teaching professions and, when in it, to performing effectively as teachers.

The Coalition of Essential Schools, with its headquarters at Brown University, and the Paideia Program that has its national center at the University of North Carolina at Chapel Hill are, in my judgment, the only two fundamental and far-reaching reforms that have been proposed in the last ten years. Neither is a quick-fix, nor can they be, because of the intransigence of the intrinsic obstacles they must overcome. Neither can be easily demonstrated; neither can produce quantitatively measurable effects; neither can be appreciated without some understanding of basic truths in the philosophy of education that correct errors widely prevalent among educators as well as in the general population.

The extrinsic obstacles are all obvious. They are so much a part of our environment that no one can fail to recognize them. But the intrinsic obstacles are hidden. Their being intrinsic means that they are integral to the needed educational reforms. If the basic philosophy and principles of these reforms are not well understood, neither will be the intrinsic obstacles that they must surmount, for these obstacles consist of impediments to accomplishing the basic changes that these reforms require. The intrinsic obstacles are no better and more generally understood than are the basic philosophy and principles of the reform programs themselves.

I doubt if there is much chance of changing this state of affairs but, in any case, I think it desirable that the good people who are engaged in the obviously meritorious efforts to overcome the extrinsic obstacles to good schooling for all should clearly understand why, in spite of the success of their efforts, the schools of this country are likely to remain as bad as they now are.

15

What I have just said about the extrinsic and intrinsic obstacles to educational reform prompts me to comment on the disastrous effect the present system of testing and grading has on the children in our schools who are not deprived and disadvantaged and thus are in a position to take advantage of Paideia schooling.

I have had two experiences that I have found instructive in this connection. One was at the Millbrook High School in Raleigh, North Carolina, when I interviewed the 50 or more candidates chosen by the school's principal in order to select only 20 for the seminars we were planning. On a sheet of paper that listed the names of these candidates, their rank in a senior class of about 400 was indicated.

The interview I conducted with each of the candidates involved asking them about what books they had read in their four years in secondary schools, books that were not assigned for reading by their teachers. I also asked them if they were planning to go to college and what reason or objectives they had in mind for doing so? Finally, I asked them to explain a brief paragraph in John Locke's chapter on the labor theory of property in his *Second Treatise on Civil Government*.

Of the twenty students I selected, only two were in the first twenty-five positions of the class ranking. The others among the first twenty-five in class rank were "good students" only in the sense that they were good note-takers and good memorizers who conscientiously boned up for the tests they had to take and managed to get high grades. They had done no outside reading; their reason for wishing to go to college and their post-collegiate aims did not betray the slightest interest in the cultivation of their minds. In addition, when confronted with a difficult text they had been assigned to read, they were at a loss to make sense of it.

In contrast, most of the candidates that I selected manifested a genuine interest in learning for its own sake; they had read books they were not assigned to read; their reasons for wishing to go to college involved other than worldly success in the rat race of the marketplace; and they applied their minds effectively to the interpretation of the text I asked them to comment on. These children had places ranked in the second and third hundred out of a class of about 400.

My second experience occurred in 1989 in Atlanta, Georgia, at the corporate headquarters of the Coca-Cola Company. The company had established, as one of its charitable endowments, a Scholars Foundation that sought to pick the top fifty college-bound high school graduates in the United States, awarding each a scholarship of $5,000—$20,000 a year for each of the four years of college. Announcing this plan, they received thousands of applications from every state in the union. By preliminary interviews, tests of various sorts, and other criteria, they eliminated all but 150 of the applicants. These chosen few, they brought to Atlanta for a three-day exercise, which involved final interviews conducted by educators the company invited to participate in this exercise. The educators were grouped in committees of 3, each committee interviewing each of 30 students.

Mebane Pritchett, whom I had known at the University of North Carolina and who had left the University to become head of the Coca-Cola Scholars Foundation, invited me to participate in this process. Urged to do so by my old friend William Friday, who for more than a quarter of a century had been President of the University of North Carolina, I accepted Mr. Pritchett's invitation.

Remembering my earlier experience in selecting twenty of sixty students at Millbrook High School in Raleigh, I used the following tactics in my part of the interviews. I asked each of the fifty or more students who we interviewed about the books they had read, which were not assigned for reading by their teachers. I asked them their reasons for going to college and what they hoped for in their careers after graduating from college. Since each of them had written a little essay about the problems that were likely to confront this country in the year 2010, I queried them about their predictions and asked them to think further about the problems they foresaw the United States would then face.

I was so shocked by the results these questions elicited, which so plainly revealed the kind of poor schooling these exceptionally bright and gifted children had received, that at the end of the three-day exercise, I promised Mr. Pritchett that I would write him a long letter setting forth my reflections about what I had learned. I did so as soon as I returned to Chicago and sent a copy of my long letter to Bill Friday as well as to him. Mr. Friday was so impressed by my letter that he had it printed in *The News & Observer* of Raleigh. Readers will find this letter as Item C in the Notes appended to this chapter.

16

A pessimistic view of Paideia's future includes one further consideration. Though it comes last, it is by no means of least importance as an obstacle to be overcome. It is the fact that the reigning values of our society are hardly congenial to the objectives of the Paideia reform.

The pay of teachers must become competitive with that of other equally demanding occupations. The professional status of the schoolteacher must be given the respect of the community in the same measure as that given other professions.

Above all, money-making and other external indices of social success must become subordinate to the inner attainments of moral and intellectual virtue. The educational revolution that Paideia is trying to promote must be accompanied and supported by revolutions in other institutional aspects of society. For that to occur ample time must be allowed.

The two major obstacles to reform have already been mentioned. One is the persistent failure of educators to recognize that a proportionate equality of results can be achieved when children who differ markedly in the degree of their educability are given the same quality or kind of schooling. The other is the persistent refusal of the educational establishment to replace the scheme of grading that puts a student in his or her niche on the bell-shaped curve by an assessment of the student's achievement, wholly in terms of that student's capacity, without reference to any other individual's achievement.

When comparative and competitive grading is replaced by individual and proportionate grading, it will no longer seem unreasonable and impractical to have the less able and more able students engage in exactly the same course of study.

Schools of education should become research institutions at the graduate level of the university and not places for the training of schoolteachers. Those planning to enter the profession of teaching should have four years of general, liberal education at the college level, and then three years of practice teaching under supervision. They, too, need coaching if they are to develop the intellectual skills involved in teaching and also learning, for the best teacher is one who learns in the process of teaching.

To become an effective Socratic conductor of seminars, to become an effective coach of the intellectual skills, and to become a didactic teacher who not only lectures effectively but is also able to engage students in discussion takes a long time even for those who have had a better education and training than most of our teachers have experienced.

At the beginning of our country's history, James Madison said:

> The establishment of a republican government without well-appointed and efficient means for the universal education of the people is the most rash and foolhardy experiment ever tried by man.

How much truer that statement is today when we now have universal suffrage. Not only the prosperity of our high-tech economy depends upon the reconstitution of our schools, but even more so the well-being of our political democracy.

Our schools are not turning out young people prepared for the high office and the duties of citizenship in a democratic republic. Our political institutions cannot thrive, they may not even survive, if we do not produce a larger and larger number of thinking citizens from whom some statesmen of the type we had in the eighteenth century might eventually emerge. We are, indeed, a nation at risk, and nothing but radical reform of our schools can save us from impending disaster.

Whatever the price we must pay in money and effort to do this, the price we will pay for not doing it will be much greater.

17

In early 1988, the Paideia Council met in Chicago to discuss the decision I had reached about transferring the furtherance of the Paideia project from the Institute for Philosophical Research to the University of North Carolina at Chapel Hill. This decision had grown out of my failure, as head of the Institute, to raise from major foundations sufficient funds needed to plan a five- or even a three-year program of Paideia activities nationwide.

It was generally known that the Institute would continue to exist only during my lifetime. Its duration was highly problematic, since I was approaching my ninetieth year. In view of that fact, how could foundations or donors reasonably be expected to give the Institute a three- or five-year grant of millions, without which I thought there was little prospect of planning an effective nationwide promotion of Paideia. It would be different if a perpetual institution, such as a great university, were to be the fund-raiser promoting Paideia's future.

At this two-day meeting, attended by representatives of the University of North Carolina who outlined what they thought could be done for Paideia if a National Center for the Paideia Program were to be established at that institution, I used part of the time to present to my colleagues the development of my thought about the three-column diagram. The original diagram had summarized the curricular framework of Paideia schools from the very beginning.

The changes that I now proposed will be found by comparing the original diagram with the revision of it proposed in 1988.

To ensure that all the important points and aspects of the revision were carefully observed, I attached to the revised three-column diagram a series of twelve "Notes on the Three Kinds of

Teaching and Learning and Their Interconnection." Readers who wish to compare the two diagrams and to study the notes will find the original diagram and the revised diagram with notes as Item A in the Notes appended to this chapter.

After prolonged discussion, my colleagues approved the revision and the notes. But in view of the projected shift of the control of Paideia activities from the Institute to the University of North Carolina at Chapel Hill, they thought it prudent to draw up a statement of Paideia principles for the guidance in the years ahead of the National Center for the Paideia Program that was to be established in Chapel Hill. That took considerable time, especially with regard to the wording of what became principle #9.

This Declaration of Paideia Principles, signed by the members of what was then called the Paideia Council, was to be attached to the contractual agreement between the Institute for Philosophical Research and the University of North Carolina at Chapel Hill. The contractual agreement between the Institute and the University was signed by the authorized parties on July 29, 1988; and the inauguration of the National Center for the Paideia Program at Chapel Hill was celebrated in September of that year.

18

The last step in this long story of my career in educational reform remains to be told. Formally established in September of 1988, the work of the next two years is a story of success and failure—success in promoting Paideia not only in North Carolina but in many other states of the nation, combined with failure in large-scale money raising for the prosecution of nationwide efforts. During these two years—1989 and 1990—the Institute continued to serve the National Center, not only with respect to schools in Chicago but elsewhere, and in the publication of the *Paideia Bulletin*. It was supported in doing so by funding from the University.

In the closing months of 1990 as my ninetieth year approached, I came to a radical decision about how I wished to spend the remaining years of my life.

I had by that time devoted a major portion of my energies for more than ten years to the work of educational reform. For more than ten years, I had transformed the Institute from an ivory tower in which purely philosophical work could be accomplished into an active, practical agency for engaging in all the trials and tribulations of the educational marketplace.

It seemed to me that I had done enough to help solve one of this country's most difficult and serious problems. It was now time for me to retire as the lead dog in the team of workers pulling the sled over difficult terrain. Donald Stedman, who had been a member of the Paideia Council for many years, had now become Dean of the School of Education in Chapel Hill, and the National Center for the Paideia Program could be operated as an agency of that school. The Institute for Philosophical Research could again become the ivory tower for me that it was at the beginning and I could now look forward to devoting a major portion of my energies in my remaining years to the pursuit of truth in philosophy, a pursuit which has no foreseeable end.

NOTES TO CHAPTER 4

Item A

Declaration of Paideia Principles*

We, the members of the Paideia Council, hold these truths to be the principles of the Paideia Program:

1. that all children can learn;
2. that, therefore, they all deserve the same quality of schooling, not just the same quantity;
3. that the quality of schooling to which they are entitled is what the

* *The Paideia Bulletin: News and Ideas for the Paideia Network*, Chicago, Institute for Philosophical Research, September/October 1990, Volume VI, Number 1.

wisest parents would wish for their own children, the best education for the best being the best education for all;

4. that schooling at its best is preparation for becoming generally educated in the course of a whole lifetime, and that schools should be judged on how well they provide such preparation;
5. that the three callings for which schooling should prepare all Americans are (1) to earn a decent livelihood, (b) to be a good citizen of the nation and the world, and (c) to make a good life for oneself;
6. that the primary cause of genuine learning is the activity of the learner's own mind, sometimes with the help of a teacher functioning as a secondary and cooperative cause;
7. that the three kinds of teaching that should occur in our schools are didactic teaching of subject matter, coaching that produces the skills of learning, and Socratic questioning in seminar discussion;
8. that the results of these three kinds of teaching should be (a) the acquisition of organized knowledge, (b) the formation of habits of skill in the use of language and mathematics, and (c) the growth of the mind's understanding of basic ideas and issues;
9. that each student's achievement of these results should be evaluated in terms of that student's capacities and not solely related to the achievements of other students;
10. that the principal of a school should never be a mere administrator, but also a leading teacher who should cooperate with the faculty in planning, reforming, and reorganizing the school as an educational community;
11. that the principal and faculty of a school should themselves be actively engaged in learning; and
12. that the desire to continue their own learning should be the prime motivation of those who dedicate their lives to the profession of teaching.

PAIDEIA COUNCIL:

George Anastaplo
Rosa Blackwell
John T. Clark
Paul A. Gagnon
Lois Haslam
Gary Hoban
Richard Hunt
Vann Langston
James G. Nelson
Cynthia L. Rutz
Donald J. Stedman
Charles Van Doren
Geraldine Van Doren
John Van Doren
Patricia F. Weiss

The Paideia Curricular Framework*
[Original Diagram]

	COLUMN ONE	COLUMN TWO	COLUMN THREE
Goals	ACQUISITION OF ORGANIZED KNOWLEDGE	DEVELOPMENT OF INTELLECTUAL SKILLS—SKILLS OF LEARNING	ENLARGED UNDERSTANDING OF IDEAS AND VALUES
	by means of	by means of	by means of
Means	DIDACTIC INSTRUCTION LECTURES AND RESPONSES TEXTBOOKS AND OTHER AIDS	COACHING, EXERCISES, AND SUPERVISED PRACTICE	MAIEUTIC OR SOCRATIC QUESTIONING AND ACTIVE PARTICIPATION
	in three areas of subject-matter	in the operations of	in the
Areas Operations and Activities	LANGUAGE, LITERATURE, AND THE FINE ARTS MATHEMATICS AND NATURAL SCIENCE HISTORY, GEOGRAPHY, AND SOCIAL STUDIES	READING, WRITING, SPEAKING, LISTENING CALCULATING, PROBLEM-SOLVING OBSERVING, MEASURING, ESTIMATING EXERCISING CRITICAL JUDGMENT	DISCUSSION OF BOOKS (NOT TEXTBOOKS) AND OTHER WORKS OF ART AND INVOLVEMENT IN ARTISTIC ACTIVITIES E.G., MUSIC, DRAMA, VISUAL ARTS

The three columns do not correspond to separate courses, nor is one kind of teaching and learning necessarily confined to any one class

* Adler, *The Paideia Proposal,* 1982, p. 23; *Paideia Problems and Possibilities,* 1983, p. 18; *The Paideia Program,* 1984, p. 8.

The Three Kinds of Teaching and Learning in a Paideia School[†]
[Revised Diagram]

COLUMN ONE	COLUMN TWO	COLUMN THREE
ACQUISITION OF ORGANIZED KNOWLEDGE	DEVELOPMENT OF SKILLS	ENLARGED UNDERSTANDING OF IDEAS AND ISSUES
by means of	by means of	by means of
DIDACTIC INSTRUCTION TEXTBOOKS AND OTHER AIDS	COACHING WITH SUPERVISED PRACTICE	SOCRATIC QUESTIONING IN SEMINAR DISCUSSIONS
in these areas of subject-matter	in the operations of	of
LANGUAGE AND LITERATURE MATHEMATICS NATURAL SCIENCE HISTORY GEOGRAPHY	READING, WRITING, SPEAKING, LISTENING, CALCULATING, PROBLEM SOLVING, OBSERVING, MEASURING, ESTIMATING EXERCISING CRITICAL JUDGMENT PERFORMING IN THE FINE ARTS	IMAGINATIVE AND EXPOSITORY LITERATURE, WORKS OF VISUAL AND MUSICAL ART, ETC.

NOTES ON THE THREE KINDS OF TEACHING AND LEARNING AND THEIR INTERCONNECTION

1. The objective or goal of didactic instruction is knowledge of the subject matters listed in Column One. But bits of information about matters of fact are not knowledge. Only facts well understood are knowledge. To fail to recognize this distinction is to confuse memorization and indoctrination with genuine learning and teaching.

   As usually conducted in our schools, in 50-minute class ses-

† *The Paideia Bulletin,* op. cit.

sions, didactic instruction is not only ineffective, but becomes indoctrination of the memory for the purpose of passing tests. To make it genuine learning, every didactic session should be conceived as a work of cooperative art in which the teacher engages the activity of the learner's mind, not just impressing the memory. A 50-minute class, for example, might be cut into two segments: the first two-thirds (or less) devoted to lecturing by the instructor, and the last third (or more) devoted to discussion with both students and teacher asking and answering questions, with the intention of producing some understanding of the factual information presented didactically.

2. The mathematical knowledge to be covered in K–12 should include geometry, trigonometry, advanced algebra, and calculus. The knowledge of the natural sciences should include biology, chemistry, and physics. Both mathematics and science should be taught in different quantities at different rates of speed to students divided according to ability. Content should be equally serious in all groups. In other subjects, grouping is unnecessary.
3. The study of literature by means of didactic instruction in Column One should be carried on differently from the reading of literature for the purpose of understanding ideas through seminar discussions in Column Three. The desired objectives are different; hence, the means should be different.
4. Coaching in the skills of mathematical operations and in the skills of scientific procedures should be integrated with the didactic teaching of these subjects. Coaching in the skills of reading, listening, and speaking should be associated with the Socratic conduct of seminars. Coaching in the skills of observing, of exercising critical judgment, and of activities connected with the fine arts should be associated with seminar discussions of paintings, musical composition, etc., in Column Three. The only skill that can be coached separately is that of writing, but that may also be undertaken in connection with seminar discussions. "Thinking" should be coached in the coaching of all other skills; it cannot be coached by itself or in itself, and in isolation from subject-matter, for it never occurs that way.
5. History should be broadly conceived as including cultural, social, and intellectual history as well as political and military history; and though stress may be laid on the history of the United States, European history and the history of other parts of the world should not be neglected.

6. Geography should be broadly conceived as including social and economic geography as well as physical and political geography. When history and geography are thus broadly conceived, these subjects subsume the so-called "social studies" subject-matter in Column One.
7. The skills of thinking are involved in forming critical judgments about what is true and false in the fields of history, science, and philosophy, especially with respect to the expository literature read and discussed in Column Three seminars. The skills of thinking are also involved in forming critical judgments about excellence in the sphere of imaginative literature and the other fine arts.
8. With regard to skill in the language arts, skill in mathematical operations, and skill in scientific procedures, students should be required to perform, under supervision, so that by repeated practice in the performance of the skill, they acquire the habit of good performance. In the fields of lyric poetry, music, and painting, performance should involve the writing of lyrics, the playing of musical instruments, the making of visual works, etc., although time limitations may restrict such activities to one or two fields.
9. Distinction should be made between *coaching* sessions and *tutorial* sessions. In the upper grades, where lengthy and difficult books of expository and imaginative literature should be studied, whole works, as opposed to the short selections that must be used in seminars, can be examined Socratically in a series of tutorial sessions. This also applies to the study of visual and musical works of fine art.
10. Understanding is an act of the intellect, and the objects most appropriate to acts of understanding are ideas and the intellectual issues concerning them. There are three ways in which ideas to be understood can be found in imaginative and expository literature and in paintings, musical compositions, etc.:
    a. They are to be found as expressed by the author of expository works of literature. They can also be found in the same way in imaginative literature; for a novelist sometimes speaks about ideas in his own voice, not that of his characters.
    b. In works of imaginative literature—novels and plays—the thought of the characters about ideas can sometimes be found in their speeches.
    c. A third way differs radically from the first two. Narrative episodes or portions of novels and plays may concretely ex-

emplify an idea; and sometimes the narrative as a whole may exemplify a number of ideas. Such concrete exemplification of ideas may also be found in other imaginative works, *i.e.*, in paintings, in musical compositions, etc. Just as there are many books, both expository and imaginative, that are inadequate for seminar discussion that aims at the understanding of ideas and issues, so too there are many paintings, musical compositions, etc., that are similarly inadequate.

11. Elements in the Paideia course of study that are not mentioned in the three-column diagram are: (a) twelve years of physical training and hygiene, associated with the coaching skills in Column Two; (b) six years of manual training (to include machine repair, plumbing, typing, computer use, cooking, sewing), not as vocational training for special jobs, but only as mind training, which is no less mind training than training in the language arts, associated with the coaching in Column Two; (c) an introduction to the world of work in grades 11 and 12, associated with didactic instruction in Column One.
12. Two things have no place in a Paideia school, except as extracurricular activities: (a) electives (subjects not mentioned in Column One); (b) particularized job-training, as distinct from the coaching of manual skills in Column Two.

THE PAIDEIA COUNCIL

ITEM B

Appendix III‡

Statement by Theodore R. Sizer, formerly Dean of the Harvard Graduate School of Education and Headmaster of Phillips Academy at Andover, and currently Chairman of a study of American high schools.

How should one begin planning for a Paideia school, or a Paideia program within a school? As no two schools will be alike, I can only make some general, procedural suggestions of steps that might be taken.

‡ Adler, *Paideia Problems and Possibilities*, 1983, Chapter 7, pp. 109–113.

Suggested first step: Make sure that all involved in the project understand it and are committed to it, however skeptical one or another might be about some of its practical aspects. Those "involved" include the teachers and principals affected. Also involved are key central office administrators, school board members, representative influential parents of prospective students in the program, and, where older students are involved, these young people themselves.

This process will take time. Many think *Paideia* is a curriculum—a set of required courses that merely have to be plugged in. They have to be persuaded that Paideia is *not* a detailed One Best Curriculum, but rather a set of principles, a framework, and a process. Those using the principles have the responsibility of crafting the critical details of the program, in ways appropriate to their own communities.

All involved have to believe that all children can be educated, that they can use their minds well, that they can be motivated and inspired to do so, and that all are properly served by the overarching *Paideia* framework. They must understand the pedagogies involved and have some experience with them. I repeat: this process takes time and patience. To rush into it, or steamroll those involved, or to impose Paideia by *ukase* is to guarantee failure.

Suggested second step: Focus on outcomes: what knowledge, skills, and understandings must be demonstrated, at which levels, and how can students most effectively exhibit their mastery? Here again the framework of *The Paideia Proposal* is a starting point, no more than that. The specifics of a particular community's objectives need to be identified and sorted out.

A good way to do this is to establish tentative "checkpoints" over the sequence of years planned for the school, and to work out examinations for each. One might select, say, the third, sixth, ninth, and twelfth grade levels (knowing full well that students will reach these different levels at different paces, and thus at moderately differing ages).

This process tends to bring disagreement about ends and fuzzy thinking about means to the surface; the very specificity of examinations focuses issues and sharpens priorities. The framework of the three columns is crucial here, as it identifies the knowledge, the skills, and the understandings to be forwarded, and it gives general guidance for the organization of subject-matter. The specifics must be done locally, as no two schools are precisely the same, nor should they be.

The process of examination-writing (which is in large part an exercise in detailed goal-setting) again takes time. It cannot be rushed, and no outside authority can do it for the staff that must use it. The traditional system of sending down from On High detailed syllabi to teachers simply will not work. If the effort is to succeed, the participants in a Paideia School must have a critical stake in its design. Outside agencies can help (just as we hope our *Proposal* helps), but they must remain the supporting actors.

Suggested third step: Once the "checkpoint" goals (in the form of tentative, prototypical examinations) are developed, the task of evolving the means to achieve them follows.

The dangers here are numerous, as the weight of tradition and the narrow, specialist education of most middle and high school teachers will conspire to force the program, at least for older students, into familiar 50-minute long sessions dominated by teacher "telling."

A good tactical protection against this is to focus first on the development of intellectual skills and the improvement of understanding. The achievement of these requires a break from many traditional modes. "Coaching" and "questioning" will lay claim to now seldom-used teacher skills and to different forms of student grouping. Once one break is made, others will follow more easily.

The labels we use for certain subjects, and the expectations behind those labels accrued over the years, present similar hazards. For example, the word "English" as used in such phrases as "English course," "English teacher," or "English department" is treacherously ambiguous. It sometimes refers to coaching writing and reading skills, and less often to the correlative skills for speaking and listening. When "English teacher" refers to a teacher of skills, it should mean coaching in all basic skills of the language arts, not just writing.

An "English course" sometimes means a course of didactic instruction in the history of English literature, and sometimes it passes from that into a discussion of important literary works in the English language. It seldom becomes a Socratically conducted discussion of all forms of literature in all fields of subject-matter—not merely poetry or imaginative literature, but also significant books in history, in philosophy, in mathematics, in natural science, and so on.

Only when "literature" stands for books of every variety, some written in English or some in other languages, does the reference to literature in Column One relate didactic instruction there to Socratic teaching concerned with the reading and discussion of books in Column Three.

Only when "language" stands for both English and a foreign language and only when the language arts include all four of the basic operations—reading as well as writing, listening as well as speaking—does the reference to didactic instruction in language in Column One relate to coaching the language arts as prescribed in Column Two.

Thus, the conventionally styled "English" teacher will find himself or herself on often quite unfamiliar ground in a Paideia school. Allowances must be made for that reality.

So, too, didactic instruction in mathematics or science, as prescribed in Column One, must be related to coaching of the operational skills in these areas of subject-matter, as prescribed in Column Two. Many of the same problems found in language and literature emerge here. Again, accommodations will be necessary.

Again, this process will take time. When there is a rush to get something "started," and only a summer, let us say, with only a part of the staff engaged in planning, the result will invariably be a botched effort. When faced with incomplete plans and ambiguous new directions, all of us naturally retreat into what we are accustomed to do—to traditional patterns.

Only a comprehensive plan, fully understood by the staff, of its own making, and specified down to a detailed, practical level, is a worthwhile effort. Some will say that this is impossible, that "there isn't time and money for planning." I respond by asking if they would take the same attitude toward the procedures in an operating room as they are being wheeled in for spinal surgery. Good planning in both schools and operating theatres simply cannot be impossible.

Suggested fourth step: Once under way, time and the means to track the progress of the program must be built in. Teachers will be threatened, inspired, exhausted, energized, and overwhelmed with the new ways of working. They will need time and opportunity to talk through what their experience is, to re-think approaches which seem not to be working as intended, and to make adjustments in the program. To assume that time for planning and planning again ceases when school starts is a mistake that will harm the program.

Such are four steps for consideration. The task can be made easier by starting with one age group—say, four-to-six-year-olds, and by planning the program for them as the years go by. Starting with a "pilot" group within a more conventional setting can also be helpful, as long as the routines of the parent institution do not critically intrude.

My advice ultimately rests on five key points. (1) Believe that all children can and want to use their minds, and that our expectations for them must be optimistic ones. (2) Pay careful attention to the three modes of learning and the three modes of teaching, and remember that the ultimate objective is to "produce" young people who know how to learn for themselves. (3) Develop a sensible local program that fits the Paideia framework, and engage in planning all those who will work in it. (4) Be patient: good school plans take time. (5) Keep a sense of humor and do not abandon your idealism.

ITEM C

A Letter from a Philosopher§

Editor's note: Mortimer J. Adler, director of the Institute for Philosophical Research in Chicago and a longtime proponent of educational reform, recently served on a committee to select recipients of college scholarships awarded by the Coca-Cola Scholars Foundation in Atlanta. Following are excerpts of an April 16 letter from Dr. Adler to Mebane M. Pritchett, the foundation's president. Mr. Pritchett is a former chairman of North Carolina's state Board of Education.

RALEIGH—This letter, which I promised you, I am writing on the Sunday morning after my return to Chicago yesterday, because I want to write while the whole experience is fresh in my mind.

First of all, I want to thank you for including me on the selection committee. I learned a great deal, both about the schools of this country and about the country itself. I wish I could say that it was all good news, but there was much that was depressing and that calls for energetic remedies.

On the positive side, all the 30 scholars that my committee interviewed were absolutely first-rate young men and women. Not only were they—all without exception—in the top 10 of their high school senior class; most of them were No. 1 in their class.

Most of them had already been accepted at the top universities of this country; all were planning to go to college and to pursue a career they had already chosen.

Quite apart from their school grades, they all clearly showed that they were highly intelligent young people: their native endowment was high. Over and above all these superlatives, they were all highly motivated super-achievers, not only well-motivated with regard to doing their school work, but also well-motivated with regard to serv-

§ Mortimer J. Adler to Mebane M. Pritchett, April 16, 1989. "A Letter from a Philosopher," *The News & Observer* (Raleigh, N.C.), April 30, 1989. Reprinted by permission.

ing the community, engaging in extracurricular activities, and performing public service. In addition, many of them held down jobs by which they earned much needed money.

All these wonderful things being so, it was all the more depressing that, with just one or two exceptions, all were poorly schooled; many of them realized they had been stuffed full of facts to be memorized in order to get good grades on tests; many of them realized that they had a large number of poor teachers; many of them criticized what they called the curriculum in their schools. But none of them, again with two exceptions, realized how seriously they had been deprived.

Their first and foremost deprivation was easy to discover. Asked what books they had read—books that were not assigned in class, not textbooks, not current light fiction—the answer was zero. The two exceptions were one girl whose parents had read to her since she was an infant; she had read one or two great novels. The other exception was a girl who went to a very small private school in Louisiana. She too had read a few great novels.

None of them had ever read an unassigned, nonfiction great book. They were all too busy to spend their time in libraries; they had no time to read what they were not required to read—textbooks. None had ever read any of the great books of Greek and Roman antiquity; none had ever read any of the nonfiction classics of modern times; none showed any understanding of the Declaration of Independence, or the Constitution, or the Federalist Papers.

To sum it up, by my standards, they were all top-notch test-takers, scoring high grades, but they were all culturally illiterate, in a more serious sense than that of Professor Hirsch of the University of Virginia.

Their cultural illiteracy will not be cured at most of the good universities and colleges at which they are going to become well-trained specialists. With the kind of schooling that they have received so far, and the kind they are going to get in most colleges, they are not likely to end up in their maturity being generally well-educated human beings.

What this country needs, politically as well as economically, are well-trained specialists in a wide variety of fields who are also generally educated human beings. Here is the most dismal failure of our education system, not only in K–12, but also in our colleges and universities.

Their cultural illiteracy is not the only defect that was glaringly apparent. Equally important was the fact that the instruction they had received did little or nothing for the training of their minds to think critically and creatively. Once you asked them a question off the beaten track, that required them to face a problem they had never faced before and think about it de novo, one drew a blank look or just a fumbling mess of words that really did not address the question posed. The look of shock on their faces when they are confronted with the task of thinking on their feet betrayed the fact that it was seldom if ever a part of their school experience.

If these top-ranking students, who were made proficient in passing subject-matter examinations with A's in every course, were poorly schooled as far as their mind's thinking abilities are concerned, their acquaintance with good literature, their use of libraries, their knowledge of history, especially American history, and their understanding of basic ideas and issues, just think—if one dares—of the mental condition of the lower three-fourths of their classmates, who are now enfranchised, who—we would like to hope—will become thinking citizens active in our political life, and who—we hope even more—will become effective members of the work force in this country's high-tech economy. What kind of future can we look forward to for this country, politically and economically, if our school system is not radically reformed in ways that the state legislatures do not have the slightest understanding of?

This is not to say that these top-ranking students were not acquainted with major contemporary problems—with the deterioration of the environment, with race relations, with genetic engineering problems, with international relations, etc. But if they were pushed to do some creative thinking about problems they recognized desperately called for solution, they were simply stumped. Nor could they follow an argument very well.

Most of them told us that the schools were not doing a very good job, but they were not very clear in telling us why they were failing so badly. They blamed the failure of the schools more upon the poor homes from which their low-achieving classmates came, than they did upon the fact that what happened in most classrooms turned students off rather than on; did not engage their minds; simply bored them. They did not realize that not just the home but also the school had to motivate students to learn; that they had to make learning a joyful experience; and that radical changes are called for in the kinds of teaching and learning that goes on in school.

It is noteworthy that most of the students in our group had one or both parents who were either teachers or in academic life. It is noteworthy that most of them were planning to go into medicine, law, engineering, or politics. Only one—one out of 30—was going to become a teacher. When they are asked about their classmates of high standing, they told us that none of them were going into teaching. Why not? Always the same answer: The pay was too low, and the job of teaching was not given much respect in our society.

One of them told us that he thought about 10 of his classmates were going into teaching. We asked him in what quartile of class rank those students stood. The answer was they were in the third quartile, one just above the bottom of the class. In other words, the very brightest students do not go into teaching because the economic and social rewards are low as compared with other occupations. The lowest ranks of the graduating class go into teaching because that looks like the only way they can earn a living. Just think of that, Mebane, and weep with me for the future of American education if we do not do something to remedy this deplorable situation.

What the Coca-Cola Scholars Foundation is doing is certainly worth doing; more corporations should follow suit. But if this is not followed up by spending a lot of money to improve our schools by changing the kind of teaching and learning that goes on there, then we are not going to solve our national political and economic problems in the next century.

CHAPTER 5

EDITORIAL WORK: THE BOARD OF EDITORS

1

Almost fifty years! While I was still on the faculty of the University of Chicago in 1943, I started doing editorial work for Encyclopaedia Britannica. Since the University received income from the company, this involved no conflict of interest.

From 1943 until 1952, I was mainly concerned with serving as Bob Hutchins' associate editor of the first edition of *Great Books of the Western World* and on the production of the *Syntopicon* to be published with that set of books. I became a member of the Board of Editors when it was established in 1948. I attended its semi-annual meetings from that point on, but I did not become actively engaged in editorial work on the encyclopaedia itself until 1965. In the intervening years, most of my editorial activities centered on the supplements to the great books set, such as *Gateway to the Great Books* and the great books annual volume, entitled *The Great Ideas Today.*

I said there was initially no conflict of interest between my connection with Britannica and my position at the University, but there soon turned out to be a conflict of time and energy.

By 1945, the direction of the large editorial staff required for the production of the *Syntopicon,* and the writing of the 102 essays on the great ideas, became so time-consuming that I took a leave of absence from my professorial post. I did continue to teach great books seminars with President Hutchins and to give lectures at the

University's downtown college until I departed entirely from academic life in 1952 to set up the Institute for Philosophical Research in San Francisco.

Throughout the 1950s and on into the 1960s until 1965, the meetings of the Board of Editors were occupied with the discussion of various proposals for a new edition, a fifteenth edition, of the encyclopaedia. The fourteenth edition had been published in 1929, and since then had undergone successive series of annual revisions, throughout all of which the encyclopaedia remained essentially the same in structure, a structure that it had had since its early editions in the eighteenth and nineteenth centuries: one sequence of alphabetically arranged long and short entries, accompanied by an alphabetically arranged index as the only means of access to its contents. The first few editions of *Encyclopaedia Britannica* did not have an index.

Bob Hutchins, who left the University of Chicago in 1951 to become Vice-President of the Ford Foundation, continued to serve as Chairman of Britannica's Board of Editors. In that capacity, he never wavered from his conviction that there was a better way of organizing the knowledge and information to be conveyed in a general encyclopaedia, other than simply by alphabetization.

The fifteen years of discussion, which occurred at the meetings of the Board of Editors, focused on the merits of alphabetical vs. topical organization. This prepared the way for the proposal in 1965 of what came to be called *Britannica 3* because its structure involved a *Micropaedia* for all the short informational entries, a *Macropaedia* for the long scholarly articles that conveyed knowledge in all the major fields of learning, and a *Propaedia,* an outline of knowledge and a topical table of contents, that would serve as a nonalphabetical finding device somewhat analogous to the way in which the *Syntopicon* served the set of great books.[1]

After almost ten years of editorial work, in which I served as Director of Editorial Planning and also as Editor of the *Propaedia,* with Warren Preece as Editor of the *Micropaedia* and the *Macro-*

1. At the initiation of the plan for the fifteenth edition of *Britannica,* I was indebted to Clifton Fadiman for his enthusiastic approval and his constructive assistance in formulating the first draft of a proposal to add a *Propaedia,* or topical table of contents, to the set.

paedia, the fifteenth edition of *Encyclopaedia Britannica* was published in January of 1974. I have told the story in Chapters 12 and 13 of *Philosopher at Large* of all the difficulties surmounted and all the intricacies that had to be ironed out. But what I could not have foreseen when I wrote that book was the complicated future developments, the major revisions and restructuring, that would take place in the subsequent twelve years. Nor could I have foreseen that there would ever be a second edition of *Great Books of the Western World,* with a revised and improved *Syntopicon.* When I wrote *Philosopher at Large* I thought that the two major editorial tasks that had occupied me between 1943 and 1974 were satisfactorily accomplished, so that they could stand unchanged in their basic structure—at least until well into the next century when advances in technology might require methods of communication other than words on the printed page.

I was wrong, innocently naive but not excusably so. In this chapter, I will complete the story of events that I did not foresee in 1974, or would then have thought most unlikely. I will deal mainly with two things. One was the struggle that led to a major improvement in the fifteenth edition of the encyclopaedia. This improvement first saw the light of day in the printing of 1985. Still further improvements did not reach completion until the early 1990s. The other was the initially aborted effort to bring the great books and the great ideas into the twentieth century. This led to the publication in 1990 of a second edition of *Great Books of the Western World,* expanded from fifty-four to sixty volumes. I will also have something to say about other sets of books that I edited for Britannica and other editorial products that I worked on.

2

Until 1949, *Encyclopaedia Britannica* did not have a Board of Editors. From 1768, it went through fourteen editions with an editorial staff and editorial consultants, supervised by an Editor-in-Chief who was responsible for planning and policy. It was Senator William Benton, who had become owner of the company in 1943 and publisher of its encyclopaedia, who established a Board of Editors in 1949 with a personnel drawn from the United Kingdom and the United States. At the same time, he appointed Robert Maynard Hutchins as its first Chairman.

Bob Hutchins had just taken leave of absence from the University when, after years of marital stress, he separated from his wife Maude and eventually sued her for divorce. It was a trying time for Bob and no one could have been more sympathetic to his predicament than his old friend and Yale classmate Bill Benton.

As the history of such events is usually reconstructed, one might be tempted to say that Benton was moved by deep reasons of policy in making this editorial innovation. That was not the fact of the matter. Bob Hutchins needed a job, an office, a title, a place to work, as well as tasks to perform in this interim period of his life before, having gained his divorce, he felt he could return to his post at the University. Making him Chairman of Britannica's Board of Editors fitted that ticket.

It also activated a genuine intellectual concern that had been present in Bob's mind ever since Benton had acquired the Britannica company in 1943 and gave the University preferred stock in the company and an annual royalty of 3 percent. From that point on, Hutchins, as President of the University, took seriously the University's obligation to improve the encyclopaedia in any way it could. Long before he became the first Chairman of its Board of Editors, he had given thought to matters of editorial revision and reconstruction. So what began as an act of friendship on Benton's part, pragmatically motivated by the occasion, very soon turned out to be a genuine employment of Bob's intellectual interests and energies.

The Board of Editors, in its first conception, was thought of as concerned with questions of editorial policy related solely to the production of *Encyclopaedia Britannica.* It later became the editorial conscience of the company with respect to all its products. Though its judgments of approval and disapproval, or its constructive recommendations, were advisory rather than mandatory in their effect on the decisions of the company's management, they were always seriously considered by management as serving to protect the good name of Encyclopaedia Britannica. Any product labeled with that name had to uphold the internationally recognized excellence associated with it.

I have been a member of the Board of Editors since its inception in 1949. One of my first acts, inspired by the work I had been doing on the *Syntopicon,* was the submission to the Board of a memorandum on how to remedy the defects of alphabetical organization if the encyclopaedia were to help those who might seek to use it in order to study in depth a whole field of subject matter. This was the first step in the long process that eventuated in the development of the plan for the *Propaedia, Micropaedia,* and *Macropaedia* of the fifteenth edition of *Britannica.*

That plan was reviewed, critically discussed, and implemented at meetings of the Board of Editors from 1965 until 1973. Then in 1974, Bob Hutchins retired as the Board's Chairman and, on his recommendation, I was appointed as his successor, a post I have held ever since. In the long period of my tenure, I have been blessed by association with friendly and cooperative heads of management—two presidents of the company, first Charles Swanson and then Peter Norton, and especially by my relationship with Robert Gwinn, who has been throughout my chairmanship of the Board of Editors the company's CEO.

3

Before I proceed to discuss the work of the Board of Editors after I became its Chairman in 1974, I think it might be informative to convey briefly my understanding of the Board's role and function, and at the same time to name its present personnel as well as the members of our University Advisory Committees. These committees were established in the early 1970s.

The most expeditious way to give readers my understanding of the role of the Board of Editors and of the University Advisory Committees is to place here a short statement that I wrote in 1989 for circulation to all the employees of the Britannica company. An excerpt from it follows.[2]

> Among the world's great encyclopaedias, many marks of distinction might be claimed for *Britannica,* but only one is incontestable.

2. Adler: "The Editorial Conscience," *KNOW,* Fall 1989, Chicago, Encyclopaedia Britannica, Inc., pp. 3–6. Reprinted by permission.

Encyclopaedia Britannica is the only truly global encyclopaedia. It is the only encyclopaedia that is distributed in all quarters of the Earth, in non-English-speaking countries as well as in English-speaking domains. It is the only English-language encyclopaedia that has major articles by contributors from many nations other than the United Kingdom and the United States, many of them translated into English from the language in which they are originally written. All of the other major general encyclopaedias, both in English and in other languages, are distributed almost entirely within the nation in the language of which they are written, and almost all of their contributors are of that nationality.

The composition of the Board of Editors and of the five University Advisory Committees is inseparably connected with the distinctive international character of the *Britannica*. This was not the case at the time of the board's establishment in 1949 and in its earlier years. But since the publication of the 15th edition in 1974, and increasingly so in subsequent years, the members of the board and of the committees are far-flung, representing the learning and scholarship of 10 great nations.

In very recent years the international character of our editorial intelligence has become more effectively integrated. The chairmen of the five University Advisory Committees attend meetings of our Board of Editors. They then report back to their committees on matters under deliberation by the board so their own deliberations can be guided accordingly.

The Board of Editors has 12 members in the United States and in the United Kingdom, 3 *ex-officio* members and the secretary to the board. There are 55 members of five University Advisory Committees from the United States, Australia, Canada, the United Kingdom and Europe. If enough space were available to describe all the scientific, scholarly and intellectual accomplishments of this assemblage, its eminence and brilliance would be difficult to surpass or overestimate.

While final decisions about all editorial productions of the company rest with its Board of Directors, the chairman of that board (who is the company's chief executive officer) and the company's president, these have always been made only after careful consultation with the chairman of the Board of Editors and with the company's editor in chief, who in turn are greatly influenced in their own thinking about all editorial matters by the consideration of the thinking of their advisers on the Board of Editors and on the University Advisory Committees. . . .

In . . . functioning [as the editorial conscience of the company], it ensures the authenticity, the authority, the accuracy and the general intellectual and scholarly excellence not only of the encyclopaedia to which the name Britannica is attached but also to all the other products that bear the Britannica name. The sterling quality of that name is the sacred trust we are pledged to preserve. Intangible as that may be, compared with the company's more bankable assets, it is, beyond all question, its greatest, its most irreplaceable, asset.

As chairman of the Editorial Planning Committee of the Board in the late '60s and early '70s, I think I can say with accuracy that the work we did to produce the *Propaedia, Micropaedia* and *Macropaedia* of the 15th edition in 1974 would not, and could not, have been done without the long preparation for it in the deliberations of the Board of Editors in the 15 years between 1950 and 1965, deliberations that explored and examined all the issues involved in going beyond the annual revision program that had been instituted shortly after the publication of the 14th edition in 1929. The result was an editorial departure from the 14th edition so extensive, so innovative and so radical as to deserve its being called not only the 15th edition but also the first genuine innovation in encyclopaedic construction in the 200 years of Britannica's history.

As chairman of the Board of Editors since 1974, I think I can also say with accuracy that the very important improvements in the 15th edition that occurred in the 1985 printing and are continuing in current annual revisions could not have been made without the editorial advice and recommendations arising from the Board of Editors and also from the University Advisory Committees that Tom Goetz [the Editor in Chief] and I met with on this continent and abroad.

Looking toward the next century as we now must, we think that any 16th edition should be as meaningful for the 21st century as the 15th edition has been for the end of the 20th. The contribution during the remaining years of this century that we can expect to receive from the Board of Editors and from the University Advisory

Committees will be an indispensable factor upon which Mr. Goetz and I and our successors must rely. . . .

Readers will find an inventory of the membership of the Board of Editors and the University Advisory Committees in the Notes appended to this chapter, Item A.

4

It was not long after the publication of the fifteenth edition of *Encyclopaedia Britannica* in 1974 that we began to discover its defects and deficiencies. At the time of its publication, flushed with the success of our achievement, we boasted that what we had produced "was more useful in more ways to more people." That was partly true, but not completely so.

We first heard complaints from librarians all over the country that the set did not have a satisfactory finding device; notably, a conventional index, and they did not regard the topical organization of the *Propaedia* as a useful fact-finding device. We had placed alphabetical indexing in the ten volumes of the *Micropaedia,* the indexing attached to the short articles therein. But ten volumes of such alphabetical indexing scattered throughout ten volumes did not serve the purpose of reference librarians.

We ourselves found other things that needed remedying. The task of producing the fifteenth edition—43,000,000 words in 32 volumes—had been a gigantic one, one done under an intense time schedule, under pressure, and without the technological advantages that have now become available.

As we reexamined the *Macropaedia* and *Micropaedia* we saw how they could be improved. In creating the original distinction between them, we had concentrated on the matter of the *length* of the articles—long for Macro, short for Micro. It now became apparent that a far more useful distinction could—and should—be made, one based not on length but upon *content.* The *Micropaedia,* while still the locus of the shorter articles, would be the place for look-it-up reference information, the who, the what, the when, the where; and it would deal with what we came to call *singulars,* individual persons, places, things, events. The *Macropaedia,* on the other hand, would deal with "why," and its articles (with some few exceptions) would cover whole fields of knowledge, so that individual subjects could be compared and contrasted and seen within a larger context. The writing of the two types of articles would also reflect their purposes and uses: the Micro descriptive, the Macro discursive. Though the *Propaedia* functioned as a topical table of contents for the encyclopaedia, offsetting its alphabetical organization, we reopened the old question that had concerned the Board of Editors in the preceding decades, the question of the comparative merits of the topical vs. the alphabetical organization of a general encyclopaedia.

The company, having spent $32 million on the production of the fifteenth edition, was inclined to proceed with greatly reduced editorial budgets in the years immediately following its publication. The deliberations of the Board of Editors were necessarily limited to the consideration of revisions that could be accomplished with such reduced editorial budgets. But after the lapse of a few years, the Board could not be restrained from reopening fundamental editorial questions about ways to improve the fifteenth edition or even go beyond it to a sixteenth edition with a radically different structure than that of the fifteenth.

In 1979, after Philip W. ("Tom") Goetz was appointed Editor in Chief, he and I came up with a plan and proposed it to the Board of Editors and to the management of the company. Why not put all the biographies in one or two volumes entitled "Persons"? Why not put all the geographical articles in a series of volumes entitled "Places"? Why not a similar treatment of all the historical articles and all the articles about things, i.e., particular monuments, edifices, institutions, organizations, all of which are designated by proper name?

Having thus disposed of all the articles about proper-named singular items that belong in a comprehensive encyclopaedia, we were left with thousands of general articles, i.e., the subjects treated in the sphere of the sciences and other fields of scholarship, as well as philosophy, law, and medicine. These we proposed to place in a series of volumes that would be entitled with the names used for the various parts and divisions of the *Propaedia*. The topical headings of the *Propaedia* could be retained as a table of contents for each of these volumes, and the *Propaedia* would, therefore, no longer be a separate volume in the set, having been replaced by a series of topically constituted volumes.

For those seeking information about particular matters of fact that would be scattered throughout the set, a one- or two-volume general index would be added as an effective finding device. But the set we thus envisaged, in addition to eliminating the need for a one-volume *Propaedia,* would also not have a *Micropaedia* and a *Macropaedia.* It would no longer be "EB 3," which was our in-house name for the fifteenth edition.

It should not be hard to imagine the storm of protests that this proposal elicited, both from members of the Board of Editors and from management, who were rightly concerned with problems of promotion, advertising, and marketability. The disputations and controversies that consumed many meetings of the Board of Editors sometimes became vehement and even vindictive.

I can remember a point at which I shocked the President of the company by suggesting that we postpone for the time being any further meetings of the Board of Editors. I regret that indiscretion on my part. At another point, I thought of resorting to FDR's device of "packing the Supreme Court" by appointing new members of the Board that might give Tom Goetz and me the majority we needed to get our radical new plan adopted.

But even if that had been done, it still would not have been accepted by the management of the company for what I believe to be sound business considerations. In retrospect, I am glad that Tom Goetz and I lost our crusade for a totally topical encyclopaedia. Out of all the wrangling and disputing came a sound and quite acceptable plan for the revision of the fifteenth edition that retained the three-part structure of the *Propaedia, Micropaedia,* and *Macropaedia,* all revised, and to which were added an extraordinarily comprehensive two-volume alphabetical index and also a one-volume statistical summary entitled *Britannica World Data.*

This improved fifteenth edition began to be published in 1985, but the completion of all the steps in its improvement did not occur until the early 1990s. Let me briefly describe all the improvements that were agreed upon by the Board of Editors, adopted and financed by the management of the company, and enthusiastically received by its sales force.

First of all, let me comment on the introduction of the volume that contained a statistical summary of the year's changes in economic and demographic data. When such matters of fact are distributed throughout the thirty volumes of the encyclopaedia, their annual updating is an extremely costly affair. Even if only one line on a page has to be changed for updating purposes, the cost of that updating is close to the cost of resetting the whole page. We were compelled to spend so much money in this updating process each year that not enough money was left in our editorial budgets to accomplish more serious scholarly revisions.

The innovation of putting all or most of the material that might need updating year after year into a single volume not only provided desirable economies; it also made it possible to enable owners of the set in a given year to keep their set up to date in subsequent years. The *Britannica World Data* is a supplementary volume bound in with the *Britannica Book of the Year.* The first section of *World Data* deals with the nations of the world individually, providing annually the most up-to-date statistics available from the various nations, and covering political, economic, and social matters in depth. The second section presents these data by subject, so that the various nations can be compared, one against another. Thus, owners of the encyclopaedia, by purchasing the yearbook, are able to maintain the statistical currency of their sets.

We improved the readability and the usability of the *Propaedia* by a radical typographical revision of its page format. By the new typography that we adopted, the user of the *Propaedia* was referred to major articles in the *Macropaedia* and to relevant parts of other articles. In addition, references to articles in the *Micropaedia* were organized under topical headings.

In the years between 1977 and 1985, the contents of the *Macropaedia* were revised by the following editorial procedures. All of the articles within a given field were gathered together into a "cluster" (as the articles piano, violin, trumpet, etc., would comprise the cluster for Musical Instruments). These clusters were sent to outside experts for review and comment, with the result that all articles were updated and/or revised, some new titles were added, some old titles deleted, errors were corrected, and so on. Internally, the editors examined the expert reviews with an eye toward maintaining the proper encyclopaedic balance between and among the various clusters. In addition, special *Micropaedia* entries were prepared (by the staff) for all subjects treated in the *Macropaedia.* These entries contain brief content—definition description—but serve mainly as an introduction and guide to the *Macropaedia* article on the subject. A great deal of cross-referencing was also added—from *Micropaedia* to *Propaedia,* to the Index, to *Macropaedia,* to the *Book of the Year,* and to other parts of the *Micropaedia* itself.

Finally, I come to the great improvement that we made in the *Macropaedia* as a result of the Board's approval of my proposal of reorganizing its articles in an "alphatopical" fashion. We thus resolved the conflict that had occurred earlier when Tom Goetz and I proposed a completely topical organization for the whole encyclopaedia. We did this by retaining an alphabetical arrangement of articles in both the *Micropaedia* and the *Macropaedia.* But, in the *Macropaedia,* we replaced the short, usually one word, titles of the articles by topical titles that were like the titles of books or essays, in which one word would operate to place the article alphabetically.

This alphatopical reorganization of the *Macropaedia* resulted in the consolidation of the many general articles that previously had been separated by a purely alphabetical arrangement. Instead of having more than 4,500 articles in the *Macropaedia,* the 1985 printing would have fewer than 700 general articles, all of the longer ones with a table of contents as a guide to its own interior structure: and each with an introductory section written in a style that would be thoroughly intelligible to the intelligent layman, even though some part of that article's content might not be so. In this way, we could more closely approximate our editorial ideal of making all the articles in the *Macropaedia* as well as in the *Micropaedia,* even articles in the field of mathematics and of the exact sciences, at least partly, if not wholly, intelligible to the curious, intelligent layman.

The reduction of 2,500 general articles to 600 involved combining articles that had been written by different authors at different times with different contexts. The combining process resulted in repetitions as well as omissions in the treatment of the subject and even some cases of apparent or real contradictions. In addition, the writing by the different authors of the articles that we combined were uneven stylistically.

The stylistic homogenization of the long 600 articles of the alphatopically organized *Macropaedia,* as well as the rectification of repetitions and omissions, could not be accomplished in time for the 1985 printing. That is why it has taken until the 1990s to complete the exacting editorial work involved in the alphatopical reorganization of the *Macropaedia.*

In the years since 1985, while the editorial department of the company completed the work described above, the Board of Editors, in addition to continuing its consideration of improvements in the *Propaedia,* was charged with the task of thinking about the shape that a sixteenth edition of the encyclopaedia might take sometime in the early decades of the next century. In its deliberations about this, the Board has been cognizant of the effect on encyclopaedia-making of the extraordinary technological advances that can be expected in the use of the computer and of the electronic media of communication in relation to teaching and learning.

That a sixteenth edition of *Encyclopaedia Britannica* will avail itself of these technological devices to combine the linear thinking and learning that occur in the use of the printed page with the nonlinear, nonleft-to-right modes of communication made available by the electronic screen, is unquestionable. But whether the electronic screen will totally replace the printed page is still highly questionable. This is the major problem that confronts the Board of Editors in the remaining years of this century.

5

In all my years as a member of the Board of Editors, even when I served as its Chairman, my predominant intellectual interest was in the great books, above that of the encyclopaedia. They were central in my life long before I started to work for the Britannica company. In fact, it was I who brought them to the attention of Bob Hutchins and Bill Benton and provoked Bill into inviting Bob and me to edit a set of great books for the Britannica company to publish.

My interest in the encyclopaedia as an object to think about came much later, and even while I was almost completely engaged in the production of the fifteenth edition, I still managed to find time and energy to conduct great books seminars and give lectures on the great ideas.

Of the two large sets of books the Britannica company publishes and sells, the encyclopaedia (EB) and the great books (GBWW), I made no bones about proclaiming the superiority of the latter as food for the mind and as an instrument of learning, just as EB is superior in matters of fact and information. In my frequent meetings with members of the sales force, in this country and abroad, I would tell them why they should always try to see the two sets of books together, not just EB by itself or only GBWW. I explained why they should do this in the following terms.

Just as food, drink, shelter, clothing, and sleep are goods of the body, satisfying its basic needs, so information, organized knowledge, understanding, and wisdom are goods of the mind, satisfying its basic intellectual needs. EB, I pointed out, provided its owners with the means to acquire information (in the *Micro*) and organized knowledge (in the *Macro*), but for the understanding of ideas and for the attainment of practical and theoretical wisdom, one had to go to the great books, with its syntopical indexing of the discussion of the great ideas. The two sets of books together covered the waterfront; neither alone sufficed.

It was not until the late sixties and early seventies that the first steps toward reconsidering the contents of GBWW first occurred. In an advertising brochure for the great books, I proposed a list of twentieth-century authors and titles that might be added to the set and solicited individuals to vote for those they approved. A little later, in 1972, Charles Van Doren and I revised *How to Read a Book,* which I had written in 1939 and which was published in 1940. The first edition contained a list of great books as an appendix. That list anticipated in large measure the list of authors and titles included in the first edition of *Great Books of the Western World.* After all, both lists had drawn heavily on the readings selected by John Erskine for his great books seminars in the college at Columbia University in the 1920s.

The list of great books that Charles Van Doren and I appended to our revision of *How to Read a Book* in 1972 went beyond the Erskine list, the list appended to the first edition of *How to Read a Book* in 1940, and the list assembled by the editors of the first edition of *Great Books of the Western World.* It not only included new authors in the period from Homer to the end of the nineteenth century, but it also included a number of authors whose works were published well after the beginning of the twentieth century.

In addition to these two early impulses toward revising and enlarging *Great Books of the Western World,* motivation in the same direction came from another quarter. When the omission of Molière's plays was called to my attention, I explained that in the 1940s no English translation of them was available. In the case of the two Homeric epics, the tragedies of Aeschylus, Sophocles, and Euripides, the comedies of Aristophanes, Virgil's *Aeneid,* and other works of Greek and Roman antiquity, we included poor translations because better translations were not then available.

For reasons difficult to explain, there was an extraordinary splurge of translating activity in the fifties and sixties. We were, therefore, quite conscious that the set published in 1952 could be improved by the substitution of better translations for the less adequate ones included in the set. The desirability of doing this was called to our attention; members of Britannica's Board of Directors urged the editorial department to consider undertaking this. With the help of Clifton Fadiman, I compiled an inventory of translations of works, both ancient and modern, that were superior to the translations included in the set. That inventory resided in my files until late 1988, when we began working on the project of a second edition of GBWW.

I was engaged in two other editorial ventures that were undertaken in the years before we seriously started on the project of improving, enlarging, and enriching *Great Books of the Western World.* Both were aborted.

In 1977 I formed a committee to work on producing a set of

books to be entitled "Great Books of the 20th Century." This committee held a series of meetings over a period of three years, out of which came a collection of memoranda from the members arguing for one or another group of twentieth-century authors and titles. At the end of three years, we finally gave up the project for the following reasons.

On the one hand, the authors about whom we could reach substantial agreement had written their books before 1930 or before the beginning of the Second World War. They themselves were nineteenth-century persons insofar as their own education, temperaments, and sensibilities were concerned. To publish a set of books restricted to their works would hardly represent the contributions most strikingly characteristic of the twentieth century.

On the other hand, we could not reach substantial agreement about books written after the Second World War by authors born in this century and representative of its most characteristic trends. It was still too early to make a reliable judgment about their worth; they were too recent to be viewed in sufficient perspective.

Out of this aborted project came articles written by Clifton Fadiman and me about our nominations for great books of the twentieth century. These were published in *Playboy* magazine, January 1966. Also *Time* magazine's issue of March 7, 1977, published an article giving my list of recommended twentieth-century authors and titles and challenging some of its inclusions and omissions. At this time, no questions were raised about female authors, black authors, and non-Western authors. Those questions were not raised until much later, beginning at Stanford University in 1988.

The other aborted venture began in Tokyo in the middle seventies. I was there to work with Frank Gibney on editorial problems connected with the publication of *Britannica International Encyclopaedia,* our Japanese encyclopaedia, and also with the Japanese branch of EB. In Tokyo at that time, the United Nations had established an international university, mainly devoted to research in pressing political and economic problems. Alexander Kwapong, who had been Vice-Chancellor of the University of Ghana, was the Vice-Rector of the United Nations University in Tokyo. He was a friend of mine through our association at the Aspen Institute. It was to him that Frank Gibney and I went with our proposal to construct a set of books to be entitled "Great Books of the World," combining the contributions of the West with those of the several cultural traditions in the countries of the Far East.

This project had occurred to me on one of my trips to Tokyo on Britannica business. I discovered a ninety-volume set of books that included, in the Japanese language, almost all of the authors and titles that were in GBWW as well as an equally large number of what were regarded as Far Eastern classics. This led me to ask myself whether it would be feasible to take this very large number of authors and titles and boil it down to the twenty-five or so works that could be regarded as of truly global significance for the whole period of recorded history from its beginnings to the present century.

Frank Gibney, Alex Kwapong, and I discussed this project on a number of occasions and drew up some very tentative nominations for inclusion in such a set of books. We thought of the United Nations University as the appropriate organization to sponsor such a project and to lend it support, financial and otherwise.

When Kwapong proposed it to the leading members of the faculty, they evinced little or no interest in it. That was one reason why the project was dropped by Gibney and me.

The other reason was my own realization that a set of global great books, combining the cultural traditions of both the West and the Far East, could not include a syntopicon that referred to one great conversation about the great ideas discussed in these books.

A great conversation of the kind that existed in the Western tradition does not exist globally. The great authors in the several cultural traditions in the Far East do not talk to one another, nor do they talk to the great authors in the Western tradition and the latter do not talk to them. There was as yet no cultural or intellectual community of global extent.

Years earlier I had discovered this on visits to the East-West Center that the government of the United States had established in Honolulu. Beardsley Ruml, who had been Dean of the Social Sciences at the University of Chicago and was then Vice-President of R. H. Macy and Company in New York, suggested that the *Syn-*

topicon should be expanded to include references to the literature of the Far East. That sent me to the East-West Center in Honolulu, where its director gathered representatives of the four or five Far Eastern cultures to discuss the great ideas I had treated in the *Syntopicon*.

To test the feasibility of Ruml's proposal, I chose what I thought were Western ideas most likely to be found in the several Far Eastern cultures: liberty, equality, and justice. Our discussion never went beyond liberty, for it revealed that that word, or its synonym "freedom," was not used univocally in the Western and Far Eastern cultures. The different Far Eastern senses of these words amounted to almost sheer equivocation, like the equivocal use of the word "pen" for a writing instrument and an enclosure for pigs.

Of course, the words "liberty" and "freedom" are used in four or five distinct senses in Western literature, as I had shown in my two-volume work on *The Idea of Freedom* (Volume I, 1958; Volume II, 1961); but I also showed therein how they all participated in one common meaning underlying the different senses of the word. This prevented them from being used in a completely equivocal manner.

One other experience that I had in mainland China confirmed my conviction that the world was not yet ready for one global cultural community or for one set of global great books in which one great conversation was going on about one set of great ideas. We have reached the stage where mathematics, the exact sciences, and their consequent technologies have become transcultural, but that is not yet true of history, the social sciences, philosophy, and religion. I was impressed with the prevalence of the idea of harmony in Chinese culture. No rendering of Chinese philosophical or religious thought could fail to focus on it. But harmony is not one of the 102 great ideas treated in the *Syntopicon*. It is not even mentioned in most of the Western great books; it is only a minor consideration in the few in which it is mentioned. It is not a major theme in the great conversation that has been going on in the twenty-five centuries of the Western tradition.

This completes my report of the experiences, the discoveries, and the aborted efforts that occurred in the years prior to 1987 when Robert Gwinn, Chairman of Britannica's Board of Directors, asked me whether we should not now consider the possibility of a revised, improved, enlarged, and enriched second edition of *Great Books of the Western World.*

My response was immediate, affirmative, and enthusiastic in the light of the background for such an undertaking that I have reported in the preceding pages. Tom Goetz, Britannica's Editor-in-Chief concurred in my reaction; and when I mentioned this as a possibility to the Board of Editors, their reaction was also enthusiastically affirmative.

Before I go on to the next section to report the steps that were taken to produce a second edition of *Great Books of the Western World,* let me state here that, at Bob Gwinn's instigation and urging, Britannica's management agreed to finance the project, setting October of 1990 as the date at which they hoped we would have the second edition ready to unveil and to distribute. How many volumes the second edition would contain; whether, in addition to new translations, we would add new authors and titles in the period between Homer and the end of the nineteenth century; whether we should also include a sampling of twentieth-century authors; how the *Syntopicon* would have to be revised—these were all questions that could be answered only after the editorial apparatus requisite for answering them had been set up and was in operation.

6

I served as Editor in Chief of GBWW's second edition and was assisted by Tom Goetz and Clifton Fadiman as associate editors; and also by Anne Long Dimopoulos, who, in addition to being secretary of the Board of Editors, served as Project Manager in the production of the set.

Goetz, Fadiman, and I worked with an editorial board that consisted of the following persons: Douglas Allanbrook, Senior tutor and Associate Dean, St. John's College, Annapolis, Maryland; Jacques Barzun, Provost Emeritus, Columbia University, and literary adviser, Charles Scribner's Sons; Norman Cousins (deceased), Professor of Medicine, University of California at Los Angeles; John Kenneth Galbraith, Professor of Economics, Harvard University; Heinz R. Pagels (deceased), Director, New York Academy of Sciences; Lord Quinton, former Chairman, The British Library Board, London, and also former President, Trinity College, Oxford.[3]

In addition to these associates, we formed an international committee of consultants to whom the nominations made by the editorial board would be sent for approval or disapproval, as well as for comments and recommendations. Readers will find this list of persons as Item B in the Notes appended to this chapter.

When we had completed a second draft of the nominations for inclusion in or omission from the second edition, the next and final step in constituting the contents of the set involved submitting this second draft for consideration to the Board of Editors and to the University Advisory Committees, the membership of which readers will find as Item A in the Notes appended to this chapter.

The editorial board met in New York in May of 1988. The members had been provided in advance with various lists of nominees for addition to the set, especially twentieth-century authors and titles. I opened this meeting by stating the criteria for selection that Hutchins and I had employed in the 1940s when we met with a similar editorial board to decide on the authors and titles for inclusion in *Great Books of the Western World*. Now as then, considerations of space played a critical role. Some things had to be rejected or eliminated to prevent the set from becoming economically unfeasible to produce, distribute, or purchase and use.

At the end of a long and, on the whole, pleasantly harmonious session, we came up with our first draft of authors and titles. Before this draft was submitted to our international committee of consultants and other groups, a footnote had to be added to it stating the authors and titles in the first edition that we proposed to drop from the second. There were four: the *Conics* of Apollonius of Perga; Joseph Fourier's *Analytical Theory of Heat;* Henry Fielding's *Tom Jones,* and *Tristram Shandy* by Laurence Sterne. The first two of these were thought to be mathematical treatises of unusual difficulty for most readers to comprehend.

3. This editorial board, especially Jacques Barzun, made many recommendations of authors and works to be included or eliminated.

We then proceeded with submitting our first draft to our international committee of consultants, to Britannica's Board of Editors, and to our University Advisory Committees. This process involved much discussion and correspondence over many months, at the end of which we came up with a final draft of the second edition's table of contents, including a list of the new and much better translations that we sought to acquire from their publishers. I have placed that list in Item C in the Notes attached to this chapter. It enables readers to see where new translations have been added, which authors not in the first edition have been added to the second, and to examine the contents of the six new volumes that we added to include the forty-five twentieth-century authors selected as a sampling of this century's writings.

Before I state the three criteria that our editorial board employed for its first draft selections and that we asked all the persons we consulted to keep in mind in judging what we submitted to them, let me say that at no point did we attain unanimity. One hundred percent agreement is too much to expect in proceedings of this kind. However, where there were unresolved disagreements, these did not exceed more than 10 percent; i.e., the items about which such disagreement occurred were less than 10 percent of the whole. That, it seems to me, is remarkable, and also sufficient to rely upon.

When all these preliminaries were completed and after the work of editorial production had begun, I found myself dissatisfied with three decisions we had made (much less than 10 percent of the whole). I regretted dropping the *Conics* of Apollonius, which was not much more difficult than Euclid's *Elements,* which we retained in the set. I thought we were wrong in dropping Fielding's *Tom Jones,* as the frequency in the *Syntopicon* of references to its contents attested, indicating its substantial presence in the great conversation. And I thought we were wrong in adding Voltaire's *Candide.* Voltaire is a great author and one of enormous influence, but by our three criteria for selection, *Candide* is not a great book.[4]

What were those three criteria of selection? The first was the

4. One other omission that was probably a mistake on our part was not including references to the Koran (qur'ān) along with the Old and New Testament in the Reference Section of the 102 chapters of the *Syntopicon.*

book's contemporary significance—relevance to the problems and issues of the twentieth century. The books were not to be regarded as archaeological relics—monuments in our intellectual tradition. They should be works that are as much of concern to us today as at the time they were written, even if that was centuries ago. They are thus essentially timeless—always contemporary, and not confined to interests that change from time to time or from place to place.

The second criterion was their infinite rereadability or, in the case of the more difficult mathematical and scientific works, their studiability again and again. Most of the 400,000 books published each year are not worth carefully reading even once; many fewer than 1,000 each year are worth reading more than once. When, infrequently in any century, a great book does appear, it is a book worth reading again and again and again. It is inexhaustibly rereadable. It cannot be fully understood on one, two, or three readings. More is to be found on all subsequent readings. This is an exacting criterion, an ideal that is fully attained by only a small number of the 511 works that we selected. It is approximated in varying degrees by the rest.

The third criterion was the relevance of the work to a very large number of great ideas and great issues that have occupied the minds of thinking individuals for the last twenty-five centuries. The authors of these books take part in the great conversation, not only by reading the works of many of their predecessors, but also by discussing many of the 102 great ideas treated in the *Syntopicon*. In other words, the great books are the books in which the great conversation occurs about the great ideas. It is the set of great ideas that determines the choice of the great books.

In a book entitled *The Great Conversation,* which is not a part of the set's second edition but which accompanies it as an introduction to the set and as a guide to its use, we have demonstrated this point by two devices. One is something that we called the Author-to-Author Index, which shows how many of each author's predecessors that author has cited in his work. The other is the Author-to-Idea Index, which shows in how many of the 102 great ideas treated in the *Syntopicon* readers will find references to that author's work on one or more topics, usually many. These two indices, along with the *Syntopicon* itself, are clear evidence of the reality of the great conversation, in which the great authors and the great books have participated.

By this criterion, the difference between great books and good books is not a difference in degree, but a difference in kind. There is not a continuum that has poor books on the far left, average books in the middle, good and very good books on the right, and a few Great Books on the far right.

As I have recently written elsewhere, the adjective "great" in the phrase "great books" derives its primary meaning from its use in the phrase "great ideas." There are many other criteria by which people make up diverse lists of the books they wish to honor by calling them "great books." But from the primary significance of the adjustive "great" as applied to the great ideas is derived the significance of that adjective as used in the phrase, "the great conversation."

In other words, we chose the great books on the basis of their relevance to at least 25 of the 102 great ideas. Many of the great books are relevant to a much larger number of the 102 great ideas, as many as 75 or more great ideas, a few to all 102 great ideas. In sharp contrast are the good books that are relevant to less than 10 or even as few as 4 or 5 great ideas. We placed such books in the lists of Recommended Readings to be found in the last section in each of the 102 chapters of the *Syntopicon*. Examples of such books will be found in the Notes to this chapter as Item D. Here readers will find many twentieth-century female authors, black authors, and Latin American authors whose works we recommended but did not include in the second edition of the *Great Books*.

To complete the picture of the criteria that controlled our editorial process of selection, it is necessary for me to mention a number of things that we definitely excluded from our deliberations.

We did not base our selections on an author's nationality, religion, politics, or field of study; nor on an author's race or gender. Great books were not chosen to make up quotas of any kind; there was no "affirmative action" in the process.

In the second place, we did not consider the influence exerted by an author or a book on later developments in literature or society. That factor alone did not suffice to merit inclusion. Scholars may point out the extraordinary influence exerted by an author or a book, but if the three criteria stated above were not met, that author or book was not to be chosen. Many of the great books have exerted great influence upon later generations, but that by itself was not the reason for their inclusion.[5]

In the third place, a consideration not operative in the selection process was the truth of an author's opinions or views, or the truth to be found in a particular work. This point is generally misunderstood; many persons think that we regard the great books as a repository of mankind's success in its ever-continuing pursuit of the truth. *That is simply not the case*. There is much more error in the great books than there is truth. By anyone's criteria of what is true or false, the great books will be found to contain some truths, but many more mistakes and errors.

As the *Syntopicon* will show anyone who uses it, in almost all of its 3,000 topics the authors cited are opposed, contradicting one another or arguing with one another for diverse views, theories, or doctrines.

There is dialectical agreement among them insofar as they are at least arguing about the same theme or issue, but there is more doctrinal disagreement among them than there is doctrinal agreement. That this is the case should not astoninsh anyone who recognizes that for every judgment that is true or correct, there can be many contrary or opposed judgments that are false or incorrect. The relation between truth and error on any point is a one-many relationship; as in the field of our conduct, the relation between what is good and evil, or right and wrong, is also a one-many relationship.[6]

5. This negative consideration applies, in my judgment, to Voltaire and his *Candide*. It also applies to the German philosopher Leibniz and his works. Just think of the influence exerted by *Uncle Tom's Cabin!*

6. Of course, what has just been said about truth and falsity, good and evil, or right and wrong, will have no significance for individuals who are relativists about such matters or who are skeptical about the objectivity of human judgments about them. But they are usually persons who are opposed to the whole business of attempting to produce a set of great books and who would have little or no interest in using the *Syntopicon*.

This fact should not be thought invidious to the worth of reading the great books or of using the *Syntopicon*. On the contrary, it is of the greatest positive importance. No truth is fully understood by anyone unless and until all the errors it corrects are understood and all the contradictions found are resolved.[7]

The *Syntopicon* was contructed with this in mind. Presenting a wide variety and divergence of views or opinions, among which there is likely to be some truth but much more error, the *Syntopicon* invites readers to think for themselves and allows them to make up their own minds on every topic under consideration.

When I wrote the 102 introductory essays for the opening section of each chapter on one of the great ideas, I think I succeeded in being dialectically objective and neutral, presenting all points of view on a given issue without tipping my hat or nodding my head in favor of any one of them.

Such dialectical objectivity consists in being point-of-view-less in the treatment of all points of view. It is a neutral detachment that can be described as dealing impartially with the partisanship of opposed opinion.

There are two other matters that I would like to mention in connection with the project of producing a set of great books.

(1) In our editorial capacity, all of us were aware of the fact that many of the authors and titles we chose for this purpose, as well as many that we did not include, are available in sets offered by other publishers, such as the Everyman Library, the Modern Library, and the Penguin Classics.

But, as Lord Quinton pointed out in his address at the Library of Congress on the occasion of celebrating the publication of GBWW's second edition, the distinctive difference between GBWW and these other collections is clear. The others are just collections of books, but GBWW is not just a collection of books,

7. Resolving contradictions is an indispensable step in the pursuit of truth; finding contradictions to resolve facilitates that pursuit because the contradiction necessarily contains the truth as well as a related falsehood. It is in the context of a plurality of errors to be corrected, and contradictions to be resolved, that the brilliance of the truth shines out and illuminates the scene.

but an integrally organized set of books, bound together by their related contributions to the great conversation about great ideas.

GBWW, in either its first or second edition, would not thus be distinctive were it not accompanied by the *Syntopicon*. Without that, it would just be another collection of books and would not serve readers, as GBWW does, to help them grow intellectually in the attainment of understanding and some modicum of wisdom.

(2) Considerations of space seriously affected the work of selection in the case of twentieth-century titles. Our choice of authors was accomplished with the same 90 percent reliability that attended our choices in the period between Homer and the end of the nineteenth century. But in order to include the forty-five authors that we thought to be a satisfactory representation of what the twentieth century had contributed, we could not, because of their length, select the titles of works that were the great works of those authors.

For example, in the case of novels, we could not choose the *Ulysses* of James Joyce, but rather chose the much shorter work, *A Portrait of the Artist as a Young Man*. In the case of Thomas Mann, we could not choose *The Magic Mountain*, but had to use *Death in Venice* instead. This applied to most of the twentieth-century writers of fictional literature. It also applied to many authors in the fields of theology, philosophy, economics, sociology, and anthropology. The two outstanding exceptions were works in mathematics and mathematical physics.

The six volumes in the set devoted to twentieth-century authors must, therefore, be viewed as a sampling of works written by authors that we felt secure in nominating for a set of books to be published in the twenty-first century, entitled "Great Books of the 20th Century." The editors of that set, using the same criteria that governed our selections, would have greater perspective than we had and, in addition, they would not be limited by considerations of space and length.

Lacking the greater perspective that they would enjoy, we also limited ourselves to works published before the mid-fifties of this century. Anything published more recently than that was too recent for us to have sufficient perspective for a sound judgment.

Adler in his Chicago office, 1988.
Photo by José Moré. Courtesy of Chicago Tribune

Adler's eightieth birthday celebration given by Encyclopaedia Britannica, Inc., at the Tavern Club, Chicago, December 1982.

Colleagues and friends attending the eightieth birthday celebration. Left to right: Charles and Geraldine Van Doren; John and Mira Van Doren.

Adler with Charles Swanson, then President of Encyclopaedia Britannica, Inc., and Robert Gwinn, Chairman of the Board of Directors of Britannica, looking through the book of congratulatory letters.

LEFT: Adler with students and teachers from Millbrook High School in Raleigh who participated in the five seminars videotaped by the University of North Carolina's Center for Public Television, Chapel Hill, 1987.
Photo by Patricia Weiss

BELOW: Adler conducting a Paideia seminar for sixth, seventh, and eighth graders at Goldblatt Elementary School in Chicago, 1988.
Photo by José Moré. Courtesy of Chicago Tribune

Dedication of the Mortimer J. Adler Seminar Room at Goldblatt Elementary School in Chicago, May 1990. Left to right: Catherine Tanner, art teacher, presenting Adler with a gift; Lillian Nash, Principal; Askia Patton, student; Roberta Brooks, Paideia Program Developer.
© Eric Werner

Adler with Lord Quinton, former Chairman of the British Library Board, and Lady Quinton at the Library of Congress Banquet celebrating the publication of *Great Books of the Western World* (2nd Edition), October 1990.
Photo by Howard L. Sachs. Courtesy of Encyclopaedia Britannica, Inc.

Clifton Fadiman.
Photo by Bob Ponce. Courtesy of Santa Barbara News-Press

Adler with Milton Rosenberg, Host, "Extension 720," WGN Radio, December 1991, discussing *Desires, Right & Wrong.*
Photo by George Burns. Courtesy of WGN Radio, Chicago

Adler with William F. Buckley, Jr., on the set of "Firing Line" discussing *Haves Without Have-Nots*, 1992. *© Jan Lukas*

Old-time friend and colleague Elizabeth Paepcke, in Aspen, 1989. She and her late husband, Walter, were founders of the Aspen Institute.

ABOVE: Adler with Larry Aldrich on a chartered yacht on the Ionian Sea, 1984.

LEFT: Adler with Henry Anatole Grunwald, then Ambassador to Austria, outside the U.S. Embassy in Vienna, 1989.

RIGHT: Adler and Philip Goetz, then Editor in Chief, Encyclopaedia Britannica, Inc., strolling through the Open Air Market in Zurich, Switzerland, on the way to the first meeting of the newly formed European Universities Advisory Committee, 1986.
Photo by Carolyn Goetz

RIGHT, TOP: Adler with Clare Boothe Luce at her home in Honolulu in April 1970.

RIGHT, CENTER: Adler greeting Associate Supreme Court Justice Harry Blackmun and his wife following *Great Books of the Western World* celebratory banquet held at the Library of Congress, October 1990.
Photo by Howard L. Sachs. Courtesy of Encyclopaedia Britannica, Inc.

RIGHT, BOTTOM: Adler with his old friend and former student, Philip Rosenthal, 1988.

Adler's sister, Dr. Carolyn Lewis, seated at the piano in her home in Kensington, California, 1988.

Adler looking on as General Robert Taylor congratulates his son Philip upon his graduation from Claremont-McKenna College, California, 1989.

Adler with his son Douglas, upon his graduation from Carnegie-Mellon University, Pittsburgh, 1986.

RIGHT: Adler with his son Michael and granddaughter Morgan in Aspen, 1990.

BELOW: Adler with his son Mark at St. John's College, Annapolis, Maryland, 1992.
Photo by Keith Harvey. Courtesy of Harvey & Harvey Photographers

ABOVE: Adler and Caroline in Aspen, 1987.
© John Lewis Stage

LEFT: Caroline with sons (Douglas on the left; Philip on the right), 1986.

Adler revising the *Syntopicon*'s Outline of Topics for *Great Books of the Western World*, 1988.

The Second Edition of *Great Books of the Western World*, 1990.
Courtesy of Encyclopaedia Britannica, Inc., Corporate Public Affairs

Adler and Bill Moyers in Aspen, Colorado, during the filming of the television programs on *Six Great Ideas* seminar, Summer 1981.
Photos by BERKO, Aspen. Courtesy of WNET.

Adler and Caroline conversing with Stephen Jay Gould, Professor of Biology, Geology, and the History of Science at Harvard University, a recipient of the 1990 Britannica Award, at the dinner held at the United Nations in New York, February 1990.
Photo by Arthur Krasinsky. Courtesy of Encyclopaedia Britannica, Inc.

Adler conducting a seminar on his book *Desires, Right & Wrong,* at the Aspen Institute, Summer 1991. *Photo by BERKO, Aspen*

Adler and Caroline sporting T-shirts given to them and participants of the Aspen Executive Seminar *The Angels and Us*, 1979.

Adler on his Amigo en route to the Aspen Institute to conduct his Executive Seminars, 1991.
Photo by Merrill Ford

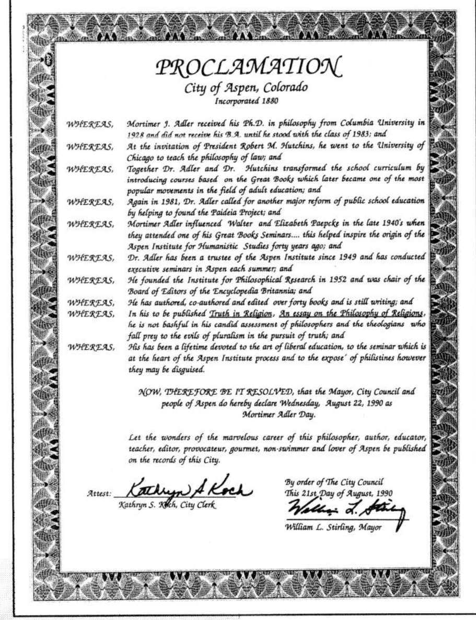

PROCLAMATION

City of Aspen, Colorado
Incorporated 1880

WHEREAS, Mortimer J. Adler received his Ph.D. in philosophy from Columbia University in 1928 and did not receive his B.A. until he stood with the class of 1983; and

WHEREAS, At the invitation of President Robert M. Hutchins, he went to the University of Chicago to teach the philosophy of law; and

WHEREAS, Together Dr. Adler and Dr. Hutchins transformed the school curriculum by introducing courses based on the Great Books which later became one of the most popular movements in the field of adult education; and

WHEREAS, Again in 1981, Dr. Adler called for another major reform of public school education by helping to found the Paideia Project; and

WHEREAS, Mortimer Adler influenced Walter and Elizabeth Paepcke in the late 1940's when they attended one of his Great Books Seminars.... this helped inspire the origin of the Aspen Institute for Humanistic Studies forty years ago; and

WHEREAS, Dr. Adler has been a trustee of the Aspen Institute since 1949 and has conducted executive seminars in Aspen each summer; and

WHEREAS, He founded the Institute for Philosophical Research in 1952 and was chair of the Board of Editors of the Encyclopedia Britannia; and

WHEREAS, He has authored, co-authored and edited over forty books and is still writing; and

WHEREAS, In his to be published Truth in Religion, An essay on the Philosophy of Religions, he is not bashful in his candid assessment of philosophers and the theologians who fall prey to the evils of pluralism in the pursuit of truth; and

WHEREAS, His has been a lifetime devoted to the art of liberal education, to the seminar which is at the heart of the Aspen Institute process and to the expose' of philistines however they may be disguised.

NOW, THEREFORE BE IT RESOLVED, that the Mayor, City Council and people of Aspen do hereby declare Wednesday, August 22, 1990 as Mortimer Adler Day.

Let the wonders of the marvelous career of this philosopher, author, educator, teacher, editor, provocateur, gourmet, non-swimmer and lover of Aspen be published on the records of this City.

Attest: Kathryn S. Koch, City Clerk

By order of The City Council
This 21st Day of August, 1990
William L. Stirling, Mayor

Proclamation declaring Mortimer J. Adler Day, August 1990.

Adler with Richard Dufallo, director/ conductor of the Contemporary Music Festival at Aspen, sporting philosophical T-shirts, 1983.
© *Charles Abbott*

TOP, LEFT: Adler with Robert Maynard Hutchins, then President of the University of Chicago, discussing the Great Books Program, 1940s.

TOP, RIGHT: Adler with Gerhard Casper, then Dean of the University of Chicago Law School, and now President of Stanford University, 1987. © *Kevin Horan*

LEFT: Adler with the University of Chicago in the background, 1987. © *Kevin Horan*

Adler at Commencement, Columbia University, Class of 1983, where he received his Bachelor of Arts degree, sixty years late.
Photo by Joe Pineiro. Courtesy of Columbia University

A gathering to celebrate Father Howell's retirement, Saint Chrysostom's Church, Chicago, December 1990. Left to right: Father Robert L. Howell, Rector, Caroline and Mortimer Adler, James McKechnie, Jr., Acolyte Master.

The Philosopher-at-Large deep in thought.

7

With fifty authors and sixty-eight titles added to the set, the *Syntopicon* had to undergo extensive revision. A fairly large staff had to be recruited and trained for the task of inserting references to passages in these works that were relevant to topics under the 102 great ideas.

Over a period of many months, I met with this staff at least twice a week to discuss a particular set of ideas, with regard to which they would raise questions about the topics under those ideas. To accommodate the thought of the new authors, especially those in the twentieth century, it was often necessary to revise the phrasing of certain topics and to add totally new topics. But it was never necessary to add any new ideas, though new terms were added to the Inventory of Terms that was a feature of the *Syntopicon*—subordinate terms the meanings of which entered into discourse about the 102 great ideas.

As I pointed out earlier, every chapter in the *Syntopicon* had a list of Additional Readings, good books relevant to that reading. These Additional Reading lists had to be brought up to date by the addition of good books published since the 1940s. But the major task in the revision of the *Syntopicon* fell to me. That was the revision of the introductory essays in each of the 102 chapters.

In the preparation of the first edition, I had written those 102 essays in twenty-six consecutive months that occupied me seven days a week, with no time off and no vacations. It was probably the most intensively concentrated, exacting, and onerous writing job that I have ever undertaken.

The work of revising these essays was even more onerous. They had been tightly written. What was now required was to find holes in paragraphs or holes between paragraphs into which could be inserted comments on points made by the new authors that had been added to the set. Attention had to be called most frequently to the disagreement of the twentieth-century authors with their predecessors, or their departure from the ground that had been covered in previous centuries and the breaking of new ground. It was especially in the essays in the chapters dealing with ideas in mathematics and in the natural sciences, as well as in philosophy, that these breakthroughs had to be stressed.

The most extensive and radical revision of the Outlines of Topics occurred with respect to the following ideas: ASTRONOMY AND COSMOLOGY, ELEMENT, EVOLUTION, MATHEMATICS, MECHANICS, SPACE, TIME, WEALTH, and WORLD. Anyone aware of the twentieth-century revolutions in the physical and biological sciences will not be surprised by this. But they may be surprised to learn that advances in economics called for new topics under the idea of Wealth, and that twentieth-century philosophical thought called for significant alterations in the topics under the following ideas: ANIMAL, CHANCE, DEMOCRACY, LANGUAGE, MATTER, PHILOSOPHY, PHYSICS, RELIGION, SCIENCE, and TRUTH.

In all these chapters, the changes in the topics required correlative changes in the essays, changes that in some cases exceeded my competence to make with sufficient precision. I am indebted to Jeremy Bernstein, to Daniel Brown, and to John Kenneth Galbraith for working with me in redrafting the essays dealing respectively with the ideas in the physical sciences, ideas in the biological sciences, and ideas in economics and sociology. I am also indebted to Wayne Moquin, Lee Kantz, W. Geoffrey Rommel, and Dennis Grumling for their assistance in revising the Outlines of Topics, the Additional Readings, the Inventory of Terms, and the Bibliography of Additional Readings. Tom Goetz, my closest associate in every phase of the editorial work, scrutinized my rewriting of all 102 essays and made excellent suggestions for their correction and amplification.

All of this work on the revision of the *Syntopicon,* I am glad to say, was accomplished on a tight time schedule in less than two years.

8

October 25, 1990, had been set as the date for the public announcement and celebration of the publication of the second edition of *Great Books of the Western World.* That took place at the Library of Congress. Three events filled that day: a press conference in the morning, a colloquium in the afternoon, and a banquet in the evening.

The colloquium was chaired by William F. Buckley, Jr. The participants in it were Prosser Gifford of the Library of Congress; Martin Marty of the University of Chicago; Robert Nozick of Harvard University; Lord Quinton, former Chairman of the British Library Board; Gertrude Himmelfarb of the City University of New York; Stephen Jay Gould of Harvard University; and science writer Isaac Asimov. The question to which the participants addressed themselves was: What had the great books of the twentieth century added to the intellectual and cultural traditions of Western civilization?

At the banquet in the evening, the guests were addressed by the Librarian of Congress, James H. Billington, by Lord Quinton, by Robert Gwinn of Britannica, and by me. That address and my speech at the press conference in the morning were not the only talks I had been scheduled to give. In those late days of October, Tom Goetz and I were interrogated on various TV and radio interviews, and I addressed a meeting of the National Press Club in Washington, D.C.

In all of these public performances, I called attention to what I regarded as the strikingly significant difference between the environment in which the first edition had been published in 1952 and the present state of affairs in 1990. Then there was no academic or public controversy about the authenticity of the canon—about the genuine worth of what long had been regarded as the classics of Western literature, the outstanding contributions to Western poetry, drama, fictional narrative, history, mathematics, science, philosophy, and theology.

Then there were no outcries about the omission from that canon of women, blacks, and representatives of the various non-Western cultures. Then there were no snide remarks or sneers about the fact that all the authors in the great books were dead white males, all European or American.

Now, in the press and on TV and radio, publication of the list of additions to the second edition of GBWW evoked protests about the fewness of the women that had been added, the absence of black authors, and the "Eurocentrism" of a set of books that was exclusively Western in its content. In addition, there were derisive comments about the significance or relevance to contemporary problems of authors in Greek and Roman antiquity in the Middle Ages, and even in modern times.

All of this brouhaha had started at Stanford University in 1988 in connection with the required readings in a survey course on the history of Western civilization. It had spread from there to other universities, in which it took different forms, especially at Duke University and at the University of Pennsylvania. It had evoked much attention by articles in the press and even by books, both pro and con. Most of it was concerned with what should be taught students in the colleges of the country.

I am not here concerned with these academic disputes and with this curricular controversy. I have dealt with that elsewhere in books and essays about the role of great books seminars not only in the college curriculum, but also in elementary and secondary schools. I wish to concentrate on the outcries from women, blacks, and non-Western groups about the authors included in or omitted from the second edition of GBWW.

In writing my editorial introduction to the second edition (in the essay entitled "The Great Conversation Revisited"), I had anticipated the angry outcries that would occur in certain quarters in response to the appearance in the public media of the list of authors added in the second edition. I must here stress the fact that none of the protestors seem to have examined the set itself or read my introductory essay, which explained the Eurocentrism of our choices and the omission of certain twentieth-century black and female authors.

I have already explained in this chapter why this set of books is exclusively Western in content. In earlier pages, I pointed out that Western and Far Eastern authors do not deal univocally with the same set of great ideas and do not engage in the great conversation with the Western authors.

No *Syntopicon* could be constructed which involved references to both Western authors and authors from the four or five cultural traditions of the Far East. That is why a set of books in which the great conversation plays a major role is exclusively Western.

With regard to questions about the omission of certain black and female writers in the twentieth century, the answer is provided by the line that divides good books from great books, in terms of the three criteria that governed our nomination of twentieth-century great books, as well as our cut-off date limiting the works to those published by mid-century. Good twentieth-century authors, who are black, female, and Latin American, appear in the *Syntopicon*'s Bibliography of Additional Readings. They are cited in relation to relatively few great ideas in the Additional Readings attached to the chapters about those ideas.[8]

In all the speeches that I gave in October and November of 1990, occasioned by the publication of the second edition of GBWW, I answered the protests that would occur in certain quarters of the academic world and of the general public. The speech I gave to the National Press Club was entitled "The Controversy About the Classics in Our Schools and Colleges"; the speech I gave at the press conference at the Library of Congress was entitled "The Great Books *Then* and *Now,* 1952 and 1990."

9

If I add up the 30 volumes of the fifteenth edition of *Encyclopaedia Britannica* and the 32 volumes of the 1985 revision of it, the 54 volumes of *Great Books of the Western World* in its first edition and the 60 volumes of the second edition, the 22 volumes of *The Annals of America,* the 10 volumes of *Gateway to the Great Books,* I get a total of 208 volumes that I have edited or co-edited for the Britannica company in the last fifty years.

That total does not include one large editorial venture that was initiated and intended for publication by a Britannica company, but ended up with another publisher. It took Charles Van Doren and me, working with a diligent staff, eight years to produce a large, one-volume book of quotations entitled *Great Treasury of Western Thought,* published by R. R. Bowker Company.

That book of quotations differed from the many books of quotations on the market with which I am acquainted. All of them contain relatively short and memorable statements arranged alphabetically. In striking contrast, *Great Treasury of Western*

8. In the Notes at the end of this chapter, Item D gives a partial listing of these black, female, and Latin American authors. There may be some highly questionable omissions from the set, but it meets our standard of 90 percent accuracy.

Thought contains much longer statements by many authors, many of whom were not included in GBWW. In addition, these quoted statements are arranged syntopically, not alphabetically.[9] I wrote the introductory notes that prefaced each chapter.

The idea for this book of quotations came out of a conversation I had with Henry Luce of *Time* magazine at the time I was working on editing the *Syntopicon*. I explained to him what the purpose of the *Syntopicon* was, how it was structured, and how it functioned. Mr. Luce applauded the idea and asked when he could expect to receive a copy of the finished *Syntopicon*. I replied: not until the whole set of great books is published, for until that happens, I said, you would not be able to look up the *Syntopicon*'s references to passages in the great books.

Harry showed visible disappointment, because his misunderstanding of what I had told him about the *Syntopicon* gave him the mistaken impression that it would contain, not references to passages in the great books, but the citable passages themselves. Remembering this conversation some years later, I broached to Charles Van Doren the possibility of producing the kind of volume that Henry Luce desired. He was attracted by the prospect and we embarked on the project, but we did not think it would take us eight years of work to finish the job in a satisfactory manner.

As I review my editorial career and my career as a writer in connection with the various editorial projects I have mentioned, I am impressed by the fact that all the ventures I undertook were extraordinarily large ones that required many years to complete—eight years on the first edition of GBWW and four more on the second edition; seven years on the fifteenth edition of *Encyclopaedia Britannica* and five years on its later recasting for the 1985 printing; eight years, as I have just said, on the production of *Great Treasury of Western Thought*, published by R. R. Bowker Company.[10]

9. The Syntopical Table of Contents of *Great Treasury of Western Thought* will be found in the Notes at the end of this chapter as Item E.

10. Not connected with work done for Britannica, but an equally extensive project was the first venture of the Institute for Philosophical Research after its establishment in 1952. More than seven years of research by a large staff and many more preceded the preceded the publication in 1958 of the first volume of *The Idea of Freedom*, and in 1961 of the second volume of that work.

Of all these extensive editorial enterprises, the production of the *Syntopicon* was, perhaps, the most exacting and innovative, the most rewarding to me intellectually. In that connection, the high point was the writing and revising of the 102 essays on the great ideas. Though that took only twenty-six months, it was by far the single most exciting intellectual job I have ever undertaken.

Some of my associates regard it as the best writing I have ever done, certainly the most unusual. That is why I am so pleased that those 102 essays, the copyright to which is owned by Encyclopaedia Britannica, Inc., will, with their permission, be published by Macmillan Publishing Company. Hitherto they have been available only to those who have purchased sets of GBWW and with it the whole *Syntopicon*. With their publication in a single volume as a trade book, they will become generally available in bookstores.

NOTES TO CHAPTER 5

Item A

ENCYCLOPAEDIA BRITANNICA, INC.

Board of Editors

MORTIMER J. ADLER, Chairman, Board of Editors. Director, Institute for Philosophical Research, Chicago.

PHILIP W. GOETZ, Executive Vice Chairman, Board of Editors. Editor in Chief, Encyclopaedia Britannica, Inc.

FRANK B. GIBNEY, Vice Chairman, Board of Editors.Vice Chairman, TBS-Britannica Company Ltd., Tokyo.

JACQUES BARZUN, University Professor Emeritus, Columbia University; Dean of Faculties and Provost, 1958–1967.

WENDY DONIGER, Mircea Eliade Professor of the History of Religions, University of Chicago.

CLIFTON FADIMAN,
writer and editor. Member,
Editorial Board,
Book-of-the-Month Club.

WILLIAM H. McNEILL,
Robert A. Millikan
Distinguished Service Professor
Emeritus of History, University
of Chicago.

MARTIN MEYERSON,
President Emeritus and
University Professor, University
of Pennsylvania, Philadelphia.

CHRISTOPHER D.
NEEDHAM, Principal Lecturer
in Library and Information
Studies, Polytechnic of North
London, 1973–1985.

LORD PERRY OF WALTON,
Vice-Chancellor, Open
University, Milton Keynes,
England, 1969–1980.

WARREN E. PREECE,
The Editor, *Encyclopaedia
Britannica,* 1964–1975.

LORD QUINTON,
Chairman of the British Library
Board. President, Trinity College,
University of Oxford, 1978–1987.

ANNE LONG DIMOPOULOS,
Secretary, Board of Editors.
Manager, Editorial
Administration, Encyclopaedia
Britannica, Inc.

Ex-officio:

ROBERT P. GWINN,
Chairman, Board of Directors,
Encyclopaedia Britannica, Inc.

PETER B. NORTON,
President, Encyclopaedia
Britannica, Inc.

NORMAN L. BRAUN,
Vice President, Public Affairs,
Encyclopaedia Britannica, Inc.

University Advisory Committees

AUSTRALIAN UNIVERSITIES ADVISORY COMMITTEE

BRIAN D. O. ANDERSON,
Chairman of the Committee.
Professor and Head,
Department of Systems
Engineering, Research School of
Physical Sciences and
Engineering, Australian National
University, Canberra.

WARREN A. BEBBINGTON,
Ormond Professor and Head,
School of Music,
University of Melbourne.

GEOFFREY BLAINEY,
Emeritus Professor of History,
University of Melbourne.

ROBERT EUGENE BOGNER,
Professor of Electrical
Engineering, University of
Adelaide, Australia.

DAVID R. FRASER,
Professor of Animal Science,
University of Sydney.

ERIC L. JONES.
Professor of Economics,
La Trobe University,
Bundoora, Victoria, Australia.
Professorial Associate,
Graduate School of
Management, University of
Melbourne.

DAME LEONIE JUDITH KRAMER, Chancellor and Emeritus Professor of Australian Literature, University of Sydney.

FRANK GRAHAM LITTLE, Reader in Political Science, University of Melbourne.

CHARLES E. OXNARD, Professor of Anatomy and Human Biology and Head, Division of Science and Agriculture; Director, Centre for Human Biology, University of Western Australia, Nedlands.

JOHN DOUGLAS RITCHIE, General Editor, Australian Dictionary of Biography; Professorial Fellow, Australian National University, Canberra.

BRITISH UNIVERSITIES ADVISORY COMMITTEE

SIR A. BRIAN PIPPARD, Chairman of the Committee. Emeritus Professor of Physics, University of Cambridge.

MAURICE CRANSTON, Emeritus Professor of Political Science, London School of Economics and Political Science, University of London.

SIR RALF DAHRENDORF, Warden of St. Antony's College, University of Oxford.

SIR GEOFFREY ELTON, Regius Professor of Modern History, University of Cambridge.

UWE KITZINGER, President, Templeton College, University of Oxford.

KURT LIPSTEIN, Emeritus Professor of Law; Fellow of Clare College, University of Cambridge.

H. CHRISTOPHER LONGUET-HIGGINS, Royal Society Research Professor (1968–1988), University of Sussex.

SIR JOHN LYONS, Master of Trinity Hall, University of Cambridge.

DONALD GUNN MACRAE, Emeritus Professor of Sociology, London School of Economics and Political Science, University of London.

DAVID A. MARTIN, Professor of Sociology, London School of Economics and Political Science, University of London; Elizabeth Scurlock Professor of Human Values, Southern Methodist University, Dallas, Texas.

DONALD M. NICOL, Emeritus Professor of Byzantine and Modern Greek History, Language, and Literature, King's

College, University of London. Director, Gennadius Library, American School of Classical Studies, Athens, Greece.

IAN G. STEWART,
Emeritus Professor of Economics; Honorary Fellow, Department of Economics, University of Edinburgh.

C. ANTHONY STORR,
Emeritus Fellow, Green College, University of Oxford; Honorary Consulting Psychiatrist, Oxford Health Authority; Clinical Lecturer in Psychiatry, University of Oxford.

SIR KEITH THOMAS,
President, Corpus Christi College, University of Oxford.

C. BARRIE WILSON, Professor of Architectural Science, University of Edinburgh; Vice-Principal, University of Edinburgh.

CANADIAN UNIVERSITIES ADVISORY COMMITTEE

WILLIAM E. FREDEMAN,
Cochairman of the Committee. Professor of English, University of British Columbia, Vancouver.

A. EDWARD SAFARIAN,
Cochairman of the Committee. Professor of Economics, Fellow of Trinity College and Massey College, University of Toronto.

J. L. BERGGREN,
Professor of Mathematics, Simon Fraser University, Burnaby, British Columbia.

FRANÇOIS DUCHESNEAU
Professor of Philosophy, Vice Dean, Faculty of Arts and Sciences, University of Montreal.

CALVIN C. GOTLIEB,
Emeritus Professor of Computer Science, University of Toronto.

PETER E. KENNEDY,
Professor of Economics, Simon Fraser University, Burnaby, British Columbia.

FREDERICK R. W. McCOURT,
Professor of Chemistry and of Applied Mathematics, University of Waterloo, Ontario.

EDWARD WATSON McWHINNEY, Queen's Counsel. Professor of International Law and Relations, Simon Fraser University, Burnaby, British Columbia. Member, Permanent Court of Arbitration, The Hague and Institute of International Law, Geneva.

JOHN T. SAYWELL,
University Professor and Professor of History and Social Science; Director, Graduate Program in History, York University, North York, Ontario.

GRANT STRATE,
Director, Centre for the Arts, Simon Fraser University. Burnaby, British Columbia. Chairman, Dance Centre of Vancouver.

A. DOUGLAS TUSHINGHAM,
Emeritus Professor of Near Eastern Studies, University of Toronto. Member, Board of Trustees, Royal Ontario Museum, Toronto; Chief Archaeologist, 1964–1979.

DONOVAN W. M. WATERS,
Professor of Law, University of Victoria, British Columbia.

UNIVERSITY OF CHICAGO ADVISORY COMMITTEE

HELLMUT FRITZSCHE,
Chairman of the Committee. Professor of Physics, The James Franck Institute.

DONALD W. FISKE,
Vice Chairman of the Committee. Emeritus Professor of Psychology.

EDWARD ANDERS,
Horace B. Horton Professor of Chemistry, Enrico Fermi Institute and Department of Chemistry.

JACK D. COWAN,
Professor of Applied Mathematics and Theoretical Biology, Department of Mathematics.

MIHALY CSIKSZENTMIHALYI,
Professor of Human Development and of Education, Department of Behavioral Sciences.

JACK HALPERN,
Louis Block Distinguished Service Professor of Chemistry.

ERIC P. HAMP,
Robert Maynard Hutchins Distinguished Service Professor of Linguistics, Behavioral Sciences and Slavic Languages; Director, Center for Balkan and Slavic Studies.

SAUNDERS MAC LANE,
Max Mason Distinguished Service Professor Emeritus of Mathematics.

JANET D. ROWLEY,
Blum-Riese Distinguished Service Professor of Medicine and of Molecular Genetics and Cell Biology.

EUROPEAN UNIVERSITIES ADVISORY COMMITTEE

HANS DAALDER
(The Netherlands), Chairman of the Committee. Professor of Political Science, University of Leiden.

MARC AUGÉ
(France), President and Professor of Social Anthropology, School of Higher Studies in Social Sciences, Paris.

MAURO CAPPELLETTI
(Italy), Shelton Professor of International Legal Studies, Stanford University, California. External Professor, European University Institute, Florence. Professor of Law, University of Florence.

MANFRED EIGEN
(West Germany), Director, Max Planck Institute for Biophysical Chemistry, Göttingen.

FERNANDO GIL
(Portugal; France), Professor of Philosophy, New University of Lisbon; Directeur d'Etudes, School of Higher Studies in Social Sciences, Paris.

JACQUES Le GOFF
(France), Professor of History, School of Higher Studies in Social Sciences, Paris.

OTFRIED MADELUNG
(West Germany), Emeritus Professor of Theoretical Physics, University of Marburg.

P. NØRREGAARD RASMUSSEN (Denmark), Professor of Economics, University of Copenhagen.

PEDRO SCHWARTZ
(Spain), Professor of the History of Economic Doctrines, Complutensian University of Madrid.

GÜNTHER WILKE
(West Germany), Professor of Chemistry, University of the Ruhr, Bochum. Director, Max Planck Institute for Coal Research, Mülheim an der Ruhr.

ITEM B

Great Books of the Western World Committee of Consultants

ISAAC ASIMOV
Science Writer; Professor of Biochemistry, Boston University; Author

DANIEL BELL
Henry Ford II Emeritus Professor of Social Sciences; Scholar-in-Residence, American Academy of Arts and Sciences

THORTON F. BRADSHAW
Chairman of the Board, RCA Corporation (deceased)

WILLIAM F. BUCKLEY, JR.
Editor-in-Chief, *National Review;* Host of "Firing Line"; Author

DAVID K. CARLSON
Partner/Director, Quality Assurance, Arthur Andersen & Company/A-Plus Tax Division

MAURICE CRANSTON
Emeritus Professor of Political Science, London School of Economics and Political Science, University of London

HUGH DOWNS
Host of "20/20," ABC News

STEPHEN JAY GOULD
Professor of Biology, Geology, and the History of Science, Harvard University

THE REVEREND THEODORE HESBURGH, C.S.C.
President Emeritus, University of Notre Dame

DAME LEONIE JUDITH KRAMER
Emeritus Professor of Australian Literature, University of Sydney

ALEXANDER A. KWAPONG
Chair, Lester B. Pearson Institute for International Development, Dalhousie University, Halifax, Nova Scotia, Canada

MARTIN E. MARTY
Fairfax M. Cone Distinguished Service Professor, Divinity School, University of Chicago

BILL MOYERS
Chairman and Executive Editor of Public Affairs Television, Inc.

HAJIME NAKAMURA
Founder-Director, Eastern Institute, Inc., Tokyo; Emeritus Professor of Indian and Buddhist Philosophy, University of Tokyo

OCTAVIO PAZ
Mexican Poet, Writer, and Diplomat

MICHEL SERRES
Professor of History, University of Paris

ITEM C

Great Books of the Western World (Second Edition)

List of Works

VOL.	AUTHOR(S)	NOTES
1	**SYNTOPICON I**	
2	**SYNTOPICON II**	
3	**HOMER**	
	The Iliad	New translation
	The Odyssey	New translation
4	**AESCHYLUS**	
	The Complete Plays	New translation
	SOPHOCLES	
	The Complete Plays	New translation

	EURIPIDES	
	The Complete Plays	New translation
	ARISTOPHANES	
	The Complete Plays	New translation
5	**HERODOTUS**	
	The History	
	THUCYDIDES	
	The History of the Peloponnesian War	
6	**PLATO**	
	The Complete Dialogues	
7	**ARISTOTLE I**	
8	**ARISTOTLE II**	
	Complete Works (in two volumes)	
9	**HIPPOCRATES**	
	Hippocratic Writings	
	GALEN	
	On the Natural Faculties	
10	**EUCLID**	
	Elements	
	ARCHIMEDES	
	Works	
	NICHOMACHUS	
	Introduction to Arithmetic	
11	**LUCRETIUS**	
	The Way Things Are	New translation
	EPICTETUS	
	The Discourses	
	MARCUS AURELIUS	
	The Meditations	
	PLOTINUS	
	The Six Enneads	
12	**VIRGIL**	
	The Eclogues	New translation
	The Georgics	New translation
	The Aeneid	New translation
13	**PLUTARCH**	
	Lives	
14	**TACITUS**	
	The Annals	
	The Histories	

15 **PTOLEMY**
The Almagest
COPERNICUS
On the Revolutions of the Heavenly Spheres
KEPLER
Epitome of Copernican Astronomy: Bks. IV–V
The Harmonies of the World: Bk. V

16 **AUGUSTINE**
The Confessions — New translation
The City of God
On Christian Doctrine

17 **AQUINAS I**

18 **AQUINAS II**
Summa Theologica (in two volumes)

19 **DANTE**
The Divine Comedy — New translation
CHAUCER
Troilus and Criseyde — New translation
The Canterbury Tales — New translation

20 **CALVIN** — New author
Institutes of the Christian Religion

21 **MACHIAVELLI**
The Prince
HOBBES
Leviathan

22 **RABELAIS**
Gargantua and Pantagruel

23 **ERASMUS** — New author
Praise of Folly
MONTAIGNE
The Essays — New translation

24 **SHAKESPEARE I**

25 **SHAKESPEARE II**
Complete Works (in two volumes)

26 **GILBERT**
On the Loadstone and Magnetic Bodies

GALILEO
Dialogues Concerning Two New Sciences
HARVEY
On the Motion of the Heart and Blood in Animals
On the Circulation of the Blood
On the Generation of Animals

27 **CERVANTES**
Don Quixote — New translation

28 **BACON**
Advancement of Learning
Novum Organum
New Atlantis
DESCARTES
Rules for the Direction of the Mind
Discourse on the Method
Meditations on First Philosophy
Objections against the Meditations and Replies
The Geometry
SPINOZA
Ethics

29 **MILTON**
English Minor Poems
Paradise Lost
Samson Agonistes
Areopagitica

30 **PASCAL**
The Provincial Letters
Pensées
Scientific Treatises

31 **MOLIÈRE** — New author
The School for Wives
The Critique of the School for Wives
Tartuffe
Don Juan
The Miser
The Would-Be Gentleman
The Would-Be Invalid
RACINE — New author
Berenice
Phaedra

32 **NEWTON**
Mathematical Principles of Natural Philosophy
Optics

HUYGENS
Treatise on Light

33 **LOCKE**
A Letter Concerning Toleration
Concerning Civil Government, Second Essay
An Essay Concerning Human Understanding

BERKELEY
The Principles of Human Knowledge

HUME
An Enquiry Concerning Human Understanding

34 **SWIFT**
Gulliver's Travels

VOLTAIRE — New author
Candide

DIDEROT — New author
Rameau's Nephew

35 **MONTESQUIEU**
The Spirit of Laws

ROUSSEAU
A Discourse on the Origin of Inequality
A Discourse on Political Economy
The Social Contract

36 **ADAM SMITH**
The Wealth of Nations

37 **GIBBON I**

38 **GIBBON II**
The Decline and Fall of the Roman Empire (in two volumes)

39 **KANT**
The Critique of Pure Reason
The Critique of Practical Reason and Other Ethical Treatises
The Critique of Judgement

40 **AMERICAN STATE PAPERS**
THE FEDERALIST
J.S. MILL
On Liberty
Representative Government
Utilitarianism

41 **BOSWELL**
The Life of Samuel Johnson, LL.D.

42 **LAVOISIER**
Elements of Chemistry
FARADAY
Experimental Researches in Electricity

43 **HEGEL**
The Philosophy of Right
The Philosophy of History
KIERKEGAARD — New author
Fear and Trembling
NIETZSCHE — New author
Beyond Good and Evil

44 **TOCQUEVILLE** — New author
Democracy in America

45 **GOETHE**
Faust (parts I and II) — New translation
BALZAC — New author
Cousin Bette

46 **AUSTEN** — New author
Emma
GEORGE ELIOT — New author
Middlemarch

47 **DICKENS** — New author
Little Dorrit

48 **MELVILLE**
Moby Dick
TWAIN — New author
Huckleberry Finn

49 **DARWIN**
The Origin of Species
The Descent of Man

50 MARX
Capital
Manifesto of the Communist Party
(with ENGELS)

51 TOLSTOY
War and Peace

52 DOSTOEVSKY
The Brothers Karamazov
IBSEN — New author
A Doll's House
The Wild Duck
Hedda Gabler
The Master Builder

53 WILLIAM JAMES
The Principles of Psychology

54 FREUD
The Major Works

The following six new volumes contain selections of works by 20th Century authors:

55 20TH C. PHILOSOPHY AND RELIGION — New authors
WILLIAM JAMES
Pragmatism
BERGSON
An Introduction to Metaphysics
DEWEY
Experience and Education
WHITEHEAD
Science and the Modern World
RUSSELL
The Problems of Philosophy
HEIDEGGER
What Is Metaphysics?
WITTGENSTEIN
Philosophical Investigations
KARL BARTH
The Word of God and the Word of Man

56 20TH C. NATURAL SCIENCE — New authors
POINCARÉ
Science and Hypothesis

PLANCK
Scientific Autobiography and Other Papers
WHITEHEAD
An Introduction to Mathematics
EINSTEIN
Relativity: The Special and the General Theory
EDDINGTON
The Expanding Universe
BOHR
Selections from Atomic Theory and the Description of Nature
Bohr-Einstein Dialogues
HARDY
A Mathematician's Apology
HEISENBERG
Physics and Philosophy
SCHRÖDINGER
What Is Life?
DOBZHANSKY
Genetics and the Origin of Species
WADDINGTON
The Nature of Life

57 **20TH C. SOCIAL SCIENCE I** — New authors
VEBLEN
The Theory of the Leisure Class
TAWNEY
The Acquisitive Society
KEYNES
The General Theory of Employment, Interest and Money

58 **2OTH C. SOCIAL SCIENCE II** — New authors
FRAZER
Selections from The Golden Bough
WEBER
Selections from Essays in Sociology
HUIZINGA
The Waning of the Middle Ages
LÉVI-STRAUSS
Selections from Structural Anthropology

59 **20TH C. IMAGINATIVE LITERATURE I** — New authors

JAMES, HENRY
The Beast in the Jungle

SHAW
Saint Joan

CONRAD
Heart of Darkness

CHEKHOV
Uncle Vania

PIRANDELLO
Six Characters in Search of an Author

PROUST
Swann in Love

CATHER
A Lost Lady

MANN
Death in Venice

JAMES JOYCE
A Portrait of the Artist as a Young Man

60 **20TH C. IMAGINATIVE LITERATURE II** — New authors

WOOLF
To the Lighthouse

KAFKA
The Metamorphosis

LAWRENCE
The Prussian Officer

ELIOT, T. S.
The Waste Land

O'NEILL
Mourning Becomes Electra

FITZGERALD
The Great Gatsby

FAULKNER
A Rose for Emily

BRECHT
Mother Courage and Her Children

HEMINGWAY
The Short Happy Life of Francis Macomber

ORWELL
Animal Farm
BECKETT
Waiting for Godot

ITEM D

A Sampling of Black Authors, Female Authors, and Latin American Authors Listed in the Bibliography of Additional Readings in the *Syntopicon*

Black Authors

Chinua Achebe
James Baldwin
Gwendolyn Brooks
Ralph Ellison
Zora Neale Hurston
Martin Luther King, Jr.
Toni Morrison
Wole Soyinka
Alice Walker
Richard Wright

Female Authors

Hannah Arendt
Margaret Atwood
Mary Ritter Beard
Simone de Beauvoir
Ruth Benedict
Charlotte Brontë
Emily Jane Brontë
Elizabeth Barrett Browning
Rachel Carson
Marie Curie
Emily Dickinson
Isak Dinesen (Karen Dinesen)
Karen Horney
Jane Jacobs
Suzanne Langer
Harper Lee
Doris Lessing
Margaret Mead
Flannery O'Connor
Sylvia Plath
Mary Shelley
Harriet Beecher Stowe
Barbara Tuchman
Anne Tyler
Simone Weil
Eudora Welty
Edith Wharton

Latin American Authors

Jorge Luis Borges
Carlos Fuentes
Gabriel García Márquez
Pablo Neruda
Octavio Paz
Mario Vargas Llosa

ITEM E

*Great Treasury of Western Thought**
Syntopical Table of Contents

* Mortimer J. Adler & Charles Van Doren, eds., *Great Treasury of Western Thought; A Compendium of Important Statements on Man and His Institutions by the Great Thinkers in Western History,* R. R. Bowker Company, New York and London, 1977. Pp. vii–xi reprinted with permission of R. R. Bowker, a division of Reed Publishing (USA) Inc.

CHAPTER 6

THE ASPEN INSTITUTE

1

This is the forty-first summer that I have spent in Aspen, a small town in the Colorado Rockies, 8,000 feet high. Aspen is the summer campus of the Aspen Institute, at which I have attended many conferences, given many lectures, conducted many seminars, and written many books. The administrative headquarters of the Aspen Institute is on the Eastern Shore of Maryland, on the Wye Plantation, and in the nine autumn to spring months, its main campus is there. I have written no books there.[1]

The relation between the Aspen Institute and the town of Aspen has not always been harmonious. After Walter Paepcke died and Robert O. Anderson became Chairman of its Board, the conflict concerning zoning restrictions on the Institute's property became so acrimonious that the Institute threatened to leave Aspen. It is against that background that I appraised the celebration of the Institute's fortieth anniversary in 1990 as a significant achievement. What David McLaughlin, the Institute's present CEO, and his executive assistant, Mona Chamberlain, did to make this an international event caused the good people of Aspen to appreciate

1. In Chapter 11 of *Philosopher at Large* (pp. 262–267) I have told the story of how the Aspen Institute for Humanistic Studies came to be established by Walter Paepcke in 1950, after the Goethe Festival in the summer of 1949, and how I came to be involved in it. But the gift to the Aspen Institute by Arthur A. Houghton, Jr., of property and buildings on his Wye Plantation occurred in 1978, and was not mentioned in that book. The story of my being instrumental in bringing the Aspen Institute to the Eastern Shore of Maryland will be told in this chapter.

the contribution of the Institute to the town. The future of the Institute's life and work in Aspen is now assured, as it was not always in the past.

At the opening session of the anniversary celebration on Thursday, August 2 (the day that Saddam Hussein's troops invaded Kuwait), there was a convocation in the music tent, to which special guests were invited, but which was also open to the public. On that occasion the principal speakers were President George Bush and Prime Minister Margaret Thatcher, both of whom Henry Catto, our Ambassador to the Court of St. James's, was instrumental in inviting. Mrs. Thatcher gave the closing address on Sunday morning. Her speech was remarkably eloquent and pertinent, both to the occasion and to world events. I am sorry that I cannot say as much for President Bush.

At the opening ceremony, the other speakers were Governor Roy Romer of Colorado, my friend Michael Sovern, President of Columbia University, and me. I was the link between Columbia University and the Aspen Institute. At the invitation of President Robert Hutchins of the University of Chicago, I brought great books seminars to that University; and finally, by the way of Walter and Elizabeth Paepcke, who were participants in a great books seminar that Bob Hutchins and I conducted at the University Club in Chicago, these seminars came to Aspen. They developed into the Aspen Executive Seminars, which made their first appearance in 1951.

In a letter that I wrote Ann Hudson, who did an excellent job chairing the planning committee for the fortieth anniversary, I pointed out that the forty years divided into two periods. In the first twenty years from 1950 to 1970, the activities of the Institute were entirely and exclusively the conduct of seminars for the leaders of industry and commerce in this country as well as for leaders in government and the professions. In the second twenty years from 1970 to 1990, the activities of the Institute expanded to include conferences on policy and governance problems. In the second twenty years, the Institute also expanded from its center in Aspen to the centers in Berlin, Tokyo, Paris, Rome, Venice, and Queenstown, Maryland.

These facts were in the background of my mind when I wrote

the speech that I delivered at the opening symposium on August 2, 1990. I started out by asserting that what was unique about the Aspen Institute was the way it functions in the field of adult education. For the last forty years it has been the only educational institution in the country concerned with the humanistic, that is, the general and liberal education, of adults, not *any* adults but those who, drawn from all walks of life, were the country's leaders. The fine extension divisions of Harvard, Columbia, and Chicago universities do not do that. In addition, with the possible exception of the University of Chicago, the Aspen Institute is the only institution involved in adult education employing the seminar method as an indispensable means for the understanding of basic ideas and issues.

I pointed out that many things are now called seminars that are not seminars at all. Before John Erskine developed the undergraduate great books seminars at Columbia, seminars in the German universities of the nineteenth century were attended by graduate students only. Oxford tutorials were conducted in a manner somewhat similar to the Erskine seminars, but they involved one undergraduate at a time, not the twenty or twenty-five who sat around the table with Erskine discussing a book that all of them had read.

From Columbia University to the University of Chicago was the first step on the way to Executive Seminars at Aspen. That was why, I told the audience, I was so pleased to have President Michael Sovern of Columbia University on the platform on this occasion.

The second step was a great books seminar in Chicago that Bob Hutchins and I conducted for leaders in Chicago, many of them trustees of the University, who were curious to find out what Bob Hutchins and I were doing at the undergraduate great books seminars in the college. Walter and Elizabeth Paepcke were in that seminar from 1943 to 1949. After the Goethe Bicentennial in Aspen in 1949, Spanish philosopher Ortega y Gasset, who had been a participant in the bicentennial, wrote a letter to Walter urging him to establish a humanistic institute at Aspen.

What Ortega meant by the humanities is *not* what that word means in our universities today. He meant a generalist—a philosophical—approach to all subjects, in order to overcome what he called "the barbarism of specialization," so rampant in our century.

As a result of Ortega's letter, Walter Paepcke invited me to come to Aspen to help him to develop great books seminars. It was through the intervention of Henry Luce of *Time* magazine, who with his wife Clare came to Aspen in 1950, that we developed, in 1951, Executive Seminars by adding to the reading list documents in our recent political and economic history and solicited attendance at these seminars from the country's leaders.

As I have already pointed out, in the second twenty years of its history, when Robert O. Anderson succeeded Walter Paepcke as its CEO, and Joseph Slater succeeded Alvin Eurich as its President, the Institute went beyond the Executive Seminars to become a conference center. I went on to say that as a conference center the Aspen Institute is not unique. There are many other conference centers that function in this country and abroad. But the Institute certainly is unique as the only educational institution concerned with cultivating the minds and deepening the understanding of this country's leaders with regard to great ideas and issues.

I concluded by explaining how I understood the radical difference between seminars and conferences. Public policy conferences are concerned with urgent economic, political, and social problems, both national and international. At them, experts in these fields usually make speeches or read papers. These papers are discussed and proposed solutions may be agreed upon. But the ultimate aim of such conferences is seldom, if ever, realized. They seldom, if ever, lead to concerted action by persons in power, without which practical problems are not solved.[2]

In sharp contrast, seminars are driven by significant texts, drawn from the last twenty-five centuries of our intellectual tradition, and the discussion that ensues, when it is Socratically conducted by penetrating questions, is controlled by these texts, or *should be* if the seminar is any good. If they are not text-driven and text-

2. The public policy programs now conducted at Aspen and at Wye may be an exception to this generalization.

controlled, they are not seminars at all, but only glorified bull-sessions.

Seminars are at their best only when they enlarge the participants' understanding of basic ideas and issues. Their purpose is purely intellectual, not practical. They are not "thought leading to action," but thought clarifying and improving itself. For that purpose they should leave the participants with unanswered questions to think about.

I had not yet shot my bolt; I had a few more words to add, pointing out that, while leadership itself is not a great idea, leaders should have a sound understanding of the great ideas, especially the ideas of liberty, equality, justice, wealth, property, democracy, and socialism.

Aspen seminars help mature leaders to become generally educated human beings, a consummation devoutly to be wished, but which cannot be hoped for in our colleges and universities, even if they were very much better than they now are, because no one can become a generally educated human being except in the closing, fully mature years of life, after fifty or sixty years of age. That is a goal to which all of us should aspire.

Plato said philosophers should be kings. I think he would have been nearer the mark if he had said that kings, or our political rulers, should become philosophers. (I hope I managed not to nod my head in the direction of President Bush when I said this.) They should become philosophers, not in the current academic sense of that term, but in the sense of understanding the great ideas. That is the high point of the ideal at which Aspen aims. I am glad I can report that President Sovern's speech, which followed, confirmed my statement about Columbia's contribution to Aspen and corroborated my encomium of John Erskine.

2

On July 4, 1977, the annual meeting of the Board of Trustees of the Aspen Institute occurred. As an Honorary Trustee, I attended the session in the morning, but decided that I would return to my study instead of going to the afternoon session. That was a fortunate decision on my part for, shortly after lunch, I received a phone call from Arthur A. Houghton, Jr., in Maryland.

Arthur and I had been friends since 1953 and my wife Caroline and I had paid many visits to Arthur's plantation at Wye on the Eastern Shore of Maryland, usually in June before we went to Aspen. Through the many conversations that we had about it, Arthur was well acquainted with the Aspen Institute, the seminars, the lectures, and the music that occurred there every summer. He also knew how enthusiastic I was about the work of the Institute and how much my Aspen experiences meant to me.

On the phone, Arthur told me about recent discussions he had had with the persons planning the distribution of his estate upon his death. Their advice to him was to make a charitable gift of his property at Wye.

With this in mind, he had first thought of giving it to the President of the United States as a vacation alternative to Camp David, but that might be superfluous. He then thought of giving it to the Governor of Maryland, but he had qualms about that in terms, I think, of the political scene in Maryland. He paused for a moment and asked me what I thought of his making a gift of the property to the Aspen Institute as a campus for its activities. How would Aspen's Board react to that offer?

After I caught my breath, I told Arthur that there was a Board meeting going on at that very moment and that the best way to find out the answer to his question was for me to return to the meeting and put the question to them. He thought that was a good idea and told me to phone him after I had done so.

I wrote a brief note to Robert O. Anderson, the Board's Chairman, saying that it was important for me to talk to him privately for a moment and asking him to leave the meeting and step outside with me. The Board was seated alphabetically and so, on returning, I took my seat next to Bob Anderson and passed him my little note. He glanced at it with a look of inquiry in his eyes, turned to Thornton Bradshaw, Vice-Chairman, and asked him to conduct the meeting, and motioned to me to go outside with him.

Outside, I told him of Arthur Houghton's offer. Not being acquainted with the nature of the property at Wye, he did not know what to make of it, but he said at once that the thing to do was to return to the Board meeting where I should tell the members of Houghton's offer.

The second piece of good fortune that afternoon was that two persons present at the meeting were Alvin Eurich and Robert McNamara, both of whom had been visitors to Arthur's plantation at Wye. After informing the Board of Arthur's intentions, I called upon them to tell the Board about the Wye property. They described the 1,400 acres of the property, the large and small houses that stood upon the land, and the camp that Arthur had established under the auspices of his Wye Institute, for the benefit of middle and high school children on the Eastern Shore, both black and white, and not from affluent homes. Eurich and McNamara were most eloquent and enthusiastic in their appraisal of the gift.

I cannot remember in detail the discussion that followed, but the general reaction of the Board was favorable and it voted to authorize Bob Anderson to meet with Arthur Houghton and to learn what financial responsibilities fell on the shoulders of the Aspen Institute to complete the transaction.

Bob Anderson and Arthur Houghton had never met before but they hit it off right from the start. The property to be transferred to the Aspen Institute consisted of 1,000 acres, Arthur reserving for his own use two parcels of 200 acres each. On the 1,000 acres stood Arthur's own magnificent dwelling, which, as later used by the Aspen Institute for seminars, conferences, living accommodations, came to be called the Manor House (recently renamed The Houghton House). There was an adjacent building, called the Library, which housed Arthur's extraordinary collection of rare books. There were also many smaller buildings in the vicinity of the Manor House that later were used to house Aspen's administrative staff. Extremely useful to Aspen were the buildings on the site of the Wye Institute's summer camp, which included a large room that could be used for seminars and conferences, many smaller cottages with sleeping accommodations, and a large dining room with kitchen facilities attached.

I was not privy to the negotiations between Bob Anderson and Arthur Houghton that, in 1978, eventuated in the charitable gift being made and in Aspen's assuming the financial and managerial responsibility for operating the property. In the years that followed, the Aspen Institute engaged in a building program that greatly enhanced the usefulness of the property for its purposes, including an elegant new seminar room dedicated to me in a very pleasant ceremony that I attended.

A year or so before all of this occurred, Arthur had started building another residence for himself nearer the Wye River. He did not complete it, but later he gave that building to the Aspen Institute which, when completed, became the River House, with living accommodations, dining room and kitchen, and seminar and meeting rooms.

In the last ten years, the Wye campus of the Aspen Institute has flourished in many diverse ways. Board meetings are held there more frequently than in Colorado. Before the acquisition of its Wye campus, the Aspen Institute operated its seminars and conferences for three months at the most—two months in the summer and one month in the ski season. Now its Wye operations are year round.

I enjoy going to Wye for at least one seminar in the spring of the year, and sometimes also for a lecture. After Arthur's death, his widow, Nina, became a member of Aspen's Board, and her interest and participation in the Aspen Institute activities have realized one part of Arthur's dream in making a gift of his property to Aspen. As it turned out, it provided Nina with an intellectually lively and engaging environment in which to live and in which to be in contact with a wide variety of influential and interesting persons who attend and participate in Aspen functions.

One more thing remains for me to mention. James Nelson, a close association of Arthur Houghton and head of his Wye Institute, became Executive Vice-President and General Manager of the Aspen Institute. Under his management, the operation of the Aspen Institute at Wye became financially self-supporting, which never was the case with the Aspen Institute's operation in Colorado.

Arthur's benefaction to the Aspen Institute should be viewed as more than a gift in land and buildings. In my judgment, the gift had another consequence of great benefit to the Aspen Institute. That was the ensuing work of James Nelson in Maryland. I think the present President of the Aspen Institute and its CEO, David McLaughlin, would agree with this judgment. David himself has turned the status of the Institute in Aspen, Colorado, in the right direction.

3

On December 28, 1982, I reached the age of eighty. In the spring of that year while I was at Aspen, the city of Aspen gave me an eightieth birthday party with a number of gifts, including a police belt-buckle and keys to the city. My relations with the city government and the members of the local community had always been more cordial than the relationship between the Aspen Institute and the city government. That had developed into prolonged town-and-gown conflict of interests.

I cannot remember the speeches made on that occasion by the Mayor and others, but I found in my files a copy of my own address in reply. When I showed a copy of that address to David McLaughlin and James Nelson, they caused it to be printed and distributed to those who attended the fortieth anniversary celebration in 1990. It was entitled "A Reminiscence . . ." and was appropriate for the later occasion because it narrated events in the early years of the Aspen Institute and in the town of Aspen.

To avoid the repetition of matters already mentioned in this chapter, I have placed appropriate excerpts from the speech as Item A in the Notes to this chapter.

One thing I did not mention in reminiscing at my eightieth birthday party. To do so would have been a jarring note on that pleasant occasion. The reading list for the Executive Seminar that we had adopted with Walter's blessing started to be revised and, in my judgment, it seriously deteriorated after his death in 1960. I was so disturbed by this corruption of the reading list that, after my friend Al Eurich became President of the Aspen Institute, I wrote him a long letter in 1964 that, at great length and in great detail, explained what a reading list for the Executive Seminars should try to accomplish and how that should be done.

I have placed excerpted portions of this letter in the Notes to this chapter as Item B.[3] From 1964, when I wrote that letter to Eurich, I have tried with successive presidents of the Aspen seminars, and also with their assistants in charge of Aspen seminars, to discard the misconceived and misdirected reading lists that other Aspen moderators preferred, and to adopt the reading list that I have been using so effectively for my own seminars for the last twenty years. *With no success*! They would hear my protests, declare that they were inclined to be persuaded by my arguments, but no corrective action ever ensued.

At last, in 1990 and 1991, substantial progress was made in the direction that I had been urging all these years. David McLaughlin and the man he put in charge of Aspen seminars, Michael Higgins, really understood my complaint about the reading list used in other Aspen seminars. They really understood why I thought my reading list should be used by all the other moderators. If they found difficulties with it, they should be trained to overcome those difficulties.[4]

The revision of the reading list, approved and authorized by David McLaughlin and Michael Higgins, now has a core of readings drawn from my reading list, with a few options left open to be chosen by other moderators. They both think that a few years hence, my reading list, with no options left open, will be required for *all* Aspen Executive Seminars. I hope they are right.

It is somewhat ironical that I succeeded in getting my reading list adopted, at least as the core assignment for the two-week Executive Seminar, at a time when I had given up moderating such seminars myself. Ten years ago I began to conduct one-week seminars in which the only assignment was a book of mine that I had recently written.

3. Readers will also find an account of the kind of discussion that occurs in a seminar using my reading list in Appendix II of my book *How to Speak/ How to Listen*. That Appendix II was, in content, identical with a speech I gave in Aspen in 1972, entitled "Pointers and Prospects from the Past: The Relevance of the Aspen Readings."

4. My friends Charles Van Doren and James O'Toole, who have been Aspen moderators, used my reading list in the seminars they moderated. They were prepared to argue the case for that reading list with the other moderators. In the spring of 1991, Charles Van Doren came to a conference of moderators and spent a whole day going over the points that should be covered in any seminar that used my reading list.

By that time I had been conducting Executive Seminars, sometimes two a summer, for over twenty-five years; and in that time I had improved my reading list to a point which I thought was perfection. But it was also true that I had reached the point of diminishing returns as far as my own earning was concerned. For each day in the twelve-day sequence, I had accumulated piles of notes stowed away in folders that recorded new points or problems that had emerged in the course of the day's discussion. It was clear that in the last few of those twenty-five years, the increment of learning had diminished to zero. It was time to stop!

In the last ten years I have used the following books of mine as the basis for six days of inquiry and discussion: *How to Think About God, Six Great Ideas, How to Speak/How to Listen, A Vision of the Future* (a book I wanted to entitle "Twelve Not So Great Ideas" but my publishers would not let me), *Ten Philosophical Mistakes, We Hold These Truths, Reforming Education, Intellect: Mind Over Matter,* and *Truth in Religion.* Some of these books were discussed in seminars at the Wye Campus of the Institute; some in Aspen; some at both.

This summer of 1991, while I am writing this book, I have so far conducted a seminar on *Haves Without Have-Nots,* and I will later conduct one on *Desires, Right & Wrong,* to be published in November of 1991.[5]

Each year, in the last decade, the Aspen Institute holds a dinner in New York at which it presents two awards. In 1986, the Corporate/Public Service Award went to Felix G. Rohatyn, and the Education/Humanities Award went to me. On that occasion, Bill Moyers was the Master of Ceremonies.

In my short acceptance speech, I told the audience that I thought I had at least become a generally educated human being, sometime

5. I did not begin this very chapter until I had concluded the seminar on *Haves Without Have-Nots.* I have found it impossible to conduct a seminar, which takes hours of preparation each day, and to write a chapter at the same time. I can take care of work for Encyclopaedia Britannica, Inc., while conducting a seminar, for that can be done by long distance phone, fax, and express mail carriers; but not writing, which requires a morning at the typewriter and an afternoon spent in "idling," by which I mean allowing the unconscious to pop into the mind sentences or insights that constitute preparation for the next day. More on this in the next section of this chapter.

after I turned seventy, and that conducting seminars at the Aspen Institute had contributed greatly to that attainment.

In fact, I said, that "for the ultimate fruits of my own life of learning, I am more indebted to the Aspen Institute than to any other institution with which I have been connected. I have come to understand more, have developed more skill, and have even attained a little more wisdom in the course of conducting seminars over the last thirty-three years than has come to me from any other source."

I added that "I can trace the brightest insights in the books I have written to the give-and-take of Aspen seminar discussions." This led me to conclude by saying that it seemed to me "that I should be giving the Institute an award for my educational benefactor—a gift of gratitude rather than standing here, proudly I admit, as a beneficiary receiving an award from Aspen, for which I am most grateful."

There is one more award that I received which, perhaps, should be mentioned here in connection with Aspen. In 1990, at the time of the Aspen Institute's fortieth anniversary celebration, Mayor William Stirling declared August 22, 1990, as "Mortimer Adler Day." This was the second declaration, the first being in honor of my eightieth birthday on April 2, 1982.

So far my account of my Aspen experiences has been on the deadly-serious side. But there have been many moments of great fun and hilarity in the process. During the week of one summer, I gave a lecture on angelology, which developed into a book entitled *The Angels and Us* (1982). At the end of that week, the participants in the seminar asked me to join them for a group photo outside the seminar building. There they all were, each in a T-shirt inscribed with the words "Mortimer's Angels" and with a T-shirt for me to put on when I joined them. That is only one of the many, amusingly inscribed T-shirts that I have received from seminar participants over the years.

Usually these presentations occur at the closing dinner on a Friday night, at which roasts, take-offs, skits, and songs enliven the evening. On one such occasion, I remember seeing a man lying prostrate on the floor and wondering why he was there in that condition. I soon found out when another man came along and asked what was wrong with him, to be told that he was suffering from "rigor Mortimer."

During the seminar itself, amusing incidents often occur. In my judgment, the laughter that follows abets the learning process. Once, during a discussion of the ring of Gyges in the second book of Plato's *Republic,* I received an answer that caused uproarious laughter. The ring of Gyges, when turned on the finger, made its owner invisible. I asked the participants to imagine that they saw, in Tiffany's window, a ring that had a card next to it, saying "Ring of Gyges, moderately priced, inquire within." Would they inquire within? Would they purchase it if it were within their means? And if so, what would they do with it? I got a wide variety of answers to this trio of questions, but finally one participant said, "Yes, I would go in, ask the price, find it within my means to buy, and then ask to try it on, and . . ." Before he could finish that sentence, the rest of the seminar got the point and roared.

In another seminar, we were discussing Machiavelli's *The Prince.* Trying to bring the discussion up to date, since there were no princes in contemporary America, I asked the seminar participants to imagine themselves New York publishers who wished to republish Machiavelli's book, with a more contemporary title to catch the eye of those engaged in the current world of business and politics. I received a wide variety of suggestions about getting into power, holding on to it, and using it in the rat-race of worldly affairs. Finally, one man spoke up and said, "Mr. Adler, I think I've got just the right title for a glossy paperback, with a curvaceous blond on the cover." I asked him for it and he replied: "The Sex Life of the Prince and Other Issues."

In the course of a long career on the lecture platform, starting in 1923 at Cooper Union in New York City, there are only three places at which I have given lectures year after year: at St. John's College in Annapolis, Maryland, since 1937; at the Aspen Institute in Colorado and in Maryland since 1950; and much more recently at Thomas Aquinas College in Santa Paula, California. I have no way of counting the number precisely, for in the course of the years, I have occasionally repeated the same lecture at several places, but I would estimate the number of different lectures to be more than 100, more than 50 at St. John's College and more than 40 at the Aspen Institute.

The subjects treated in most of these lectures have later entered into the composition of books that I have written. This is particularly true of the lectures I have given in Aspen since 1950 and of the thirteen books that I have written in my summers since 1979. That is a large number of books to write—at the rate of one a year, not to mention a few other books in the same period that were not written in the summer months in Aspen.[6]

Readers may naturally wonder how writing so many books in a relatively short time and in an otherwise busy life is accomplished. I think I have a very special technique for doing so. People who have read my *How to Read a Book* have often suggested that I write a companion-piece entitled *How to Write a Book*. I have not done that because it does not need a whole book to do it. In relatively few pages, in the next section, I can explain how I write a book in less than a month of writing days each summer at Aspen.

4

The title of the brief disquisition to follow should not be "How to Write a Book," but rather "How I Write a Book," for I am sure that one's method of composition is idiosyncratic. For all I know, I may be the only person in the world who writes books this way, or there may be a very small number of us. Nevertheless, it may be of general interest, so here goes.

I should add before I start that I did not always write this way. It is the method I developed when I started writing books in Aspen and after I wrote *Philosopher at Large* the year my family and I lived in London.

In an otherwise very busy life, writing is a task that can be easily set aside or postponed. I make sure about any book I am planning to write that I am morally obliged to produce it and have the manuscript ready for delivery at a fixed date. To impose that

6. The first installment of my autobiography, *Philosopher at Large,* was written in London in 1974–1975; *The American Testament,* co-authored with William Gorman, was also written there. The three Paideia books were written in Chicago. In any case, my literary output was greater in the last fifteen years than at any period of my life.

obligation upon myself, I first think of the title of the book I want to write (a tentative title seldom changes very much in the course of writing), outline a table of contents for the book, and write a brief description of its general theme or points of interest. This I send to my publisher and ask for a contract that carries with it a small advance royalty on signing.

When that comes through, the publisher sets the date for delivery of the manuscript (when the rest of the royalty advance will be paid) and also the date when the book will be published. That is usually a little more than a year later; for example, if I sign the contract for a given book in late spring of 1986, it will probably call for delivery of the manuscript in September of 1987, with publication six or seven months later in March or April of 1988. That gives me about a year to think about the book from late spring of one year to the beginning of the next summer, when I will go to Aspen mid-June or early July and start writing.

Getting a moral obligation to discharge is the first step; but the time schedule that follows from it is essential to my scheme of writing. That time schedule involves a sharp division between thinking and writing. I try to do all the thinking necessary to write a book before I ever start writing.

In my judgment, those two operations are better not mixed. I have found from long experience that whenever I combine thinking with writing, neither is very well done. One should have all one's thoughts in order before one starts to write, for if they pop into one's head in the course of writing, they are likely to be out of order and the writing will suffer in consequence.

Authors who think while they write often have to do a great deal of rewriting to iron out the blemishes that result from disorderly thought and from writing that stumbles back and forth. My first draft may undergo a number of revisions before it is set in type, but I have never had to rewrite a book, or even one or more chapters of it.

In the early autumn of the year in which I have previously signed a contract for a book, I start to jot down notes of the thinking evoked by my general idea of the book to be written. As these relatively random notes accumulate, I then become more systematic and have my secretary provide me with a set of file folders, each labeled with a chapter number and title, according to my provisional table of contents for the book. With that done, I then start dropping the notes that record my thinking on this or that point in the file folder to which this or that point appears to be relevant.

This process goes on for many months, in which I may do some reading that is germane to my subject; in which I may have to look up a questionable fact or two (though that is infrequent because the kind of philosophical books I write are seldom concerned with research about matters of fact); or in which I may engage in conversation with my associates at the Institute for Philosophical Research or with other friends to test out one or another line of argument that I have been considering for inclusion in the book.

All of this is part of the intellectual process of planning the book before writing it, and it is usually a year-long process. When it is performed adequately, the book is potentially done before I sit down to the typewriter; that is, it is written in my head so far as all or most of the thought process is concerned, and all that remains is to find the right words and sentences and their proper ordering, which is the task of actualizing what, before that, is only a potential book in my mind.

The more adequately the thinking is done before the actual writing begins, the more attention can then be paid to all the rhetorical and grammatical problems of writing, for the basic logical problems have all been solved. In short, my separation of thinking about the book to be written and actually writing it accords with a separation of logical questions from considerations of grammar and rhetoric that are so different.

Exceptions often occur to the procedure I have just outlined. Sometimes, when my family and I go away from Chicago for a winter vacation, I will take a typewriter and a few files of notes with me, in order to start writing a chapter or two before I go to Aspen in the summer. Having made that early start somehow facilitates and encourages the continuation of the writing process, instead of having to start from scratch when I get to Aspen.

Sometimes in the course of writing one chapter, I think of points or arguments to put in later chapters and, then, of course, I put notes of such thinking (that occurs during the days of writing) in the appropriate file for the later chapter. To this extent, the required thinking may not be completely done before I reach Aspen; but, for the most part, that is not the case.

The file folders that I take with me to Aspen, along with other relevant materials to which I may need to refer, such as earlier books of mine, contain the book *in potentia*. The task that remains is only that of putting words, sentences, and paragraphs on paper, which I do by typing them out on an old standard manual Royal typewriter. I cannot use an electric, and I have a more than efficient secretary, Marlys Allen, who has been with me for almost thirty years. That makes a word processor unnecessary. Instead, as will be seen presently, the only device that serves my purpose is a Xerox machine.

Let me explain how this works. First, an essential ingredient in my method of writing is to write every successive day once I start writing, with no time off on Saturday or Sunday, no breaks at all. The only exception to this, as I pointed out earlier, is the break in my writing on a week when I am conducting a seminar. That is why I prefer, when other factors make it possible, to get to Aspen fairly early in June, so that I can start writing and even finishing the book before my first seminar of the summer in mid-July. In the last decade this has fortunately been the case in most of my Aspen summers.

With the exceptions noted above and with this plan of work, I can usually complete the writing of a chapter of ten or fifteen pages in a day or, at the most, two days. That is accomplished in three or four hours of writing, beginning at seven in the morning and finishing well before noon. Accordingly, the first draft of a book of fifteen or twenty chapters will be completed in less than a month of successive days.

Each day, after I have pulled the pages out of the typewriter, I sit down either before lunch or immediately after, and write corrections by pen onto my poorly typed manuscript, correcting not only typographical mistakes but infelicities of phrasing or sentence structure and sometimes even an additional sentence or two. I also put paragraph signs in order to turn a long paragraph into a number of shorter ones, because I believe short paragraphs are easier to read.

With this done, I send post haste a corrected manuscript to Marlys in Chicago, who makes a clean copy, Xeroxes it, and sends the Xerox copy back to me for further corrections. At the same time, she sends Xerox copies of that first draft to a number of colleagues and friends who have become accustomed and responsive to my request for their recommendations of revisions to be made in the first draft.

With not much delay, they give these to Marlys or send them directly to me. What always amazes me about this process is that the overlapping in their revision suggestions is slight as compared with the quite different recommendations they make. They even call my attention to different typographical mistakes. I put all of the corrected and revised or commented on pages in the file folder for that chapter; and when I have finished writing the book early in the summer, I devote later weeks of it by doing a second draft of each chapter, incorporating in that revision not only all the typographical corrections but also all the suggestions for substantive or stylistic improvements that I have found acceptable. Changes in the main lines of my thinking—its insights or arguments—seldom if ever occur.[7]

The time schedule that I have outlined enables me to finish the writing of a first draft and also its first revision in plenty of time for Marlys to send a clean copy of the revised manuscript to the publisher, either on or before the day in September appointed for the delivery of the manuscript. My editors at Macmillan have told me that I am one of a very few authors, or even the only one, that is punctilious about delivering the manuscript on its due date.

Subsequently there are several months in which further revisions occur, made by my editor, made by the outside copy editor to whom the manuscript has been sent, and even by me when I see the copy-edited manuscript before it is set in type. This, moreover,

7. The process I have just described does not apply to this book that I am now writing; in the first place, because it is an autobiographical, not a philosophical, book; in the second place, because its relatively small number of chapters are much longer than the chapters in my philosophical books, which I try to keep relatively short; and in the third place, because writing an autobiography involves a large number of factual matters on which I had to do extensive research, resulting in a large amount of autobiographical documents that I had to bring to Aspen in many file boxes in order to write this book. As for the philosophical books I have written, some well, some not so well, I shall have more to say on this subject in Chapter 8.

does not preclude further editorial revisions that I cannot resist making when I read both galley and page proofs, because, for reasons I will never understand, reading what you have written in print rather than in typescript enables you to perceive infelicities of expression or *lacunae* of thought that you have missed on all previous readings of the manuscript. Even the change from the look of the galley proofs to the look of the page proofs causes such discernments.

One more, not unimportant, detail remains to be added. It concerns what I always do in the afternoon of any day in which I have spent the morning hours writing and correcting the manuscript to send to Chicago. After lunch, and sometimes after a short nap, I spend several hours in what I call "idling."

I have defined idling in an earlier book, in which I dealt with the six activities that consume all of our life's time—sleep (and other biologically necessary functions such as eating, cleansing), play, economically necessary toil or work, truly leisure pursuits, rest, and last, but not least, idling.[8]

Human idling is like the idling of an automobile engine when it is turned on, but not put into gear to move in some determined direction. We idle when we are awake, but do no purposeful thinking, thinking driven by some aim or goal. If one has done highly concentrated and purposeful work in the morning, such as writing a chapter, that concentration and purpose cause things in the fringe of your conscious mind to be shunted into your unconscious. Then when you relax in the afternoon to spend an hour or two idling, those things, buried in your unconscious, come alive in your conscious mind.

Sometimes they are phrases or sentences to use in the chapter you are going to write the next morning or on some subsequent day that week. Sometimes they are an addition to the thinking process that you had assumed was completed before you started writing.

The writing of the chapter in the morning did not include the thought or two that pops into your mind while idling that after-

8. See Adler, *A Vision of the Future: Twelve Ideas for a Better Life and a Better Society* (1984), pp. 8–34.

noon. It was shunted out of your conscious mind into your unconscious because your attention was so concentrated in the morning on the task of writing. Knowing this, I never sit down for my afternoon hours of idling without paper by my side on which to take note of the words or thoughts that idling always produces.

The usefulness of idling in the process of writing a book is not peculiar to that process. It will occur in the busy life of professional persons, such as lawyers, physicians, or engineers, as well as in the busy life of top executives in commerce and industry.

It will occur, but only if they allow it to occur, which means they must *avoid being busy* all the hours of their waking life. Especially if they work hard in the morning, they should manage to find an hour or two for idling in the late afternoon or evening of the very same day. Postponing it for some other day or later in the week will not do. What was buried in the unconscious by concentrated attention to the tasks of the morning must be permitted to revive in the afternoon or evening of the same day. Idling delayed is idling deprived of its efficacy.

5

Summers at the Aspen Institute in Colorado provided another facet to my life—the world of TV interviews on PBS. This began when Bill Moyers and his wife Judith conducted an Executive Seminar. Bill invited me to talk to his seminar on the day that they were discussing the *Communist Manifesto*. This led to his videotaping an interview with me in the garden outside the seminar room. I cannot remember whether that interview was ever broadcast, but I suppose it was.

A couple of years later—in fact, in 1978 after my book *Aristotle for Everybody* was published—Bill arranged for the videotaping of an hour-long seminar on that book. There were about twenty participants in the discussion that took place around the seminar table. I played the role of Aristotle, explaining his doctrines in response to a wide diversity of questions and challenges. That videotape was broadcast at that time, and I know that it has been rebroadcast more recently.

The big event came a few years later after the publication of my book *Six Great Ideas,* in 1981. The management of the Aspen Institute talked to Bill Moyers about taping one of my Executive Seminars to spread information about them to the TV audience. The plan turned instead to doing a week-long seminar on my *Six Great Ideas,* one idea a day.

At an early stage of the planning, the participants were to be the random selection that any ordinary Executive Seminar draws. But as things developed, Joseph Slater, who was then President of the Institute, nominated a group of VIPs from abroad as well as from this country, leaving it up to Bill Moyers and to me to name the others who were to sit around the table.[9] It turned out to be an impressive group of persons, with a diversity of credentials. They were sent the book to read well in advance of the seminar and arrived in Aspen for a get-together on the Sunday evening before the first seminar on Monday morning.

That evening I became a little apprehensive about the truculence of some of the VIPs that Slater had invited. They were manifestly indisposed to behave like ordinary participants in an Executive

9. *Seated on my right were:*
Alan Bullock, Aspen Institute Trustee and Senior Fellow; Fellow of the British Academy, Oxford, England
Francis Mading Deng, Ambassador of the Sudan to Canada; Aspen Institute Trustee, Ottawa, Ontario, Canada
Betty Sue Flowers, Vice President and Dean of Graduate Studies, University of Texas at Austin, Austin, Tex.
Jamake Highwater, Writer and Artist, New York, N.Y.
Joseph E. Slater, President, Aspen Institute for Humanistic Studies, New York, N.Y.
Soedjatmoko, Aspen Institute Trustee; Rector, United Nations University, Tokyo, Japan
Rüdiger von Wechmar, Aspen Institute Senior Fellow; Ambassador of the Federal Republic of Germany to Rome, Rome, Italy

Seated on my left were:
Jeremy Bernstein, Department of Physics, Stevens Institute of Technology, Hoboken, N.J.
Robin C. Duke, New York, N.Y.
Shirley Hufstedler, Aspen Institute Trustee; Hufstedler, Miller, Carlson, and Beardsley, Los Angeles, Calif.
Alexander A. Kwapong, Aspen Institute Trustee; Vice Rector, United Nations University, Tokyo, Japan
Ruth B. Love, General Superintendent of Schools, Chicago, Il.
Robert A. Mosbacher, Aspen Institute Trustee, Houston, Tex.
Jon O. Newman, U.S. Circuit Judge, U.S. Court of Appeals, West Hartford, Conn.
Gus Tyler, Aspen Institute Senior Fellow; Assistant to the President, International Ladies' Garment Workers' Union, New York, N.Y.

Seminar. Bill Moyers sensed the same thing, and he admonished them in a short talk about the performance he expected from them the next morning.

He told them that the final product that would be broadcast would run for fifty-five minutes. The discussion in the seminar room would go on for two hours. But only twenty or twenty-five minutes of what was filmed would be finally used, the rest of it dropped on the cutting-room floor, because in the other thirty minutes of the film to be broadcast, Bill and I would be conversing, one-on-one, about that idea in various outdoor locations in Aspen. That being so, would they all speak briefly and keep to the point in answer to the questions that I would ask. Lengthy speeches on their part would simply be deleted, so if they wished to appear on the screen, they had better follow his advice.

The largest of the seminar rooms the next morning was a sight to behold. At the far end of the room opposite to where I would be sitting was the bank of technical equipment used in filming—the sound equipment, the lights, three cameras, the crew, Bill Moyers, and his technical director. The participants sat at opposite sides of the octagonal table, seven or eight on my left and the same number on my right. There was room at the back for a small number of auditors who were given permission in advance to attend the sessions.

That Monday morning, as on every other morning of that week, Bill Moyers and I met at some visually attractive location, to converse about the first of the six great ideas. Truth.[10] To take advantage of the softness of early morning light, we started at seven, though our conversation did not actually start then because it took almost an hour for all the equipment to be made ready for shooting.

That done, Bill and I assembled with the participants in the seminar room at nine forty-five where Bill once more repeated his admonitions to them of the night before. It fell on deaf ears, totally unheeded. The VIPs present, who sat on my right side, paid little or no attention to the questions I asked them. They appeared not to have read the chapter assigned for discussion that day. Each,

10. The other ideas in sequence were Beauty, Goodness, Liberty, Equality, and Justice.

interrogated by me, instead of answering the question I posed, made a long speech about matters dear to his or her heart, and scarcely relevant to the subject under discussion. It was a patently exhibitionistic performance on their part. The performance of the participants on my left side, most of whom had been chosen by Bill Moyers or me, was better, but still not up to snuff.

After two more hours of filming on outdoor locations with Bill Moyers and me conversing, I went home that first day greatly depressed about what had happened that day in the seminar room. Could I stand five more days of that? How could I get them to discuss the ideas assigned in the light of what the book they were supposed to have read said about that idea? The telephone rang, and Bill Moyers told me he had to talk with me at an early breakfast the next morning before we started to film on location.

He was as upset as I was about what had happened in the seminar room the first day, but he was most upset about the look of agony and despair on my face as he watched my performance on the camera through which he viewed me. From now on, would I please try to smile and looked relaxed, regardless of what the others said or did not say. Would I bear in mind that in the editing of the film, all those long irrelevant speeches would be cut out and only the relatively brief and lively interchanges would be retained?

I promised and managed to do so. As the days succeeded one another, the performance of the VIPs improved slightly, but never that of the more exhibitionistic among them. The participants on my left hand, chosen by Moyers and me, did substantially better and that helped to make what was retained on the edited film more like a lively discussion of the ideas treated in the book, which they had read as the VIPs opposite them had not.

For me, it was an exhausting week, beginning early in the morning on outdoor locations every day, then two trying hours in the seminar room, followed by two or three hours of more outdoor filming in the late afternoon, and an evening of preparation for the next day. Nor did it end with six days, but required a seventh and eighth day of filming on outdoor locations to produce an apt beginning and ending for the sequence of six days in the seminar room.

In the course of all this, some amusing interludes occurred. One day, while the seminar was in process, I felt someone, under the table, pulling on the bottom of my slacks. I managed to look down and there was the girl on Moyers' staff whose job it was to attach my audio equipment every morning. She had been sent under the table by Moyers so that her transit from him to me would not be in the eye of the camera. She handed me a note from him that said: "Please stop pounding the table when you want to stress a point!"

All was not over when Moyers and the crew had a merry farewell party with Caroline and me after the eight or nine days of filming. It took thirteen months to edit the films from three cameras. Out of more than 250,000 feet of film in the cans, only a little more than 50,000 feet were saved for the final product to be broadcast; and I must say, the skillful editing by Bill Moyers and Sage Ewing achieved a result that I was delighted to see when, one day over a year later, I spent six hours in the viewing room at PBS (WNET–Channel 13) in New York, looking at the six TV programs in succession. The improvement in performance of the participants from the first day to the last was plainly visible.

In between the day in the studio in New York and the filming we had done in Aspen, there was a year of hard work in promoting the series with the press before it was broadcast. Bill Moyers and I traveled around the country to be interviewed; and we also visited ARCO headquarters in New York, Philadelphia, and Los Angeles to show them snatches of the final product, for it had been Thornton Bradshaw, President of ARCO and also Vice-Chairman of the Aspen Institute Board, who had persuaded Bill Moyers to engage in this venture and had persuaded ARCO to underwrite the cost of doing it. The highly favorable comments in the press, both before and after the films were broadcast nationwide on PBS, fill a bulging folder in my files. Since then the six programs have been rebroadcast many times.

Bill Moyers has told me that the response to the broadcast films received by Channel 13 in New York was unusually large, and there was also an exceptionally large demand for the printed transcripts of them. But, for both him and me, the most extraordinary response came from some construction workers (mostly plumbers) in Utah, in the form of letters that told us how viewing the six films on TV and then reading my books, changed their lives. I have placed two of these letters in the Notes to this chapter as Item C.

My own recollection is that I first appeared on William F. Buckley, Jr.'s program "Firing Line," in 1980 when Buckley interviewed me on my book, *How to Think About God,* published that year. I have been appearing on "Firing Line" on books that Macmillan Publishing Company has published ever since; all in all, sixteen times.

Though they differ greatly in style, I have enjoyed all the TV work I have done with both Buckley and Moyers. They both do their homework by reading the book in question very well before we get in front of the cameras, Moyers then asking me questions that he thinks the audience would like to ask, and Buckley questioning me in a manner that goes beyond the book in review to its underlying implications.

Also differing in their style of interrogation are Milton Rosenberg on "Extension 720" (WGN Radio, Chicago) and Larry King on his nationally syndicated radio talk show. Both of these are two-hour-long radio interviews, with listeners to the program calling in and asking me questions in the second half. I think I have talked with Milt Rosenberg about as many of my books as I have done on TV with Bill Buckley.

6

I have not reported all the incidental benefits that have accrued to me as a consequence of my work done for the Aspen Institute in Colorado, as well as the associations I have formed there. I cannot remember them all, but there is one I can hardly forget.

It concerns my getting my Bachelor of Arts degree from Columbia University in 1983, a full sixty years after I completed my undergraduate courses in the college in 1923. In *Philosopher at Large,* I have told the story of how the Dean of the College called me into his office the Friday before Commencement on a Tuesday in May 1923, to advise me that I would not receive my diploma because I had not completed all the requirements for graduation, though I had already received my Phi Beta Kappa Key for passing, with high honors, 135 points of course credit when only 120 points were required for graduation.[11]

Seeing the puzzlement on my face, the Dean explained that four years of physical education and passing a swimming test were requirements for graduation. My failure in attendance and performance on both counts was the reason I would not receive my diploma on Tuesday.

The story of my withheld diploma has been mistold by many chairmen who have introduced me on the platforms from which I have given lectures in the years to follow. They always stress the fact that I did not get my B.A. because I could not swim. That is partly true. I still cannot swim and I have persistently turned away persons who have tried to teach me. The other, and more important part of the truth, was that I attended gym and the running track only a few times in my first year in college. I disliked the business of exercise, and also of dressing and undressing in between other classes. After those first few times, I never went to gym again.

How does Aspen come into this story, many years later in the 1980s? The answer is the intervention of friends that I met at Aspen—Leonard and Evelyn Lauder, of the cosmetic company that bears the Lauder name. Leonard is an Aspen Institute trustee of long standing, an enthusiastic supporter of Aspen seminars, and Caroline and I have spent many pleasant hours with Leonard and Evelyn.

On one of these occasions, I must have told the Lauders about not getting my B.A. at Columbia in 1923. They were greatly amused, and it was Evelyn, I think, who decided that something should be done to rectify that academic defect in my career.

I cannot remember the steps she, and also Leonard, took to get Columbia to award me a much-delayed bachelor's degree, in view of the fact that 1982 was the year of my eightieth birthday. Their efforts obviously prevailed, because I received a letter from the Dean of Columbia College asking me whether I would accept the diploma if it were offered to me at commencement the following May.

11. See *Philosopher at Large*, pp. 21–23.

I answered in the affirmative, saying that I prized the bachelor's degree more than the Master of Arts degree (which I did not work for), and the Ph.D. degree that Columbia had awarded me in 1928. I did not mention the fact that, in the intervening years, the University of Seattle had given me an honorary B.A. and that St. Mary's College, in Moraga, California, had given me an M.A., *honoris causa.* I told the Dean that I valued what I had learned as an undergraduate student in the college much more than all the instruction that I had received—or avoided—in the graduate school.

That commencement Tuesday in May of 1983, was a gala day for me. President Michael I. Sovern honored me at a luncheon he gave for the trustees and for the recipients of honorary degrees. I was interviewed before the commencement exercises by a host of reporters, including representatives of the major wire services. At the exercises themselves, I marched with the undergraduates, wearing my Ph.D. gown and hood. And after the commencement was over, Caroline and I attended a party at the Lauder home, at which I was given graduation gifts, including a pair of bright red swimming trunks.

My old friend, Henry Anatole Grunwald, who, in 1952, had written the *Time* cover story about me, and had now become the Editor-in-Chief of Time Inc., was a guest at the Lauder party. He caused *Time* to do a story in its next issue about my long delayed B.A.

That was a very small part of the journalistic response to the event. Stories about it appeared in newspapers all over the country. I even ran into one in an English newspaper in Seoul when Caroline and I went to Korea a month or so later. Though it was hardly the most important event in my life, or an achievement of any real significance, it received more attention in the press, as well as on radio and TV, than anything else that I have ever done or that has ever happened to me.

7

My Aspen years have enriched my life with many friends. I have so far mentioned only Leonard and Evelyn Lauder. Then there is Dr. Emmanuel Papper and his wife Pat with whom Caroline and I have been friends for many years. Dr. Papper was Dean of the School of Medicine at the University of Miami and is one of the world's leading anesthesiologists. He has participated in many of my seminars and as his interests go beyond medicine to philosophy and literature, our conversations have covered many subjects.

Among the Music Associates, I have enjoyed knowing two conductors of the orchestra—James DePreist, resident conductor of the Oregon Symphony Orchestra in Portland and visiting conductor at Aspen, and several times a seminar participant; and Larry Foster, conductor of the Monte Carlo Symphony Orchestra, as well as music director of the music festival at Aspen.[12]

Edward and Ann Hudson of Fort Worth, Texas, have been close friends of mine and of Caroline's with whom we have enjoyed many spirited evenings. Ed is a director of the Kimbell Art Museum in Fort Worth and is also connected with the Whitney Museum of American Art in New York City. Ann has become a member of Aspen's Board of Trustees. As in the case of the two conductors mentioned above, and of the Pappers, our conversations with them go beyond philosophy to many other fields of humanistic interest.

This summer of 1991, while I am writing this book, we are living in the new house that Merrill Ford and General Robert Taylor built for themselves last year. As a great kindness to us, they vacated it so that we could occupy it, moving for the summer months to another house nearby in Snowmass. General Taylor served as an agent of the CIA, and Merrill Ford is a director of the International Institute of Design and President of the Board of the Aspen Art Museum. Merrill and Bob have been our friends for years, as also have been Larry and Wynn Aldrich, encountered many years ago through Larry's attendance at an Executive Seminar. We have traveled with them in Europe, in Greek waters, and in the Caribbean, along with Bob and Merrill.

With two exceptions, I will not mention by name the many

12. This summer at the behest of Larry Foster, the conductor, and of Robert Harth, who is now President of the Music Associates of Aspen, I have helped to arrange a series of seven talks for the music students and faculty, on a variety of subjects that are aimed to engage those present in an extended question and answer period. This harks back to the early days of Aspen when the musicians and seminar leaders, with fewer demands on their time, interacted to the profit of both groups.

persons with whom we have become personal friends through their repeated participation in the seminars I have conducted in the last ten or fifteen years. Caroline and I refer to them fondly as "Adler groupies,"

Robert H. Matt of Omaha gave up business for philosophy as a result of his Aspen experiences and in recent years he has, against my advice, tried to pursue the study of philosophy at the University of Chicago. While this has been going on, we have met frequently in Chicago and I think I have finally persuaded him to pursue his interest in philosophy outside of academic circles.

James O'Toole, who is a professor at the Graduate School of Business Administration at the University of Southern California in Los Angeles, and his wife Marilyn came to Aspen in the early 1970s, and we have been close friends ever since. Our children have grown up together. Jim has been associated with me in the Paideia educational reform and also with editorial work for Encyclopaedia Britannica. Recently he, along with Charles Van Doren, has helped to train moderators to use the readings I have recommended for the conduct of their seminars.

Last, but by no means least, there is Walter Paepcke's widow, Elizabeth, with whom I first came to Aspen in 1950. She is three months older than I am, from which vantage point she feels privileged to scold me for my excesses. She has been a friend of mine since the 1930s and an intimate friend of Caroline's since we were married in 1963. It was in that year that Caroline first came to Aspen.

In the past decade, I have taken the opportunity afforded by my seminars, to give the participants a special afternoon talk about the deplorable state of the country's schools and about the proposed Paideia reform of them. Doing this has served to elicit help from the business community and to get a number of top businessmen to assist in the financing of the Paideia reform movement. Among them was Michael Tobin, until recently Chairman and CEO of the American National Bank and Trust Company of Chicago. His generous contribution of funds from the American National Bank Foundation enabled us to turn the Goldblatt Elementary School in an all-black Chicago ghetto and the New Sabin Magnet School in an Hispanic neighborhood with a high rate of juvenile delinquency into model elementary schools.[13]

Douglas and Philip Adler, two sons born to Caroline and me, now twenty-eight and twenty-six years old, have spent almost all of their summers in Aspen. They first came here by train when they were infants in baskets and they have been summering here ever since. During their college years they have been employed by the Institute to help set up seminar rooms and other things. They, like their parents, have made many friends here.

I should also mention that one of my two adopted sons from my first marriage, Michael Adler, lived in Aspen after he left the Rocky Mountain School in nearby Carbondale; and now, with his second wife Pam and their daughter, Morgan, live nearby in Glenwood Springs. My other adopted son, Mark Adler, came to Aspen with Michael in the early 1950s. Mark spent his honeymoon here with his wife Nancy and they, with their sons, have visited us in Aspen in recent years.

All in all, Aspen has been not just a workplace for me. For my family and me it has been a humanly rich and varied experience during the years of our mature lives.

NOTES TO CHAPTER 6

Item A

Excerpts from Eightieth Birthday Address/ Mortimer J. Adler Day Aspen, Colorado, April 2, 1982*

Ladies and Gentlemen: I am deeply appreciative of the honor you have bestowed upon me this day and I am most grateful to all of you who are here this evening to help celebrate the occasion.

This is a great event in my life, coming as it does on the edge of my

13. See Chapter 4, *supra.*

* *A Reminiscence* . . . (Speech published on the occasion of the 40th Anniversary of The Aspen Institute), The Aspen Institute, August 1990.

80th birthday. I am delighted that I can share it with my wife Caroline and with three of four sons, Michael, Douglas, and Philip, who are here with me. Since I am probably the oldest Aspenite in this room tonight, I feel privileged to reminisce about earlier days when none of you were here.

Receiving this honor is much better than receiving an Oscar, even if it is an Oscar for best picture of the year, because the winner is after all only one of five nominees for the award and the four others are breathing down his neck. I stand here quite alone.

It is also better than receiving an honorary degree, for then you are only one of six or eight to be honored on the occasion. I stand here quite alone.

But I would rather not stand here quite alone. Oscar winners on the stage of the Academy Awards affair often express a wish to call their co-producers and other associates to the platform with them. That's what I would like to do if I could. I would like to have here with me tonight

Walter and Elizabeth Paepcke
Herbert and Joella Bayer
and
two persons you may not have heard of
Robert Hutchins, of the University of Chicago, and
Ortega y Gasset, of the University of Madrid

They were the main actors at the start of the story I want to tell you. It begins in 1945 when the Paepckes decided to create a ski resort in Aspen. Though the Paepckes were close friends of mine, that action on their part did not interest me, because I did not ski and knew that I never would. A man who cannot swim and cannot ride a bike should certainly never put himself on skis.

The new Aspen, the modern Aspen, the rejuvenated ghost town, was born on snow and on skis in 1945. It might have remained a winter resort and grown mightily as one, if it had not been for Bob Hutchins. Prompted by a request from two professors at the University of Chicago—Arnold Bergstrasse and Antonio Borgese—to celebrate Goethe's bicentennial in 1949, Bob Hutchins went to his old friend Walter Paepcke, who was a devoted fan of Goethe, and together they decided to celebrate the event at Aspen rather than at the University of Chicago.

I do not have to tell you what a great success the Goethe Festival was in the summer of 1949. That is well-known history. But I must remind you of one thing. Ortega came from Spain, delivered a fine address about Goethe, and then wrote Walter Paepcke a letter about the humanities. This inspired Walter to decide to establish the Aspen Institute for Humanistic Studies. . . .

. . . In the summer of 1949, with lectures by scholars from all over the world and with music by the Minneapolis Symphony Orchestra, the new Aspen had its second lease on life and began the development of what it has become in the last thirty-two years and, I hope, will always continue to be, a great cultural center, nourished and sustained by poetry and music, by the visual arts, by the dance and by theatre, and above all by philosophy and by ideas—great ideas. . . .

In April 1950—just about thirty-two years ago from this evening—Walter and Elizabeth took me to Colorado for my first visit to Aspen. My first impression was far from bright. There were no paved streets. The spring thaw had begun and the thoroughfares were seas of mud, alarming to one who could not swim or even wade. Nevertheless, the Paepcke hospitality, their lovely house, the good meals at the renovated Hotel Jerome, the company of the Bayers and other friends of Walter's, and the promise of the future, overcame my initial distaste for this as yet unreconstructed ghost town. After all, I was a city boy who, twenty years earlier, had refused Bob Hutchins' invitation to join him at the Yale Law School, because I could not imagine giving up Manhattan and living in a small village like New Haven.

We planned that first summer of the Aspen Institute in the Schweitzer cottage that April in 1950. It was not a great success. Great books seminars did not quite work out because the participants were seldom there for more than a week or two and the great books seminar plan called for continuous participation over a period of at least twelve or fourteen weeks. The music was wonderful; some of the lectures were good; but the facilities were somewhat primitive.

I gave the opening lecture on the nature of man on July 1 in the tent, at ten in the morning, to an audience of about 150, with stray dogs walking across the platform, with birds picking at my notes on a music stand, and with gusts of wind often blowing the notes off the stand.

Seminars were held on the grounds of the Paepcke home, on the porch of the Four Seasons Club where the Music School now resides, and around the edge of the Jerome swimming pool.

Lectures were given in the Blue Lounge of the Hotel Jerome, in the burned out auditorium of the Wheeler Opera House some evenings, and some mornings in the tent.

Audiences were very small by present standards, but they usually included most of the resident musicians who had very much lighter schedules than they have now.

There was no health center, and other than the dining room of the Jerome, the Red Onion, and the Golden Horn, there were almost no restaurants to speak of. Shops there were few, and motels there were none at all.

Miraculously, the Institute survived all these hardships, largely through the courage and dogged obstinacy of Walter Paepcke. Through the wise intervention of Henry Luce of Time, Inc. (a classmate of Walter's at Yale), we decided to give up Great Books seminars and substitute something that slowly grew into seminars for business executives with readings drawn from the two-volume collection of documents used at the University of Chicago, called *The People Shall Judge*.

With the help of Clarence Faust, then Dean at the University of Chicago, I drew up the first reading list that was to develop into the readings for the Aspen Executive Seminars; and, as I recall, I conducted the first of these seminars with Meyer Kestnbaum as my associate. Meyer was President of Hart Schaffner and Marx in Chicago and a good friend of Walter's.

By 1955, the facilities were somewhat improved. The Aspen Meadows complex was built, but with only one chalet at the beginning. We had the Paepcke Auditorium* and the seminar building, with the ideal seminar rooms designed by Herbert Bayer. We had the tent, and that was about all we had.

But by this time, the Executive Seminars began attracting national attention, though I must add that expenses and fees for conducting them never moved from the red into the black during Walter's lifetime. He always had to pass the hat among his friends and dig deep into his own pocket to finance the deficits.

The years from 1950 to 1955—before the streets were paved—were nevertheless great years. I can remember coming back from a trail ride in the hills and coming down dusty Main Street to the Hotel Jerome on horseback. Elizabeth Paepcke took my picture when I dismounted, knee-sore and saddle-weary. You could see Pyramid Peak through the ellipse formed by my bowed legs. She still has the picture, on which she inscribed the words "Hopalong Adler."

* This was an error on my part. The Paepcke Auditorium was not built until after Walter's death in 1960.

Between 1955 and 1960 the number of executive seminars increased, the Health Center was built, the concerts flourished under the management of the Aspen Music Associates, the lectures were followed by two-hour forums the next morning (because the schedule still allowed everyone plenty of time for reflection and talk), but there was none of the innovations that came later and gave Aspen the beginning of its outreach to a larger world.

That beginning was inaugurated when Robert O. Anderson succeeded Walter Paepcke as Chairman (at Walter's instigation) and when Joseph Slater became the Institute's President. Since the 1960s, the Institute that bears the name of Aspen has grown steadily in many directions—both geographically and intellectually—not only to other places in this country, but also to locations abroad, and by adding other programs and seminars to what is and will always remain the backbone and center of the Institute—the Aspen Executive Seminar.

The Institute is now operative all over the world. It is now engaged in many intellectual and cultural activities at Aspen and elsewhere. And as the Institute has reached out into the world beyond Aspen, it has also brought the whole world to Aspen. That is what Bob Anderson and Joe Slater have done for the city of Aspen, for which the city owes them an inestimable debt of gratitude.

Let me be sure that one thing is crystal clear. Just as the Aspen Executive Program will always be the backbone of the Aspen Institute's varied and far flung activities, so the City of Aspen will always be the heart and home of the Institute. The Institute owes a debt to the City that cannot be paid in any other way.

Aspen is the place to which people from all over the world will come in the summertime. No other location, no matter how scenic, can ever replace it during those months, because no other place is likely to be able to offer all the attractions, cultural and otherwise, that have developed in the vicinity of Aspen during the last thirty years.

No matter how far and wide the Institute may spread itself, no matter what activities it conducts elsewhere in the other nine months of the year, Aspen will always be—in June, July, and August—its dominant center, the center from which its world-wide influence emanates, an influence always carrying the name of Aspen.

That is why I have repeatedly said that Aspen deserves to be acknowledged the Athens of America—a great cultural center not only for our own country, but also for the whole world.

Let me conclude by telling you a story about my wife Caroline. When she first came to Aspen with me in the early sixties, we often drove down the road past Basalt to Carbondale and Glenwood Springs. For some reason, she was struck by a sign pointing to a little town called Emma across the Roaring Fork. She expressed the wish to be known as Caroline Adler of Chicago and Emma. I regret to say that I have never gratified her wish.

I have a much higher ambition. You have started me off on its gratification. You have made me an honorary citizen of Aspen.

I have lived parts of my life in New York, Chicago, San Francisco, and London, but they haven't done for me what you have done.

Moreover, I have written more books in Aspen, given more lectures in Aspen, conducted more seminars in Aspen, and, with Bill Moyers, made more films for television in Aspen than anywhere else.

Aspen is clearly my intellectual home, no matter where else I pay my taxes and hang my hat.

And since all the world comes to Aspen for what it has to offer intellectually, I would like to be known as Mortimer Adler of Aspen and the world.

Item B

LETTER TO ALVIN C. EURICH

March 2, 1964

Mr. Alvin C. Eurich
Ford Foundation
477 Madison Avenue
New York City, New York

Dear Al:

The memorandum from Bob Murray about the Executive Seminar program for the summer of 1964 arrived. I assume that this is what you had in mind when you told me some weeks ago that a "composite list" would be made up from the suggestions of the several moderators taking part in the program this summer.

It would serve no purpose for me to try to conceal from you that I am unhappy with the list as it stands. When you told me that you were going to pool suggestions from the several moderators, I feared it might turn out this way. A good reading list—one that has thematic unity or unities, order, coherence, and development—cannot, in my judgment, be constructed by piecing together the separate nominations of a number of people. Like any work of art, it must be seen as a whole first and the parts must be defined and related in terms of the conception of the whole.

You said that you would welcome my criticisms and suggestions after I had examined the "composite" that resulted from pooling the recommendations received from four or five hands. I'm afraid I cannot be very helpful—*constructively.* I cannot improve the present list by saying "substitute this for that," "drop this," and "add that." To proceed in that way would not and could not result in the kind of change which, in my judgment, must be made if the reading list is to perform the function it should for an Aspen Executive Seminar.

The only way in which I think I can be helpful is to set down as carefully as I can the principles I would have in mind in constructing a reading list. Clarence Faust, Met Wilson, and I had such principles in mind when, in the middle fifties, we constructed the first reading list for the Executive Seminar; and we followed these principles in subsequent years as we gradually improved the original list. The turning point came after Walter Paepcke died and Bob Craig radically revised the list, departing from these principles, or worse—going in the opposite direction. . . .

I could not . . . get a good sequence of seminars out of the Craig hodge-podge. . . . My seminar last summer, as you know, had a different reading list from the one used by the other seminar leaders.

It was my impression that you regretted that I had not sent you a copy of my list in advance of your coming to Aspen last summer, because you would have much preferred to teach the list I used—the old-fashioned Aspen list—instead of the Craig list. It was also my impression that Bob Anderson applauded the resuscitation of the old Aspen reading list. It was in terms of his enthusiasm for the kind of seminars it produced that first he and I, and then you and I, talked about (1) the possibility of publishing a set of Aspen readings constructed along the lines of the list I used last summer, and (2) the possibility of getting out a moderators' manual which would give the seminar leaders precise directions for the conduct of seminars to make the most effective use of the Aspen readings. We talked about doing these things last August. I talked with Bob Anderson about them again on the phone in the Fall when the good news of your appointment came through. And I talked with you about them subsequently—both on the phone and in New York.

I mention all this to explain my great surprise at the reading list that Bob Murray sent me last week. If this kind of material is right for the Aspen seminars, you could not possibly publish a set of Aspen readings or devise a moderators' manual. If the direction in which I moved away from the Craig list last summer was the right direction in which to move—and I certainly thought this was your opinion at the time, as well as Bob Anderson's—then I cannot understand why the present list seems to be moving sharply in the opposite direction again. . . .

. . . What is at stake here is a set of general principles, not a particular reading list. I am willing to accept any one of a number of reading lists if they all conform as closely as possible to the principles; and among alternative reading lists I would also choose the one that conformed most closely to the principles.

Now I am quite prepared to be told that my conception of the Aspen idea is incorrect, or that I have not correctly stated the Aspen principles. You'll have to forgive me for saying in advance that I find it hard to believe that I have misunderstood what we were trying to do all those years. But maybe I did. Or maybe it is now time to change the Aspen idea and operate on a new set of principles. If so, I would like to have the idea defined for me and the principles explicitly formulated, so that I can understand how a reading list—any reading list, including the one now in hand—puts those principles into practise. But if I correctly understand the Aspen idea, and correctly state the Aspen principles—and I am still hoping that this is the case—then it seems to me that we must do something about constructing a proper reading list—one that conforms. And I am pretty sure that cannot be done by pooling suggestions from various sources. It can, of course, be done by a committee—as it was originally done by Clarence, Met, and me—but only if the members of that committee work closely with one another, sit around a table, discuss each item, and work together with the kind of unity that is necessary to produce a coherent result.

With all this said, I am now ready to state my understanding of the Aspen idea, and my understanding of the Aspen principles.

I. *The Aspen Idea of an Executive Seminar*

A. Negatively, the Executive Seminar is not a great books discussion group. (We started out that way in the early fifties, and we soon realized that this was the wrong approach for the type of person we hoped to reach in these executive seminars.)

B. Negatively also, the Executive Seminar is not a course in the humanities, of the type set up by the Bell Telephone Company at the University of Pennsylvania. The aim is not to read literary classics for their own sake.

C. And, negatively, it is not a course in business management of the kind that goes on at the Harvard summer school of business administration.

D. Positively, on the side of substance, it is an effort to acquaint the leaders of our industrial democracy with a small number of basic ideas that are directly germane to the problems our kind of society faces today; and it aims to do this by means of a series of readings that reveals the role these ideas have played in the development of our national life and the role they are playing, quite crucially, today.

E. Positively, on the side of method, it is an effort to get top business men and industrialists to read more carefully—more analytically and critically than they are normally accustomed to—and also to get them to become clearer and more articulate in the expression of their own views, as well as more receptive to the views of others. It tries to inculcate the disciplines of the liberal arts by sticking closely to the texts read, by demanding that discussion follow the precepts of sound logic, by controlling the interchange of views so that relevance and cogency are maintained at all times.

F. It was said above that a small number of ideas should dominate the two weeks—the twelve sessions—of the Aspen Executive Seminar. In the course of two weeks, it is difficult to explore and come to grips with much more than two basic ideas, and they should be the ideas most central to our national life, ideas that are most directly involved in the social, economic, and political policies which the business man, industrialist, or labor leader confronts both in the conduct of his own corporation and in the relation of his corporation to the community at large.

1. The two basic ideas that for many years we thought supreme for this purpose were the ideas of democracy and capitalism, not simply in themselves but in all their complex ramifications, including all their antitheses.
2. These over-arching ideas involve a number of related ideas—the ideas of liberty, equality, justice, rights, progress, human dignity, human happiness, and the general welfare. These ideas have social, political, economic, and ethical connotations.
3. We recognized the difficulty of doing an effective job with this small number of basic ideas; but we also always found it possible to awaken some understanding of them in the executive participants, and to arouse a continuing interest in understanding them better, but only on condition that we concentrated all our time and effort on these few ideas and no others, by making all the readings and all the discussions revolve around them, never allowing either the readings or the discussions to stray far from the set of ideas which constituted the core of our program. . . .

II. *The Aspen Principles by which I mean, the principles for constructing a reading list that conforms to the Aspen idea.*

A. The readings should form a developmental sequence which leads the discussion on from day to day, so that matters discussed on Monday of the first week lead directly into matters discussed on Tuesday, and so on for at least the whole of the first week. It may be necessary to make a fresh start on the second Monday, in order to develop a second sequence of discussions, but there should not be more than two sequences in the course of the two weeks, and the second sequence should be closely connected with the first, so that matters discussed during the first week are carried over into the discussions of the second week.

B. The one or two developmental sequences should be primarily sequences in the development of the few central ideas that constitute the core of the program. They may, but need not, be readings arranged in an historical order of development. But anyone attempting to construct one or two developmental sequences will find that a series of texts in historical order is very effective for the purpose. Departures from the historical order are certainly justifiable, but they need to be justified on the ground that they help the discussions to get to more fundamental ground in the discussion of the central ideas. This, for example, is achieved by introducing Aristotle, Plato, or Machiavelli into a series of readings that for the most part involve texts of more recent vintage—from the 18th century on.

C. Not only should a high degree of relevance, coherence, and continuity obtain in the order of the readings in the sequence of twelve days—or in the two six-day sequences—but these qualities should also be present in any set of readings chosen for a particular day. Thus, if more than one author is read on a particular day, the two or more authors read should *all deal with the same general theme;* they should express divergent or conflicting points of view; the set of readings should provide materials for constructing issues and for observing how such issues are or can be debated.

D. With very few exceptions, the readings for a single session should not be longer than thirty pages. Again, with few exceptions (Machiavelli is the only one I can think of), they should never be book length—certainly not a book of over 150 pages.

   1. They can be whole works, such as a short dialogue of Plato, or a short piece like the *Communist Manifesto* or like Thoreau's *Civil Disobedience*.
   2. Or they can be short parts or short selections from whole

works, such as Book I of Aristotle's *Politics,* or a short set of selections from Tocqueville's *Democracy in America.*

3. Or they can be papers, documents, pamphlets, essays, such as the kind of material collected in *The People Shall Judge.*

E. The required brevity can be violated only with the most unhappy results. It may be said that much longer readings can be assigned because the readings are sent out well in advance and the participants can be expected to read them before they come to Aspen. Maybe yes, maybe no. But even if they do, it is still absolutely necessary for the participants to re-read or closely review what they have read in the hours just before the seminar begins—that very morning or the night before. If they don't do that, the moderator will not be able to conduct the seminar by asking searching questions about the text; the discussion will degenerate into bull sessions; it will take off from the book and leave it far behind. In addition, the participants will be given no discipline in reading, in marking texts, in bringing the marked text to class to use in discussion, in following an argument, in sticking to the point, etc. These important things can be accomplished only if the text assigned is short enough to be re-read carefully and in entirety in the period just before it is discussed.

F. In addition to consisting in a small number of pages, the readings must be tightly packed with substance—with material to be analyzed, with ideas to be discovered, with important positions taken or opposed, with arguments advanced for or against them, etc. The more that a particular selection can pack into a small number of pages, the better it is for the purposes of an Aspen seminar. The best examples of combined density and brevity are, of course, such writings as a dialogue of Plato, 25 or 30 pages of Aristotle, a set of PSJ selections amounting to about 30 pages, or something like the *Communist Manifesto.* One paragraph of the Declaration of Independence packs enough substance to support a whole hour's discussion. But books written in the 20th century, running for 200 pages or more, are usually very thin; I have tried them out again and again and have learned that they don't say enough to support even one hour of good discussion, much less two. Some of them, as for example Kennan's little book on American foreign policy, may be interesting to read, are hardly discussable at all. In any case, examples aside, the principle should be to choose readings which say the most in the fewest pages, for this will provide materials that are not only worthy of maximum attention and care in reading, but also capable of being read in a short time; and such materials have the power to support exciting cross-table discussion for the full two hours without allowing the discussion ever to wander from the texts or the themes they present.

G. Two negative injunctions should be added to the foregoing:

1. Secondary works should be avoided wherever possible, and it should always be possible to avoid them in favor of primary documents—the great seminal texts. (If what I have in mind is not clear here, let me refer to such things as Bronowski's *Science and Human Values,* Heilbroner's *The Worldly Philosophers*).
2. Imaginative works—plays, novels, etc.—should not be included unless they somehow contribute to the discussion of the very same ideas that are dealt with in the expository readings. In other words, they should not be included for their own sake, no matter how good or great they are.

If I am wrong about these principles, then I am probably wrong in my reaction to the reading list just sent out. But if I am right about the Aspen principles, it is difficult to see how that reading list can be regarded as acceptable.

Taking the two weeks as a whole, there is no developmental sequence at all—neither in the twelve sessions, nor in two sets of six sessions, nor for that matter *in any two* successive days.

Taking particular sessions, most of the combined readings put together writings that have little or no relevance to one another, even when the writings, taken separately, are quite good: for example, *The Book of Job* and *The Prince;* or *Antigone* and selections from *The Republic;* or a poem by Wallace Stevens, *Babbit,* and the *Education of Henry Adams.*

The list includes works that, in my judgment, don't fit into the Aspen picture, such as Huxley, J. Bronowski, Paine, Macaulay, Henry Adams, Sinclair Lewis, Robert Heilbroner, Bernard Shaw, Henry Miller. . . . My negative judgment differs, of course, item by item, but each of the aforementioned items falls, on one count or another, to provide us with the kind of materials we need for Aspen seminars. A few of the aforementioned items might be restored, if they were added to a list that gave them the kind of relevance they should have; but this could be done only with a few. . . .

Finally, let me say just once again that my negative reaction to the list as a whole, to most of the particular sessions, and to many of the particular readings, has nothing to do with the merits of the particular writings mentioned. Most of them have some merit; many of them great merit; *but in other connections or for other purposes.*

My negative reaction to the list as a whole and its organized parts is based on the set of principles which I have always thought were, or should be, the guiding criteria for constructing an Aspen reading list: the fewness of the central ideas; the ordering of the twelve sessions into one or at the most two developmental sequences; the relevance of each day to the next, and of the first week to the second week; the close coherence of the items to be read in any single session, based on the fact that they all deal with the same theme; the brevity and compactness of the readings assigned; and the primacy of the pieces assigned—all for the sake of producing well-disciplined discussions; preventing loose talk and bull sessions; cultivating good habits of reading, listening, and speaking.

Of one thing I am absolutely sure: a good reading list will never in the world be constructed by pooling the recommendations of the moderators, most of whom do not bother very much to understand the purpose or method of the Executive Seminar, and some of whom seem to have little sympathy with it.

I will anxiously await word from you about the next steps to be taken. My time—as much of it as you may need—is at your disposal.

As ever yours,

Mortimer J. Adler

MJA:mab
CC: Mr. Robert Anderson
Mrs. Elizabeth Paepcke

ITEM C

LETTERS FROM DAVID M. CALL ON BEHALF OF A GROUP OF CONSTRUCTION WORKERS

March 13 and April 10, 1985†

Dear Mr. Adler:

I am writing in behalf of a group of construction workers (mostly, believe it or not, *plumbers*!) who have finally found a teacher worth listening to. While we cannot all agree whether or not we would hire you as an apprentice, we can all agree that we would love to listen to you during our lunch breaks. We have been studying your books for over a year now and have put together a sizeable library of your writings, the Institute's and Britannica's.

† David M. Call to Mortimer J. Adler, March 13, April 10, 1985. Reprinted by permission.

The Conditions of Philosophy
Philosopher at Large
Six Great Ideas
How to Speak/How to Listen
A Vision of the Future
Aristotle for Everybody
How to Think About God
The Angels and Us
The American Testament
The New Capitalists
The Common Sense of Politics (my favorite)
The Paideia Proposal
The Paideia Program
Paideia Problems and Possibilities
How to Read a Book
Great Treasury of Western Thought
The Idea of Progress
The Idea of Justice
The Idea of Happiness
The Idea of Love
The Annals of America
Gateway to the Great Books
Great Books of the Western World
Great Books Reading Plan
Encyclopaedia Britannica

I am sure that it is just due to our well-known ignorance as tradesmen that not a single one of us had ever heard of you until one Sunday afternoon we were watching public television and Bill Moyers came on with his show Six Great Ideas. We listened intensely and soon became addicted and have been ever since. We never knew a world of ideas existed.

The study of ideas have completely turned around our impression of higher or lower education. We only wish we had not wasted 25 to 35 years in the process. But we do have you to thank for the next 35 to 40 years that we have before us to study and implement the great ideas into our lives and into the lives of our communities. Since reading and discussing your numerous books we have all become devout Constitutionalists. We have grown to love the ideas behind our Country's composition. We thank you and we applaud you. We are certain that the praise of a few plumbers in the State of Utah could hardly compare with the notoriety that you deserve from distinguished colleagues, but we salute you just the same.

Despite the numerous books that we have read and collected we still are not satisfied that many of your writings have escaped us, particularly *The Idea of Freedom* (vols. I & II). We have sent away for them several times and have not been able to purchase them. We have searched used book stores across the west from Washington to Arizona and still have come up empty handed. We will never be satisfied until we have these writings to study and discuss. The following are the books that we anxiously miss:

* *The Time of Our Lives*
* *The Difference of Man and the Difference It Makes*
** *The Idea of Freedom* (2 Vols.)
* *The Capitalist Manifesto*
What Man Has Made of Man
Saint Thomas and the Gentiles
* *Problems for Thomists: The Problem of Species*
How to Think About War and Peace
The Revolution in Education
A Dialectic of Morals
Art and Prudence
Crime, Law and Social Science
Dialectic
* *Research on Freedom* (2 Vols.)
Some Questions About Language

The books with the asterisk are the books that we are very nervous about. If we cannot get hold of these books we will never be satisfied. We are also very disappointed that the *Idea of Equality* has not made it to publication as of yet. It is, for us particularly, an important aspect of American thought. Are there any other books published by your Institute? *The Idea of Religion*? etc. that are available?

Another important desire on our part is to obtain the video's of you and Bill Moyer's Program Six Great Ideas. There are many of the workers who missed the programs and try as we may they cannot be found in any Library or Public Television Library. Are they available?

One last comment. We do indeed have Mortimer Adler as a teacher during our Lunch break, thanks to a little book that we found at a used book store called *Great Ideas from the Great Books*. These series of questions and answers are the perfect size for our lunch hour. The only thing we regret is that it makes our lunch hour turn into two if we are not careful.

Again we thank you. We also hope that any help you give us in locating any of these books will not be a further burden to your busy career. Also, do you ever visit the State of Utah? Probably not.

One last thought, we may be plumbers during the day, but at lunch time and at night and on weekends, we are Philosophers at Large! God bless you Dr. Adler!

Respectfully Yours,

David M. Call

P.S. It just came to my attention on a second reading of your Autobiography that there is a very important addition to *The Annals of America* which we are currently studying called *The Negro in American History* (3 vols.); *The Makers of America* (10 vols.). These would be eagerly devoured also, if only they were available. Could you help us? Also, how many of your articles are still available? We apologize for overwhelming you with this long list of books, but you must remember we have been intellectually starved for 25 to 35 years now and can hardly contain our appetite.

Dear Dr. Adler:
It is impossible for us to thank you for your kindness and generosity. We have received your books and pamphlets and have already begun examining them with great delight. We had no idea that you would respond so favorably towards us, needless to say, if it is possible for a man to be immortalized before he is dead, you have accomplished that feat in our eyes!

My brother Mark and I enrolled into a philosophy class last semester at the University of Utah. We wanted to know if plumbers could philosophize on a College level and pass with a "C" or better. Much to our surprise we not only succeeded but excelled. This was a great boost to our confidence. So proud were we that we are sending you a copy of the five papers that we wrote for the course. We received an A+, A, A, A−, & A−.

We are not sending these papers to boast of our achievements but rather to give credit where credit is due, and to applaud you, not ourselves! Besides, we are not even sure you would agree with everything that we wrote, but whether you do or not, you will have to agree that we tried. Nevertheless, we have you to thank for any success we enjoy and we wanted you to know that.

Incidently, at the end of each paper the teacher consistently asked what our sources were. We thought, wouldn't Mortimer be pleased with us had we simply wrote "common sense derived from every day experience" as our source material.

We also thought you might be interested in knowing what it is like to philosophize on a construction site. One instance will serve as an example: Several days ago my brother and I were discussing free-will and determinism within the hearing distance of a group of brick layers. They were busily laying their brick but could not help but overhear our philosophical arguments. Finally, one of the brick layers could take it no longer and shouted over to us: "I've got a philosophical question!" Surprised, we inquired as to what it was, to which he responded: "What is your philosophy on getting a good orgasm?"

All of his fellow brick layers were quite delighted in his question and were celebrating with many chuckles and jeers when I responded: "Let me ask you a question, then!" As soon as the brick layers noticed that I was taking them seriously they all stopped and turned around to see what I would ask. I addressed the bricker who had started the whole affair and said: "Tell me, would you, which it would be better to be—a pig satisfied or a man dissatisfied?"

After a *very* short discussion among themselves (and not wanting to concede my point) they heartily agreed that it would be much better to be a pig satisfied, to which I retorted "Well you 'gentlemen' ought to be thankful that you have both the power and the ability to choose the level of life you wish to live, a pig doesn't." And so you see, Dr. Adler, they had entered our discussion of free-will and determinism afterall!

Incidently our group has countered all of the "Coors," "John Deere," and "Michelob" hats with "Great Idea" hats. Maybe if we change the label at the top of our heads we might also be able to change our image. We are sending you a "Great Idea" hat in case you ever have the misfortune of entering a construction site.

We do not wish to burden you with this letter but there is one other incident that might be of interest to you. I had my Strongs Bible Concordance on my family room floor and my youngest boy (9 yrs. old) was thumbing through it when I noticed that he was having difficulty finding the word that he was looking for. Wanting to help, I asked him what word he was looking for, to which he responded: dinosaur! I related this incident to our group and no one seemed to catch the humor of irony behind looking up the word dinosaur in a bible concordance, after I explained that this incident typified the tragic conflict between science and religion and the fact that each and every new generation appears to be saddled with the same contradictions and conflicts that their parents struggled with, they still failed to see the significance of the incident, to which I sharply replied "Well Mortimer would!"

Again, we salute you and thank you and beg your forgiveness for infringing upon what has already been a very busy and productive life.

Respectfully Yours,

David M. Call

P.S. Would it be pushing it too far to request a personalized and autographed copy of your Autobiography? I would cherish it greatly, much in the same way, I imagine, that you would have cherished a personalized copy of John Stuart Mill's *Autobiography.* We do have our idols.

I am sending my copy of your Autobiography in the hopes that you will favor my request.

P.S.S. Included with these papers is a political question that our group is struggling with. We have all agreed that if any one could cut through this "Gordian knot" it would be you, any response would be relished.

PART THREE

Reflections About My Life as a Whole

CHAPTER 7

TEACHING AND LEARNING

1

In an earlier chapter I reported my lifetime engagement with educational reform in our colleges and public schools; and in the preceding chapter I stressed how much I have learned as a result of conducting seminars at Aspen. Here in a relatively brief chapter, I wish to say a few things more about my own education and how one becomes a generally educated human being in the mature years of one's life.

At the end of Chapter 4, I confessed how weary I had become with being involved in educational reform and how tired I was of thinking about the problems of education, but my zest for teaching and learning is as strong as ever.

Professional educators—in fact the whole educational establishment, especially its schools of education—are preoccupied with a host of practical problems (administrative, economic, and sociological problems, problems of testing and grading). They give cursory and peripheral attention to what lies at the heart of the educational process—teaching and learning. That is why Bob Hutchins used to say that education was a dull subject, but he never lost interest in teaching and learning. So, too, my colleague Jacques Barzun recently wrote a book entitled *Begin Here*. It is a book mainly about teaching and learning, but one that pays critical attention to some of the agitated educational problems that occupy the attention of most people, especially the educational profession.

2

I have said again and again that no one becomes a generally educated human being in school and college, or even in the graduate schools of our universities. There are two reasons why that is so. One is that youth is an insuperable obstacle to becoming a generally educated person. Schools and colleges would be at their very best, as they seldom are, if they were to prepare the young for a lifetime of learning after they have completed their stay in educational institutions, fully realizing that the diplomas and degrees they have acquired do not signify that they have completed their education.

The second reason is that, with the elective system regnant in most of our colleges, they have become places devoted largely to special education, serving the professional or occupational aims of their students. There are very few colleges in this country devoted solely or even largely to general education—the kind of study that anticipates the need for a lifetime of further study if anyone is ever to become generally educated. Specialized education prevails in the graduate schools of the university, whether they are directed to training for one of the learned professions or to training and research in the humanities, the arts and sciences.

Some years ago I wrote a book entitled *A Guidebook to Learning*. In its closing chapters, I argued that the three fields of subject-matter that constituted the realm of general education were poetry (by which I meant not just lyrics, but the whole of imaginative, narrative literature in prose or verse), history, and philosophy. I omitted the special sciences because they did not have the transcendental character of history and philosophy. There can be a history of history and a philosophy of history; a history of philosophy and a philosophy of history; and, of course, a history and philosophy of science; but there is no science of philosophy, no science of history, and no science of science.

When we use phrases such as "the science of physics," "the science of chemistry" or "the science of mathematics," the meaning of the word "of" has changed. In the phrase "philosophy of history," the "of" means that history is the object being studied philosophically; whereas in the phrase "science of physics" it means that physics is the name of a particular, specialized body of scientific knowledge; in other words the phrase "the science of physics" translates into "the science *which is* physics."

The particular, highly specialized branches of scientific knowledge belong in one's pursuit of general learning *only* when they are approached historically and philosophically; which is to say, from the standpoint of the generalist, not the specialist. The same general themes that philosophy treats abstractly and intellectually, poetry deals with concretely and imaginatively. While history deals with every aspect of our human experience in terms of what has actually happened to the human race on earth, poetry enriches our insight into that experience by going beyond the actual to the possible, telling likely stories about what might or could have happened in the lives that human beings live.

After they leave their formal or institutional schooling far behind, the chief leisure pursuit of mature human beings should be the study of poetry, history, and philosophy, year after year. Such continuing study on the part of adult men and women should be interminable. It does not come to an end; it is not completed by the award of a diploma or a degree. The only certification of its completion in this life is a death certificate.

Thus understood, it is quite different from what is usually called "adult education" or "continuing education," in the extension divisions of our universities. For the most part, the courses that adults take there, sometimes for credit, sometimes not, are efforts toward their special, not their general, education, compensating for or supplementing instruction they did not receive in earlier years of their lives. What I mean by adult education or continued learning that aims at becoming generally educated does not involve taking courses of any kind. Getting credit is no part of its motivation. That arises from the joy of learning for its own sake; never for any pragmatic reason or practically useful result. It is, in short, the learning of the autodidact—the person who learns without intervention or help on the part of others who are professional teachers.

How should the autodidact proceed? First of all, that word "autodidact" is a misnomer; for autodidacts do not teach themselves—no one can do that. But the learning of the autodidact does not exclude teaching, for one learns a great deal by one's self in the process of teaching others. I have experienced this in the course of conducting seminars. Teaching others, I have found, is one of the most effective means of learning what cannot be taught by others.

Apart from teaching others, what should an autodidact do to continue learning throughout his or her adult life? In the closing pages of *A Guidebook to Learning*, my answer was summed up in three words: "Read and discuss." Reading the great books alone will not do. I said many years ago, after I had written *How to Read a Book*, that solitary reading is as undesirable as solitary drinking. To enrich one's understanding of what one has read, one must discuss it with others who have read the same book, with or without the guidance of someone who is a better reader than most of us are.[1]

Nor will discussion itself serve the purpose, without any control by or reference to topics or themes developed in the great conversation to be found in the great books. Without that control, discussion usually degenerates into superficial chatter, after-dinner chitchat, or what is worse, a bull-session that is nothing but an exchange of opinions with everyone speaking in turn without anybody listening to what anyone else has said.

The regulative maxim for the autodidact is "read *and* discuss" with emphasis on the word "and" to signify that the two activities must be done in planned conjunction with each other, not each in the absence or deprivation of the other.

If I were called upon to add anything to that maxim as advice to the autodidact, I would add only one more word of counsel. I would admonish individuals to travel as much as they could in their mature years; only then can they benefit by direct acquaintance with the diversity of peoples and cultures, as enlightening to their understanding of the specific, common human nature that all of us share alike, especially the sameness of the human mind that is to be found in all human beings.

1. That is the reason why well-conducted seminars discussing great or good books lie at the heart of the Paideia proposal for the reform of basic schooling. It is also the reason why the seminars offered by the Aspen Institute are so important—I would almost say indispensable—in the realm of adult learning.

3

At the invitation of Dean Michael Shinagel of the Harvard Extension School, I delivered the Lowell Lecture at Harvard University on April 11, 1990. My title was "The Great Books, the Great Ideas, and a Lifetime of Learning." I thought it appropriate for the occasion to begin in an autobiographical vein. On rereading the opening paragraphs of my address, I find them to be of relevance here and so I quote them below.[2]

> I was a drop-out from high school. I wanted to be a journalist, and went to work on the old, very great *New York Sun* under editor Edward Page Mitchell. I thought that I should have a little more schooling than I had, having had only two years of high school, so I enrolled in extension courses at Columbia—took a course in Victorian Literature and a course in Wordsworth and Coleridge, of the century before. In the course in Victorian Literature I was assigned to read John Stuart Mill's *Autobiography*. I discovered, to my amazement, that John Stuart Mill could read Greek at the age of three, had read the dialogues of Plato in Greek at the age of five, and by eleven had read most of the books that I later discovered were the *Great Books*. At eleven he edited his father's history of India. At twelve he edited Jeremy Bentham's *Rationale of Judicial Proof*. And I was now fifteen and had read none of these.
>
> So I decided to buy a set of Plato, which ruined me. I decided I could play the Greek game of Socrates—a game with one's mind. I had impressed Frank Allen Patterson, who was Director of the extension school; he taught [the] course in Victorian Literature. He got me a three-year scholarship at Columbia. And I did go there for three years—sophomore, junior and senior year—but unlike what Dean Shinagel told you, I did not graduate in 1923, though I did get a Phi Beta Kappa key. . . . I got my Bachelor's degree in 1983—sixty years after I had my Ph.D.

2. They repeat stories I told in the first chapter of *Philosopher at Large*. "The Great Books, the Great Ideas, and a Lifetime of Learning" (The Lowell Lecture delivered April 11, 1990, Harvard University), Major Issues of the 1990s Lecture Series, Sponsored Jointly by the Lowell Institute of Boston and Harvard Extension School, 1990, pp. 5–11. Reprinted by permission of the Lowell Institute of Boston and Harvard Extension School.

I reminded my audience of the basic distinction among all the phases of schooling—from kindergarten up to the graduate degrees (which are terminated by diplomas, degrees, and certifications) and the one phase that is truly interminable, the phase that is genuinely adult learning.

> We normally have eight years of elementary school, four years of high school, four years of college, three or four years of medical school, law school, engineering school. Degrees, diplomas, or certificates honor the completion of these phases of schooling. It is proper for a person to say "I've completed my college program" or "I completed my professional training." It is similarly proper for a person, enrolled in extension courses, to say "I have now completed the specialized education that I did not complete in college or professional school." But it is totally improper for an adult to say, "I have now completed my adult education."
>
> No more preposterous words can be uttered than for someone to say—at the age of thirty, forty, or fifty—"I have now completed my adult education." To that, the only response should be: "Are you ready to die? What are you going to do with the rest of your life?"
>
> Adult learning, for the sake of becoming a generally educated human being, once begun, is interminable. Our minds, unlike our bodies, are able to grow and develop until death overtakes us. Unless it declines because of serious mental illness, the mind is not like a muscle, bone, or bodily organ that begins to decline when youth ends, but it is a vital instrument that, if properly exercised, continues to improve. The only condition of its continual growth is that it be continually nourished and exercised. *How nourished? By reading the great books year after year. How exercised? By discussing them.*

I then proceeded once again in the autobiographical vein.

> Permit me to digress for a moment by speaking to you autobiographically. I became an undergraduate in the college of Columbia University in 1920. At Columbia two strokes of good fortune befell me and changed my life. The great books seminars were invented

by John Erskine, of whom I was a student in 1922 and 1923. My first stroke of good fortune was to be asked to teach one of those seminars with the poet, Mark Van Doren, from 1923 to 1929. I would have supposed, under other circumstances, that I had read the great books and understood them, and would not have to read them again. What I learned by having to teach them Socratically the year after I graduated from college was that I did not really understand them.

This gave me the insight that the great books are endlessly re-readable and that the attempt to understand the great ideas to be found in them is an interminable pursuit. That insight was reinforced by the years of teaching great books seminars at the University of Chicago with President Robert Hutchins, between 1930 and 1950, by the teaching of adult seminars in Chicago and at the Aspen Institute ever since, and by all the work I did in editing *Great Books of the Western World* for Encyclopaedia Britannica, and all the work I did in producing the *Syntopicon* of the Great Ideas.

I concluded my address by saying:

Generally educated persons are those who, through the travail of their own lives, have enough experience to assimilate the ideas which make them representative of their culture and the bearer of its traditions. . . .

Autodidacts who read, year after year, the great books of history, philosophy, and poetry, and discuss them with their peers, are on the road to becoming generally educated persons before they die, and to have lives that are enriched by a lifetime of learning.

The question period after the lecture was vigorous and penetrating. It was a thoroughly enjoyable occasion, proceeded by a dinner hosted by my old friend and colleague Professor Richard Hunt, and attended by notable members of the Harvard faculty, including Professor David Riesman, with whom I was glad to renew my acquaintance, harking back to the days when we lived in adjoining houses on the campus of the University of Chicago.

4

Rick Hunt had been an associate of mine at the Aspen Institute. He also was and is on the Board of Directors of my Institute for Philosophical Research, and he was a founding member of the original Paideia Group that sponsored *The Paideia Proposal* (1982). Adele Simmons, then President of Hampshire College, and now President of the John D. and Catherine T. MacArthur Foundation, was also a member of the original Paideia Group. I had known her since her childhood, for she is the daughter of Hermon Dunlap Smith, as Trustee of the University of Chicago and a member of the Board of the Institute for Philosophical Research when it was established in 1952.

I mention these facts to explain the background of the affair they arranged at Harvard in the fall of 1985. The previous spring, the three of us had had lunch together in Cambridge, Massachusetts, and I must have aroused their sympathies by complaining about the difficulties I had experienced in obtaining charitable grants from foundations to support the ongoing work of the Paideia reform. They never told me this, but I think this is what led them to host a banquet to cheer me up, to which they invited friends of mine from all over the country, among whom were Douglass Cater, then President of Washington College in Chestertown, Maryland; Fred Drexler from San Francisco, the Chairman of the Board of the Institute for Philosophical Research; Louis O. Kelso, also from San Francisco, with whom I had co-authored *The Capitalist Manifesto* in 1958; Gail Thomas and Donald Cowan from Texas, with whose Dallas Institute for Humanities and Culture, I had been associated; Mary Tyler Cheek from Richmond, Virginia; Tom Goetz, the Editor in Chief of the *Encyclopaedia Britannica*; my close associates at the Institute for Philosophical Research, Charles, Geraldine, and John Van Doren; and my wife Caroline.

I recall the witty and amiable speeches made on this occasion by Tom Goetz, Louis Kelso, Charles Van Doren, and, of course, by Adele Simmons and Rick Hunt. The foibles, follies, and idiosyncrasies of Mortimer J. Adler gave them plenty of material to make jokes about. One thing in particular sticks in my mind. Among the encomiums that Rick Hunt heaped on me, he called me "a born teacher."

Whether he was right or not, I have always immodestly taken pride in my ability as a teacher. But what is meant by calling anyone "a born teacher"? Are teachers born, not made? What is the innate gift of temperament—certainly not intellectual endowment—that predisposes an individual to be good at teaching.

As I have reflected about this, it seems to me that being a born teacher is something like being a born actor. Think of the countless young men and women who go to drama schools year after year and seek training for a career on the stage. How many of them end up recognized by the public as stars of the theatre, or even as chosen by theatrical producers for bit parts in the plays they put on the stage? The selection process that winnows a very small amount of wheat from a large amount of chaff must have something to do with the native endowment, not the training of the few who succeed in their ambition to be actors or actresses. Is the same true of the many who go to schools of education to prepare themselves for the teaching profession and the few who turn out to be really good teachers? Does it also explain why some who never went near a school of education, and would not be caught dead doing so, turn out to be very good teachers? If I am a good teacher, I am one of them. And what is the innate temperamental gift that underlies this result?

I think I can answer this last question, and the answer may throw light on the similitude between teaching and acting. The temperamental endowment is a love of thinking combined with a sympathetic concern for the thinking of others and for the improvement of their intellects—the growth of their understanding. The born teacher is one who is motivated not just to think, but to think with others in order to help them think, and also to teach, thereby to learn.

The born actor or actress is likewise one who is endowed with a temperament for projecting the personality he or she portrays so that an audience can empathize with the character of that personality. The born teacher has the ability to project his own thinking in a way that engages the thinking power of others. Whether these reflections are sound or not, I have always deeply enjoyed teaching and will go on doing it whenever the opportunity for doing it is afforded me.

5

For me, teaching is the most effective means of learning. If everyone who wished to learn something was engaged in teaching it to others, he or she would learn more than the individuals being taught. The best teachers are those who learn the most from teaching, and those who learn nothing in the process of teaching are hardly teachers at all. They should be called indoctrinators who impress the memories instead of developing the minds of their students.

I said earlier that I have learned more from the seminars I have conducted in the last seventy years than from any other source. I have also learned a great deal from the lectures I have given and from the books I have written, insofar as my intention in lecturing and writing was wholly or partly that of teaching.

As compared with conducting seminars, lecturing is an inferior form of teaching. It was wittily remarked by someone that lecturing is the process whereby the notes of the teacher become the notes of the student without passing through the minds of either. That is as true of public lectures as of classroom lectures. The only way to correct this miscarriage of teaching is to hold a forum after the lecture—if possible, a protracted question and answer session. Then the lecturer learns from the questions he is unable to answer on the spot and takes away for later reflection.

In a long career on the lecture platform, I have always insisted upon a question and answer period after the lecture. When that is not possible or permitted, lecturing is not teaching at all, at least not for me, because it is not a learning experience.[3]

3. I remember the year before I wrote *How to Read a Book*. That book originated in a lecture I gave to assembled alumni of the University of Chicago. I spoke from notes I had made on the two sides of a three-by-five card. As I gave that lecture again and again in the months to follow, the questions I received from a diversity of audiences enlarged my notes until the file of notes I compiled gave me, in outline form, the book I wrote at the end of that year.

The nub of the matter lies in the questions the teacher is asked that he or she cannot answer at once and profits from keeping in mind and returning to for subsequent reflection. The easy questions that the teacher can answer at once can be dismissed from mind. Not so, the difficult—the perplexing—questions. Therein lies the learning that results from teaching, more so from conducting seminars than from lecturing, but especially from conducting seminars about one's own books, as I have done in recent years at the Aspen Institute.

Socrates is the model teacher. The Socratic method of teaching is by questions and answers. The dialogues of Plato should be read as an account of the process by which Socrates learned in the course of questioning others, and also answering questions raised by others. That may be why my first reading of a few early Platonic dialogues in my teens awakened in me the desire to teach. I was so inspired by the Socratic performance that I tried to engage my friends in mimicry of it, with me playing the role of Socrates.

In the first twenty years of my teaching experience, I taught young adults in college classrooms, either conducting seminars Socratically or giving lectures, accompanied by questions and answers. In the last forty years I have lectured to adult audiences and conducted seminars, in Chicago, Aspen, and elsewhere, for mature adults. For the same reason that mature individuals are better able than the immature to learn what is requisite for becoming generally educated persons, one is also able to learn more from trying to teach them than one can learn from teaching the young, the immature.

The difficult questions mature individuals ask in terms of experiences they have acquired in their mature years go to the heart of the matter. Trying to answer their questions is more rewarding than answering questions raised by students in college. In short, trying to teach one's peers in the mature years of one's own life is teaching and learning at its best.

CHAPTER 8

THE VOCATION OF PHILOSOPHY

Philosophy has been my vocation since 1917 when at the age of fifteen (and before going to college), I made the acquaintance of Socrates by reading Plato's *Euthyphro*. I was stung to the quick as a result of learning from John Stuart Mill's *Autobiography* that he had read all of Plato's dialogues in Greek by the age of five, and here I was fifteen.

For seventy-five years I have been driven by the love and pursuit of philosophical truth—the truth that can be discovered by reflection and thought, without moving out of an armchair or while sitting at a desk, not the truth sought by scientific research or historical scholarship. Unlike the other activities that I have reported in earlier chapters—educational reform, editorial work, and Aspen Institute functions (activities in which I have been engaged at different periods of my life)—teaching and learning and the pursuit of philosophical truth have been lifelong occupations.

The philosophical books I have written since *Dialectic* in 1927 do not conform to my present conception of how philosophical books should be written. With the possible exception of the extensive notes that I appended to *What Man Has Made of Man* in 1937 and of *A Dialectic of Morals: Towards the Foundations of Political Philosophy* (1941), the other books written before 1976 were written mainly for an academic audience, though I unsuccessfully tried to write them also for the general run of readers who might have enough curiosity about philosophy to read them.

It was not until 1965, when I wrote *The Conditions of Philos-*

ophy, based on lectures that I delivered at the University of Chicago, that I arrived at a mature understanding of the line that divided philosophical thought from mathematics, from the investigative, empirical sciences, and from historical research. However I find clear anticipations of that understanding in the most important notes that I added to *What Man Has Made of Man* in 1937.[1]

I also find anticipations of another book that was based on University of Chicago lectures (*The Difference of Man and the Difference It Makes,* 1967) in the notes appended to the earlier book. The same is true in the field of practical (i.e., moral and political) philosophy. The aforementioned *A Dialectic of Morals* anticipates two more books that were based on University of Chicago lectures: *The Time of Our Lives: The Ethics of Common Sense* (1970) and *The Common Sense of Politics* (1971).

Though my understanding of philosophy had matured in the four books I wrote from 1965 to 1971, I still had not achieved the right style for writing philosophical books. I was still trying to write them with all the paraphernalia of footnotes and extensive scholarly bibliographies to win the attention of a professorial audience, while at the same time trying to use the language of ordinary speech and avoiding so far as possible all technical jargon. This double effort on my part fell between two stools. The books were too complicated for the general reader and, for reasons I shall mention later, they were seldom reviewed in the technical philosophical periodicals.

I resolved this dilemma by the time I wrote *Aristotle for Everybody* in 1978. If, as this book declares in its opening pages, philosophy is everybody's business and is not the special province of university professors of philosophy and their graduate students, then philosophical books should be written in a style that is popular—intended for the general public, not for professors of phi-

1. *What Man Has Made of Man* was based on four lectures that I gave at the Institute for Psychoanalysis in Chicago in the spring of 1936. The subtitle of the book, when it was published in 1937, was "A Study of the Consequences of Platonism and Positivism in Psychology," which showed why I felt it necessary to add 100 pages of notes to the book when I prepared for publication the four lectures that I had given to the assembled psychoanalysts. In an Epilogue to the book, I said that I wrote the foregoing 62 Notes as a philosophical—and Aristotelian—commentary on the errors of Platonism and positivism. At the end of the book, I presented an itemized inventory of the 62 Notes. I have placed this inventory as Item A in the Notes appended to this chapter.

losophy. The latter have wrongly dismissed these later books of mine as "popularizations" of philosophy, which they are not.

Philosophy is the only academic subject listed in college and university catalogues that, in varying degrees, should be the vocation of everyone.[2] Everyone should not aim to be a mathematician, a physicist, a molecular biologist, an economist, or an historian. These and most other subjects listed in college and university catalogues are fields of academic specialization as philosophy has, unfortunately, also become in the twentieth century. Unlike all these fields of specialization, philosophy, properly understood, is the vocation of all thinking human beings who confront fundamental problems and issues about the world in which they live, about human society, and about themselves and their place in nature. If confronting these problems, they are inclined to think about them, they are involved in philosophical thought.

It is this fact that distinguishes the seven or eight major philosophical books I have written since *Aristotle for Everybody* in 1978 from the books written by professors of philosophy in the same period. The books they have written, like the articles they write for the technical journals of philosophy, are written for their peers (i.e., other professors of philosophy). In contrast, the books I have written attempt to restore philosophy to its proper place in our society and culture.

In the twenty-five centuries of Western philosophical thought, it is only recently, with Kant and other German philosophers after him, that philosophical books were written by men who held university professorships of philosophy.[3] I do not think that I would, or could, have written the books I have produced since 1978 had I been a professorial philosopher, concerned with the esteem of other professors of the subject. Instead, philosophy has been my lifelong vocation and I have at last learned how to write, not for

2. The only other vocation that resembles philosophy in being the vocation of everyone is that of being a humanist. Both aim at making us generalists rather than specialists.

3. Though not professorial by occupation, the great philosophers of earlier epochs (e.g., Plato, Aristotle, Epictetus, Descartes, Spinoza, and Locke) did not write their books for an academic audience, as most modern professors of philosophy, but neither did most of them write for the general public.

professors of philosophy, but for other human beings who have the same vocation in some degree.

2

The phrase "common sense" in the titles of books that I wrote in the late 1960s indicates why philosophy is everybody's business—a common human vocation. Philosophical reflection about what we all know by common sense deepens and enriches our understanding of our common-sense knowledge. It seldom runs counter to or challenges common sense; it almost always enlarges it. That is why philosophical discourse should always use the language of common speech and avoid, wherever possible, all technical jargon.

I learned this from George Santayana fairly early in my life. In his *Skepticism and Animal Faith,* the following passage occurs.

> For good or ill, I am an ignorant man, almost a poet, and I can only spread a feast of what everybody knows. Fortunately exact science and the books of the learned are not necessary to establish my essential doctrine, nor can any of them claim a higher warrant than it has in itself: for it rests on public experience. It needs, to prove it, only the stars, the seasons, the swarm of animals, the spectacle of birth and death, of cities and wars. My philosophy is justified, and has been justified in all ages and countries, by the facts before every man's eyes. . . . In the past or in the future, my language and my borrowed knowledge would have been different, but under whatever sky I had been born, since it is the same sky, I should have had the same philosophy.[4]

This insight about the relation of philosophy to common sense was later confirmed for me when I read Jacques Maritain's *Introduction to Philosophy,* in which he pointed out that this was what distinguished being an Aristotelian. I had this in mind when I wrote *Aristotle for Everybody* and declared that Aristotle was the only one of the great philosophers whose thinking was for every-

4. George Santayana: *Skepticism and Animal Faith,* New York, Charles Scribner's Sons, 1923, pp, ix–x. Before Santayana, William James made somewhat the same point in *Pragmatism* (1908).

body because of its relation to what everyone knows by common sense. This could not be said of Plato, Descartes, Spinoza, Leibniz, Hobbes, Locke, Hume, Kant, Hegel, and Schopenhauer.

Where Santayana refers to public experience as the empirical basis of his philosophical thought, I used the term "common experience" in *The Conditions of Philosophy* to make the same point; for it is our common human experience that is the source of our common-sense knowledge.

By "common experience" I had in mind two things. In the first place, it is the experience all of us have every day of our waking, conscious lives, as distinguished from the special experience that investigative scientists have when they collect the data of research they find in response to the specific questions that govern their investigations. Our everyday common experience does not occur in answer to controlling questions of any kind. *In the second place,* it is "common" in the sense that, at its core, it is the same for all human beings at any time or place.

3

One professor of philosophy and member of the American Philosophical Association, Paul Weiss, has commented favorably on my philosophical books.[5] That may be explained by the fact that Paul and I are old friends, going back to the 1920s when he and I wrote for *The New Republic* and the *Nation* respectively, the only adversely critical reviews of Will Durant's *Story of Philosophy.* When Paul became a professor of philosophy at Bryn Mawr College and at Yale University, he invited me to give lectures to his students there.

As I have already pointed out, my books have been dismissed out of hand by the professorial philosophers in our secular uni-

5. There are a few other exceptions to which I should call attention. In this country, at the instigation of Jacques Barzun, Professor Charles Hartshorne of the University of Texas at Austin wrote a commentary article about my philosophical work for *The American Scholar* (Spring 1972). And in the United Kingdom, I have received favorable comments from Anthony Quinton when he was fellow of New College, Oxford, and later President of Trinity College; and also from Professor Maurice Cranston of the London School of Economics and Political Science.

versities, either because they are deemed mere popularizations having no technical merit, or because they are so Aristotelian in tenor, or simply because I am not a member of the professorial fraternity and so can be disregarded. It cannot be because what I have written is manifestly misguided and erroneous or because I have not considered their professorial opinions and dealt critically with them.

My recent philosophical books have been acknowledged to have merit by fellow Aristotelians and Thomists in the American Catholic Philosophical Association. They know that I am not a Roman Catholic, though in the period that I wrote articles and books that commented on the thought of Thomas Aquinas, I became a member of the American Catholic Philosophical Association in 1932 and participated in its meetings, not always to good effect. My articles and books were thought by the conventional orthodox Thomists of that day to be radically and unreasonably revisionist on points of Thomistic doctrine.

In 1976, I was awarded the Aquinas medal by the American Catholic Philosophical Association. I believe that I am the only individual to receive that award who was not a Roman Catholic and was also not a university professor of philosophy.

The recipient of the award is expected to make a brief response when given the medal. Mine was entitled "The Bodyguards of Truth" and, in summary fashion, pointed out the ancient truths that should be borne in mind to safeguard us against errors in modern philosophical thought that have occurred as a result of either ignoring or misunderstanding the cumulative wisdom of antiquity and the Middle Ages. Since the first part of my address on that occasion was autobiographical, I think it fitting to reproduce its opening paragraphs below.

> My serious study of [philosophical thought] began when, at Columbia University in the early twenties, I took a course in the history of philosophy taught by Professor F.J.E. Woodbridge. Just before Christmas in 1921, I received as a Christmas gift, a copy of the Oxford translation of Aristotle's *Metaphysics*, with an inscription from Professor Woodbridge that read as follows: "To Mortimer Adler who has already begun to make good use of this book."

I owe to Professor Woodbridge, for whom, as for Thomas Aquinas, Aristotle was "the Philosopher," my early sense of the number and variety of the truths that might be found by a careful study of Aristotle's works, as well as a recognition of the soundness of Aristotle's approach to philosophical problems and his method of philosophizing. But I owe to Thomas Aquinas, whose *Summa Theologica* I discovered a few years later, the instructive example of a powerful use of that method, together with the direction and guidance one needs not only in the study of Aristotelian philosophy, but also in the application of it to problems not faced by Aristotle himself.

With one or two exceptions, all the fundamental philosophical truths that I have learned in more than fifty years, to which I am now firmly committed, I have learned from Aristotle, from Aquinas as a student of Aristotle, and from Jacques Maritain as a student of them both. I have searched my mind thoroughly and I cannot find in it a single truth that I have learned from works in modern philosophy written since the beginning of the 17th century. If anyone is outraged by this judgment about almost four hundred years of philosophical thought, let him recover from it by considering the comparable judgment that almost all modern and contemporary philosophers have made about the two thousand years of philosophical thought that preceded the 17th century. In view of the fact that philosophy, unlike science, does not advance with each succeeding generation of men at work, it should not be deemed impossible, or even unlikely, that the first two thousand years of philosophical thought discovered a body of truths to which little if anything has been added and from which much has been lost in the last four hundred years.[6]

In the next section of the address, I went on to talk about what I had learned from studying the history of philosophy. This is also autobiographical and I think it worth reproducing below.

The pre-modern career of philosophy contains errors as well as truths. As I have already intimated, the truths, for the most part, have been contributed by Aristotle and by Aristotelians. Even the tradition of Aristotelian thought is not without faults—deficiencies

6. Adler, "The Bodyguards of Truth," *Proceedings of the American Catholic Philosophical Association,* 1976, p. 125. Reprinted by permission.

and errors. In the course of my own work as a student of Aristotle and Aquinas, I have, from time to time, uncovered such faults and tried to correct them. Such efforts on my part, may I say in passing, especially essays and books that criticized the traditional theory of species, the traditional view of democracy, and traditional formulations of the proofs of God's existence, were not universally applauded in the late thirties and early forties by my fellow-members in the American Catholic Philosophical Association. Whether, if reviewed today, they would be differently appraised, I cannot say. To win tolerance for such fault-finding, I did try to say then, as I would say now, that in every case the correction of an error or the repair of a deficiency in the philosophy of Aristotle and Aquinas rests on the underlying and controlling principles of Aristotelian and Thomistic thought. In fact, the discovery of such errors or deficiencies almost always springs from close attention and leads to a deeper understanding of those principles.

Here lies what for me is the remarkable difference between the faults I have found in modern philosophy and the faults I have found in the tradition of Aristotelian and Thomistic thought. The errors and deficiencies in this or that modern philosopher's thought arise either from his misunderstanding or, worse, his total ignorance of insights and distinctions indispensable to getting at the truth—insights and distinctions that were so fruitful in the work of Aristotle and Aquinas, but which modern philosophers have either ignored or, misunderstanding them, have dismissed. In addition, the errors or deficiencies in the thought of this or that modern philosopher cannot be corrected by appealing to his own most fundamental principles, as is the case with Aristotle and Aquinas. On the contrary, it is usually his principles—his points of departure—that embody the little errors in the beginning which, as Aristotle and Aquinas so well knew, have such serious consequences in the end.

To say, as I have said, that I have not learned a single fundamental truth from the writings of modern philosophers is not to say that I have learned nothing at all from them. With the exception of Hegel and other post-Kantian German philosophers, I have read their works with both pleasure and profit. The pleasure has come from the perception of errors the serious consequences of which tend to reinforce my hold on the truths I have learned from Aristotle and Aquinas. The profit has come from the perception of new but genuine problems, not the pseudo-problems, perplexities, and puzzlements invented by therapeutic positivism and by linguistic or analytical philosophy in our own century.

The genuine problems to which I am referring are questions that have been generated under the cultural circumstances characteristic of modern times, especially the effect on philosophy of its gradually recognized distinction from investigative science and from dogmatic theology, as well as the effect on it of certain developments in modern science and certain revolutionary changes in the institutions of modern society.

The profit to be derived from the perception of these problems (of which Aristotle and Aquinas were not aware or were only dimly aware) is the stimulus it gives us to try to extend their thought in response to them. I have always found that I could solve such problems within the general framework and in the light of the basic principles of their thought. They may not have faced the questions that we are obliged to answer, but they nevertheless do provide us with the clues or leads needed for discovering the answers.

Many years ago, in our early days together at the University of Chicago, my friend Professor Richard McKeon once quipped that the difference between the members of the American Philosophical Association and the members of the American Catholic Philosophical Association was that philosophers in our secular universities specialized in very good and novel questions, to which the scholastic philosophers did not yet have the answers, whereas the scholastics had a rich supply of true principles and conclusions but usually failed to be aware of many important questions to the answering of which they could be applied. My own experience has confirmed the wisdom as well as the wit of that observation. . . .[7]

In recent years I joined the American Maritain Association, motivated by my indebtedness to Jacques Maritain, from whose books I have learned so much, as well as from my personal association with him when he visited the University of Chicago and when he became associated with the Institute for Philosophical Research.

7. Ibid., pp. 125–126.

In 1987, the Maritain Association held a three-day symposium, entitled "Freedom in the Modern World," in which various participants read papers on the contributions to that subject by Jacques Maritain, Yves R. Simon (a student of Maritain, who has written many books of philosophical magnitude and merit), and Mortimer J. Adler.

I would be glad to report here if I could, all that was said about my two-volume work, *The Idea of Freedom,* the first product of the Institute for Philosophical Research. That took eight years of work to produce; the first volume was published in 1958; the second in 1961.

One address at that symposium does have a direct bearing on matters here being considered, particularly the Roman Catholic evaluation of my contribution to philosophy, so different from the evaluation of me by professors of philosophy in our secular universities. That was an address by Professor Ralph McInerny, entitled "Adler on Freedom." Most of that address was not about Adler on Freedom, but about Adler as a philosopher.[8] I hope I may be excused the immodest delight that I took in the judgment of me that Professor McInerny delivered, as well as in the stories he told about me. His address is too long to reproduce here, or even to excerpt here, so I have placed an excerpt from it as Item B in the Notes to the chapter.

4

The English rendering of the Greek work *"philo-sophia,"* translated literally, is "love of wisdom." There is precious little of the love of wisdom in philosophy as taught in our universities and colleges, whether they are dominated by the linguistic and analytical philosophy that is regnant at Oxford and Cambridge, or by the positivism, existentialism, phenomonology, structuralism, and semeiotics that are current on the continent of Europe.

For those of us who still think, as I do, that philosophy goes

8. Ralph McInerny: "Adler on Freedom," in *Freedom in the Modern World* (Jacques Maritain, Yves R. Simon, Mortimer J. Adler), edited by Michael D. Torre, American Maritain Association, Notre Dame, Ind., University of Notre Dame Press, 1989, pp. 65–72. Reprinted by permission.

beyond common-sense knowledge to understanding and to wisdom, the latter comes at the end of the trail. Practical wisdom is to be found in the ultimate ends that are understood to be the first principles of moral and political philosophy; and theoretical or speculative wisdom lies in the principles of metaphysics and philosophical theology.

Wisdom may lie at the culmination of philosophical thought when it is properly conducted, but throughout it is driven by the love of truth. If, for any reason, truth were unattainable, philosophy would be a worthless enterprise. This would have to be said, of course, of scientific and historical research as well. They might still be pragmatically useful, but they, too, would be intellectually worthless.

The definition of truth as the comformity of what we think to the way things are in reality goes back to Plato and Aristotle. This common-sense conception of truth is employed in all business negotiations and in judicial tribunals, trying questions of fact, when juries are asked to bring in verdicts that are true judgments, either beyond a reasonable doubt or by a preponderance of the evidence.

I have always thought it important to bear the following points in mind. The meaning of "true" and "false" as applied to the judgments we make gives us our definition of what truth and falsity are, but that definition does not give us the criteria by which to tell whether or not a particular judgment is true or false. It is here that William James's pragmatic theory of truth comes in, as well as other theories of how to verify or falsify the judgments we make.[9]

In the pursuit of truth, Aristotle tells us, "it is necessary to call into council the views of our predecessors, in order that we may profit by whatever is sound in their thought and avoid their errors."

And in another place, Aristotle tells us:

9. There are very few self-evident, necessary truths, which are undeniable because it is impossible to think the opposite. These are the only philosophical truths that are in the realm of certitude—beyond the shadow of a doubt. All the rest are in the realm of doubt—either beyond a reasonable doubt or probable by a preponderance of the evidence. None of these probable truths are incorrigible. Their probability is forever subject to change as new evidence or rational arguments correct earlier judgments about their degree of probability.

> The investigation of the truth is in one way hard, in another easy. An indication of this is found in the fact that no one is able to attain the truth adequately, while, on the other hand, we do not collectively fail, but every one says something true about the nature of things, and while individually we contribute little or nothing to the truth, by the union of all a considerable amount is amassed.

There have always been skeptical denials that truth is attainable. They existed in antiquity; they exist today. Complete skepticism of the kind proposed by the ancient Pyrrhonists is refutable as self-contradictory. More limited forms of skepticism (such as that which concedes some measure of truth attainable by empirical science and historical research, while still asserting that none can be found in philosophical thought) are more difficult to deal with. Those of us who regard philosophy as an intellectually respectable enterprise must deal with the positivism so prevalent in our day.

Until this century, anyone engaged in teaching and learning acknowledged an aspiration to get at the truth, whether in history, science, or philosophy. But today "truth" has become almost a dirty word in academic circles. In a recent book, *Truth in Religion*, I have pointed out how those who appear to deny truth in religion, also appear to lack any understanding of what truth is.[10]

Commitment to the pursuit of truth is unfashionable in academic circles. Making unabashed judgments about what is true and false is considered academically impolite. It tends to pit professors against one another in a public display of antagonism, which is to be avoided for the sake of peace and harmony in the professional fraternity.

So far as philosophy is concerned, let us consider the case of Isaiah Berlin. He is often mistakenly regarded as an eminent contributor to twentieth-century philosophical thought. But he tells us explicitly in a recent book, *The Crooked Timber of Humanity: Chapters in the History of Ideas*, that he gave philosophy up for history because he could not embrace Plato's and Aristotle's "assumption"—he should have said "conviction"—that philosophers

10. See Adler, *Truth in Religion: The Plurality of Religions and the Unity of Truth*, 1990.

can succeed in the pursuit of truth. Though he was trained in philosophy, Berlin decided on being instead an historian of ideas rather than a philosopher. He is quoted as saying "Philosophy is a wonderful subject, but it is necessarily unfinished and unfinishable. You can't really solve anything. At the end of my life, I wanted to know more than I did at the beginning. And I couldn't get that from philosophy."[11]

The history of ideas, to which Isaiah Berlin has devoted his life, is not a philosophical clarification of them. Only that is a contribution to the understanding of our mind's intelligible objects. I think I have made that kind of philosophical contribution in *The Idea of Freedom,* which explained in its opening pages why it was not a history of that idea but rather a dialectical propadeutic to geting at the philosophical truth about human freedom.[12]

The many forms of characteristically modern idealism—the central tenet of which is that there is no knowable reality independent of the human mind—are another departure from the pursuit of truth in philosophy. Unless there is a reality independent of the human mind—that is what it is, whether we think about it or not, and also regardless of how we think about it—there can be no pursuit of objective truth in philosophy, or for that matter, in science. In another recent book,[13] I have severely criticized the current form of philosophical idealism in this country, called "constructivism" by its leading exponents, such as Jerome Bruner, Nelson Goodman, and Richard Rorty.

I am and always have been a philosophical realist since the days of my youth when, as a college student at Columbia University, I read a book entitled *The New Realism,* written at that time by six American professors of philosophy. Times have changed since then.[14] All philosophers in antiquity and the Middle Ages were realists; none was an idealist in epistemology or metaphysics.

11. Suzanne Cassidy, "I Think I Hear Them Talk," in *The New York Review of Books,* March 24, 1991, p. 30.

12. Adler, *The Idea of Freedom,* Vol. I, Garden City, N.Y., Doubleday & Company, Inc., 1958.

13. See Adler, *Intellect: Mind Over Matter,* 1990, Chapters 7 and 8.

14. Ibid.

5

In 1990, Clifton Fadiman, one of my oldest friends, with whom I first became acquainted when he was a student of Mark Van Doren's and mine in a great books seminar at Columbia in 1923–1925, told me that he had been asked by Doubleday to edit a book of essays entitled *Living Philosophies: The Reflections of Some Eminent Men and Women of Our Time.* He invited me to contribute a short essay of about 2,500 words to that volume. The required brevity made the task difficult, but I did it within the space limits specified.

Since that essay is autobiographical and since the first part of it is highly relevant to the considerations of this chapter, I think it is useful to reproduce it here.[15]

> I dream of a postmodern era maturing in the next century, one in which the viability of the planet is ensured, in which world peace is established and becomes perpetual, and in which a better culture emerges, fostering an intellectual climate that is more congenial to philosophical thought than the philosophically deprived and recessive culture against which I have struggled during my lifetime. . . .
>
> The vocation of a philosopher is the pursuit of truth about God, the physical cosmos, and the human world—man's nature and culture. With respect to human life and society, philosophy seeks not only descriptive truths, but also truths that are prescriptive and normative. The latter are statements about how we *ought* to conduct our lives, privately and socially, and what we *should* do to constitute a just political and economic order.
>
> I regret that I have been compelled to say that the twentieth century has not been a felicitous time for philosophy. In my judgment, philosophy has reached its lowest level in a steady decline since the seventeenth century. My most fundamental conviction is that the manifold mistakes in modern philosophical thought began in the seventeenth century with little errors in the beginning that have led to disastrous consequences in the end. Instead of correcting

15. With the permission of the publishers, of course. Mr. Fadiman tells me that, for one reason or another, the book as published was not widely circulated. That is all the more reason for reproducing an excerpt from my essay here.

these errors, modern philosophers in successive centuries have tried to solve the puzzles and paradoxes to which they gave rise.

Since the days of Descartes, Hobbes, Locke, and Hume, these initial errors have gone uncorrected, and their consequences have been multiplied in the centuries that followed, especially in German thought—in Kant, Hegel, Schopenhauer, and Nietzsche—at the end of the eighteenth, and in the nineteenth century.

The cause of these errors and their consequences was the ignorance, misunderstanding, or neglect of the philosophical wisdom to be found in antiquity and in the Middle Ages. Only two of the mistakes that have plagued modern thought have come down to us from antiquity and have been perpetuated in modern times—the atomistic materialism that we find in Hobbes and the Platonic dualism (mind *and* body) that we find in Descartes.

To the baleful influence on twentieth-century philosophy of Hobbesian materialism, Cartesian dualism, and German idealism and transcendentalism must be added the mistake made by Russell and Wittgenstein in our own century. This was the mistake of supposing that symbolic and mathematical logic, together with a psychological theory of knowledge, lies at the basis of all philosophical thought.

I must confess to having made the same mistake in my early twenties, but fortunately I grew out of it. By the time I was thirty, I began to grow up philosophically and corrected the error of my immaturity by looking to metaphysics for the foundations of philosophy—a metaphysics that has its roots in common sense and is in no way affected by the findings of modern mathematics and science.

With this controlling conviction about the history of philosophy, I have devoted my intellectual energies to restoring the neglected and misunderstood truths that have been lost in modern times and trying to add some things to the foundations they provide. With few exceptions, mainly William James, George Santayana, Jacques Maritain, and Etienne Gilson, I have learned little or nothing of value from those who have come to prominence in the last fifty years, especially not from those whom the contemporary world has honored as the philosophical eminences of this century—Ludwig Wittgenstein and Martin Heidegger.[16]

Another characteristic of the twentieth century that makes it inhospitable to the philosophical enterprise as I conceive it is the uncritical and unfounded assumption that, for solid truth about anything, one must go to science. The truths attained by the exact sciences in the study of the cosmos, physical nature, and man are seriously limited to what can be known by measurements yielding numbers that can be fed into mathematical equations. The many important aspects of reality that are immeasurable lie beyond the reach of exact science.[17]

In four successive generations, great scientists such as Einstein, Bohr, Heisenberg, and Hawking have allowed themselves to slip from saying "what is not measurable *by* physicists has no reality *for* physicists" to saying "what is unmeasurable has no reality." Immeasurable simultaneity, the immeasurable reaches of infinite time, the determinate but indeterminable velocity *and* position of electrons do not exist in the physical world.

Not only do the immeasurable aspects of reality lie beyond the world of the physicist, but also, if there are truths to be learned about God, they are to be learned by philosophy, not by science. In addition, science cannot establish a single prescriptive truth about how we *ought* to conduct our affairs.

The moral problems we face in the twentieth century are in all essential respects the same as those faced by our ancestors in antiquity. The many technological and institutional changes we have experienced in this century do not make the problem of leading a morally good life more or less difficult to solve. The best philosophical guidance we can get is to be found in Aristotle's *Ethics*, written in the fourth century B.C. The last three centuries have contributed little or nothing of value in ethics.

16. My further reflections about Wittgenstein can be found in the next section of this chapter.

17. Since Descartes, it would be difficult to name a first-rate scientist who is also a first-rate philosopher. Most of them are exponents or adherents of positivism, the intellectual error most of them are addicted to.

With respect to political theory, the situation is different. Here contributions have been made by modern thinkers—by Locke's *Second Treatise on Civil Government* and by J. S. Mill's *Representative Government* and his essay *On Liberty.*[18]

6

I read Ludwig Wittgenstein's *Tractatus Logico-philosophicus* (1922) when I was a graduate student at Columbia University immediately after it was published in this country in the same series in which my first book *Dialectic* was published in 1927. This series was edited by C. K. Ogden under the title *International Library of Psychology, Philosophy and Scientific Method.*

I can still remember and will never forget the stunning last sentence, numbered 7, of the *Tractatus,* which read "That whereof one cannot speak, thereof one must be silent." In his later career as a philosopher, Wittgenstein practiced what he preached. He substituted *showing* for *telling* with regard to matters about which silence should be maintained, because no attempt should be made to make statements in propositional form that are not susceptible to logical proof or disproof.

I also remember I was so impressed by that stunning last sentence of the *Tractatus* that I was inspired to give a series of ten lectures on the philosophy of silence. Looking over my notes for those lectures still in my files, my present judgment is that they were an immature effort on my part. I am glad that I did not try to turn them into a book for publication.

I have read in the last year, Ray Monk's biography of Ludwig Wittgenstein. I noted the many similarities between Wittgenstein's youthful career in philosophy and my own—his dissatisfaction with twentieth-century culture, so dominated by science and technology; his criticism of modern philosophy for taking science and mathematics as models to imitate; his contempt for most of his professorial contemporaries, whom he called "philosophical jour-

18. Adler: "A Philosopher Looks Back and Forward," *Living Philosophies: The Reflections of Some Eminent Men and Women of Our Time,* edited by Clifton Fadiman, New York, Doubleday, 1990, pp. 272–277. Reprinted by permission. I have placed the rest of my essay in the Notes to this chapter, Item C.

nalists"; his youthful addiction to logic and grammar as the indispensable foundation for philosophical thought; and his concern with the meaning of meaning.[19]

The similarities noted above do not necessitate any retraction on my part of the statement made in the preceding section about my not having learned anything from Wittgenstein. We were both wrong in our youthful addiction to logic as the foundation for philosophical thought. If I were to add any exception to my statement that I learned nothing from Wittgenstein, it would be with respect to his distinction between what he called "family resemblances" and what in Aristotelian philosophy are treated as generic and specific samenesses and differences.

Ray Monk's biography of Wittgenstein contains a number of statements that confirm the parallelism that I have noted between Wittgenstein's attitude toward academic life and toward professors of philosophy and my own.

Monk writes that, for Wittgenstein, "academic life was detestable." I think I would use the word "intolerable" instead. Monk tells us that Wittgenstein congratulated his friend Maurice Drury for being "saved from becoming a professional philosopher." Monk quotes a passage from a letter that Wittgenstein wrote to Moritz Schlick in which he said ". . . from the bottom of my heart it is all the same to me what the professional philosophers of today think of me; for it is not for them that I am writing."[20] To that I say "Amen."

How divergent my mature work in philosophy is from that of Wittgenstein—and why it should be obvious to anyone that I have

19. *The Meaning of Meaning* was the title of a book written by I. A. Richards and C. K. Ogden, which influenced me to write a juvenile essay on the philosophical and psychological problems of meaning, which I delivered before the Graduate Philosophy Club at Columbia University while I was still an undergraduate student in the college there (see *Philosopher at Large,* pp. 39–40). The problems I had not solved in that early essay remained unsolved for me until, in 1976, I wrote *Some Questions About Language: A Theory of Human Discourse and Its Objects*. In that book, I criticized the grave deficiencies and errors in the theories advanced by Bertrand Russell and Ludwig Wittgenstein (see the Epilogue to that book in the new paperback edition, 1991).

20. Ray Monk, *Ludwig Wittenstein: The Duty of Genius,* New York, The Free Press, 1990, pp. 323–324.

not learned anything from him, for better or worse—can be seen by reading *Some Questions About Language, How to Think About God, Ten Philosophical Mistakes, Intellect: Mind Over Matter, Truth in Religion,* and *Desires, Right & Wrong,* all books written since 1976.[21]

Let me sum up the difference between being a professional philosopher and the few of us who strive to make philosophy their life's vocation by writing philosophical books while not teaching philosophy in academic institutions. We are generalists in philosophy, thinking in all four of its dimensions and pursuing the truth in all four. The professors of philosophy in our academic institutions tend to be specialists, as college and university catalogues reveal, teaching courses in this or that branch of philosophy but seldom in all, and usually about the history of ideas and not about the ideas themselves as intelligible objects of philosophical thought. This is a dimension of philosophy that is neglected by most academic specialists. I think the list of my philosophical books show that my thinking covers—perhaps not adequately—all four dimensions of philosophical discourse.

21. In a conversation with M. O'C. Drury, Wittgenstein confesses: "Here I am, a one-time professor of philosophy who has never read a word of Aristotle!" That confession may also explain the divergence between my mature philosophical work and that of Wittgenstein (see *Recollections of Wittgenstein,* edited by Rush Rhees, Oxford and New York, Oxford University Press, 1981, p. 158).

NOTES TO CHAPTER 8

Item A

What Man Has Made of Man*

List of Principal Notes

[1] Schools of Psychology and Controversy in Other Sciences

[2] Formal and Material Logic

[3] Materialism and Cognition

[4] Psychology and Cognition

[5] Common and Special Experience

[6] Common Experience and the Status of Philosophy

[6a] The Different Utilities of Philosophy and Science

[6b] The Positive Distinction between Philosophy and Science

[7] Conflicts Between Philosophy and Science

[8] Infra-intelligible and Supra-sensible Objects

[8a] Questions of Existence in History, Science and Philosophy

[9] The Divisions of Philosophy: Grades of Abstraction

[10] The Proper Sphere of Investigation

[10a] Relations Between Philosophy of Nature and Natural Science

[11] Mathematical Physics as a Mixed Science

[12] Applicative and Inductive Use of Experiment

[13] Science and Causality

[16] Modern Philosophy Before and After Kant

[16a] The Positive Contribution of Positivism, and its Negativism

[17] The Fact of Understanding and Logical Positivism

[18] Imagination and Intellect

[19] Dependence of Understanding on Sense and Body

[20] The Word "Cosmology"

[20b] Monism, Dualism and Modern Philosophy

*Adler, *What Man Has Made of Man*: *A Study of the Consequences of Platonism and Positivism in Psychology*, Intro. by Dr. Franz Alexander, New York and Toronto, Longmans, Green and Co., 1937. To be reprinted under the title *The Consequences of Platonism and Positivism in Psychology*, New Brunswick, N.J., Transaction Publishers, Rutgers University, 1993.

[21] Dialectical Materialism: Aristotle, Aquinas, Marx

[22] The Basic Principle of Realism, and Idealistic Errors

[23] Hierarchy of Substances and the Order of the Sciences

[24] Human and Animal Psychology

[25] Philosophy of Science and Philosophy of Nature

[28] Marxian and Formal Materialism

[28a] The Significance of Human History for Materialism

[29] Interior Sense in Animals and Man

[30] The Utility of the Intellect

[31] Continuity in Nature

[32] Scientific and Philosophical Accounts of Rationality

[32a] The Uniqueness of Psychology: The Order of its Questions

[33] Distribution of Psychological Topics in the Ancient and Mediaeval Tradition

[35] Virtuality and the Plurality of Forms

[36b] Positivism and the Histories of Psychology

[36c] The Subject-Matter of the *De Anima*

[38a] Aristotle and Aquinas as Aristotelians

[39a] Kantian and post-Kantian Psychology

[39b] Freudian and Thomistic Critiques of Modern Psychological Subject-Matter

[39c] Rational and Empirical Psychology: Wolff, Kant and thereafter

[43] Gestalt and Behavioristic Psychology

[45] The Inductive Fertility of Psychometrics and Psychoanalysis

[45a] The Subject-Matter of Scientific Psychology

[45b] The Significance of the History of Psychiatry

[46] The Doctrine of Faculties in Psychometrics and Psychoanalysis

[47] The Different Logics of Science and Philosophy in Relation to their Different Problems

[48] The Meaning of "Hypothesis"

[50] Psychoanalysis and Aetiology

[51] The Metapsychology of Freud

[52] Topography of the Psyche: Reification of Powers

[54] Need and Desire: Kinds of Appetite

[55] The Conscious, the Unconscious, and Repression

Item B

Excerpt from "Adler on Freedom" by Ralph McInerny in *Freedom in the Modern World*

When I was asked to prepare this paper I saw it as an opportunity to pay tribute to a man whose philosophical work over the years, while it has had a tremendous effect, has not yet had anything like the effect it deserves. There are various reasons for this, some quite incidental, but one at least is a trifle unsavory. You know the story of Thales who, in order to show that the philosopher could be an entrepreneur if he chose, cornered all the olive presses and made a killing at harvest time. We easily imagine the reaction of the olive growers. But ask yourself what Thales' fellow philosophers would have thought.

Mortimer has borne with Stoic dignity the burden of being the most highly paid philosopher in the United States. Thales would have been proud of him. But perhaps academic philosophers, nursing economic and other grievances, have been less receptive to what Mortimer Adler had to say. For the best of reasons and highest of motives of course. . . .

When I accepted this assignment, I imagined myself writing the paper in the warm confines of the Maritain Center on the seventh floor of the Hesburgh Library, to which we shall all repair after this session. There the *opera omnia* of Adler would be at my elbow as well as those of Jacques Maritain and Yves R. Simon. As one does when such projects are but a twinkle in the mind's eye, I imagined coming before you on this occasion with a comprehensive overview of Adler's discussions through the years on the concept of freedom. To do this well, it would be necessary to take up allied topics and I would be able to show and not simply assert that some of his books that seem to have been mere by-blows of a collective effort are all but definitive treatises. I remember thinking, when *Some Questions About Language* came out in 1976, that here was a book which, better than any other book in that seemingly overworked field, laid out the issues, indicated solutions, and would define subsequent discussion. (The book was dedicated to Jacques Maritain.) Similar praise can be heaped on other works of Mortimer Adler, and I hoped to use this occasion to do some heaping.

This is not the paper I had hoped to deliver. When I sat down to write, I found myself, not on this campus and in the Maritain Center, but high above Cayuga's waters warming the Kaneb Chair in Catholic Studies. Cornell has an excellent library, but nothing like the Maritain Collection here, with its repository of Adleriana gathered in grand indifference to the Library of Congress, to say nothing of the Dewey Decimal system. I do not mean to suggest, of course, that if I had stayed home I would have written the paper I hoped to write, one that would be worthy of Adler's work. But perhaps the distance between cup and lip would have been somewhat less. . . .

To pick up any work of Mortimer Adler, early, middle, or late, is to be called to order. One imagines him looking at his watch, waiting for us to settle down, and then, when he has our complete attention, beginning. He is a schoolmaster, a *scholasticus*. There is work to be done and we are here to do it.

Consider the 1965 volume *The Conditions of Philosophy* with its subtitle: "Its Checkered Past, Its Present Disorder, and Its Future Promise." At the very outset, Adler acknowledges that he seems embarked on a tiresome, even trite, exercise. How many dozens of attempts have been made over recent centuries to overcome the so-called "scandal of philosophy"? That is, the undeniable fact that the history of philosophy presents us with a cacophony of voices, endless disputes, seemingly no generally accepted solutions.

This situation leads some to take on the burden of remedying the problem by constructing out of whole cloth, as it seems, a worldview. Others become disciples of these sturdy souls so that we have not simply Descartes, Locke, Leibniz, Hume, Kant, and Hegel, but Cartesians, Lockians (Turnkeys), Leibnitzeans, Humeans, Kantians, and Hegelians.

I think it fair to say that Adler from the very outset of his studies at Columbia was struck by this scandal. And, going by the excerpts from his youthful writings he gives us in *Philosopher at Large*, he meant to do something about it. The confidence he showed not only in his own reason, but in human reason itself, to move through and beyond this dissonance and uncommunicating diversity fairly lifts from the page. The issues philosophy addresses are simply too important to be left in this parlous condition. This state of affairs cannot be allowed to continue. But how to remedy it?

Mortimer Adler seems never to have been tempted by the prospect of inventing an Adlerian worldview. Nothing could be farther from his outlook than the Cartesian willingness to wipe the slate clean, to pick the lint from his own navel, and, madly to mix more metaphors, forge in the smithy of his soul the uncreated conscience of his race. What Adler did, instinctively at first and then with growing awareness of the method, was to look for clues within the diversity of philosophical positions as to how the situation could be bettered.

In short, he became a dialectician in the Aristotelian sense. Like Aristotle, he refused to think that intelligent human beings were simply in disagreement with one another on basic issues. Like Aristotle at the outset of most of the treatises, e.g., the *Physics,* the *De anima,* the *Metaphysics,* Adler wants us first to acquaint ourselves with what has been said. He has an Aristotelian confidence that beneath the surface disagreements will be found at least tacitly held common ground. But if this approach has Aristotelian origins, the task in the mid-twentieth century was enormously different from what it was in the mid-fourth century B.C. . . .

Book One of Volume One of *The Idea of Freedom* is a masterful statement of the method Adler hit upon. His Institute's approach to the study of any controverted issue, in this case of freedom, is characterized as follows:

- it is a non-historical study of ideas;
- it is a non-philosophical approach to philosophical ideas;
- it strives to achieve a non-partisan treatment of philosophical positions or views;
- it tries to approximate comprehensiveness in scope;
- it limits itself to what is explicit or implicit in written works.

Adler and his team would dare to ask precisely what disagreement and controversy are and what sort of agreement he envisaged.

It is the distinction between dialectical and doctrinal agreement that will surely catch the eye. What Adler hopes to achieve is agreement that the issue has been fairly and accurately stated, and this provides the context within which future discussion can take place. He cites this comment of Jacques Maritain on the neutrality of the language of dialectical formulation. In order to be neutral, Maritain wrote, it must be

> "echoless," i.e. strictly limited to what is barely stated and deprived of any further doctrinal overtones or connotations. Just because such assertions or formulas, having no actual philosophic life of their own, are, so to speak, only in potency in regard to some philosophical wholeness or totality, every philosopher in the group concerned can subscribe to them; but in doing so each will infuse into them the connotations or overtones peculiar to his own entire doctrine, and foreign to the doctrine of his colleagues (*The Idea of Freedom,* I, 68).

Taken just as such, this would not seem to be worth it. Indeed, it echoes with some of Maritain's hopes for the Universal Declaration of Human Rights. In that case, he might seem to be saying that an agreement can be had on statements even though there is radical disagreement as to the meanings of the terms in the statements. Of course, he did not mean anything so vacuous, and we can be sure that Adler does not either. What Maritain meant and what Adler went on to say he meant was that it is "only through the medium of constructed formulations which are neutral in language and intent that philosophers can be brought to the recognition of their dialectical agreements as well as of their doctrinal agreements and disagreements. Without this medium as a *tertium quid,* each philosopher tends to remain in the world of his own thought and is conversant there with other philosophers only in the guise which he gives them when he imports them into his own world" (Ibid., I, 68). . . .

I don't think we should pass quickly over this point. The success of Adler's effort cannot be likened to, say, a poet who works in obscurity producing his oeuvre, which is then effectively ignored by mankind. Reception apart, the poetry either is or is not good. And, should this ultimately be recognized, say on the order of the discovery of Catullus or the belated reputation of Hopkins, they are welcomed into a traditon of poetic work.

But Adler did not seek simply to make his own contribution to the ongoing tradition of philosophy. His was the far more ambitious task of introducing order into the philosophical community so that its future might be different from its past. There is a thematically practical aim underlying his effort. His success will be measured in terms of how much or how little he has effected what he sought to effect. And I suggest that, to date, the results are not favorable.

One of the greatest obstacles has been the obscurantist disinterest among professional philosophers. I recall reading a review of Walker Percy's collection of essays on language in which a professional philosopher condescendingly offered to provide Percy with a reading list if he wished seriously to get into the problem of language. Adler, of course, has all the appropriate academic credentials, he has been on the faculty of two of the best universities in this country, but some professional philosophers regard him as something of an interloper. This is unfortunate and one can only hope that the work of the Institute for Philosophical Research will find a warmer welcome in academe than has been the case till now.

Fortunately, if the jury is still out on the success of the Institute's effort to restructure the way philosophical controversy is conducted, there is another side of Adler's effort that can be pronounced successful here and now. . . .

The original sin of Adler's academic career was that he wrote a best-seller, *How to Read a Book*. This made him as welcome among philosophers as Barbara Tuchman is among academic historians. I once heard a young historian say of Philip Hughes, the great church historian, that he wasn't a real historian. It wasn't simply that Hughes was readable; he didn't have a pedantic bone in his body. Adler gets a firm grip on his reader's lapels from the first sentence, but from that point on it is the flow of the narrative that holds the reader. Mortimer Adler has the great knack of communicating difficult ideas in a jargonless language understandable by any intelligent reader. This is unforgiveable.

Not only that, what he communicates is both his own confidence in reason and arguments that enable the reader to share that confidence. For contrast, look at Thomas Nagel's *What Does It All Mean?* Here we have a professional philosopher of great talent writing a book for the masses on the main issues of philosophy. Of Nagel it can be said, he's no Mortimer Adler. I don't mean that he gives us philosophical jargon; the problem is the same as that of Bertrand Russell in his popular efforts. The answer Nagel gives to his question is: probably nothing but it doesn't really matter. The jaded skepticism of academic philosophy makes even thinner gruel when it is freed from the protective garb of jargon.

Brand Blanshard was among those who praised *The Idea of Freedom* for its fairness and objectivity. Adler the dialectician does not load the case. But when Adler does philosophy he profits from that vast dialectical working up of 2,500 years of philosophy—he may be more knowledgeable than any other living philosopher about philosophy's past—and he provides his reader with the elements of a substantive answer to the great questions. . . .

Let me conclude with the remark that there is something quintessentially American about Adler's work. His *Paideia* program aims at enabling his fellow citizens to fulfill their tasks as members of a free society. The sturdy confidence that led him through the thickets of philosophical controversies over 2,500 years toward a clarification of the points at issue was meant to lead on to the resolution of the major differences. The practical importance of this is that a society such as ours cannot function as it should if there is fundamental confusion about the concepts and truths on which it is founded. So it is that Mortimer Adler became a public philosopher, an intellectual who dared to engage in the great conversation all his fellow citizens, in the conviction that common sense is indeed common. That it is uncommon for a philosopher to say such things nowadays is a sign of how grateful we should be for Mortimer Adler.

Item C

Excerpt from "A Philosopher Looks Back and Forward," in *Living Philosophies*

[Let me conclude:] two facts about the twentieth century . . . hold out promise for the postmodern age that lies ahead. The word "democracy" has been misused for many things, but we have at last come to use it strictly for constitutional government with truly universal suffrage (disfranchising only infants, the mentally incompetent, and felonious criminals) and with all natural, human rights secured, economic as well as political. Political democracy and, inseparable from it, socialism in the economic order came into being for the first time in this century and so are still feeble and fragile.

The other fact is that this is the first century in which there has been in any society a privileged majority and oppressed minorities. In all societies before 1900 there was a privileged minority and an oppressed majority. This extraordinary shift, like the crossing of a great divide, augurs well for a future in which the ideals of democracy and socialism will be more fully realized. Only then will be see the elimination of all oppressed minorities.

What is now happening under Gorbachev's regime in the Soviet Union leads me to think, and also to hope, that in the next century the two major economies that have been pitted against one another will converge to produce a worldwide economy that we cannot at present fully envisage but in which the *difference* and the *antagonism* between the two forms of capitalism—state capitalism and private property capitalism—will cease to exist in a completely industrial world that is everywhere capital intensive.

If in the next century a new economic order emerges that combines efficiency with justice and that provides the economic underpinnings of political democracy, then another hope of mine may be realized. The insuperable obstacle to world federal government has been the heterogeneity of the major powers in their political and economic institutions. That obstacle would be removed if the economic and political institutions of the major powers were to become essentially homogeneous, differing only in detail.

Without a world federal government replacing a relatively impotent United Nations, I can see no hope for this planet as a viable place for vegetative, animal, and human life. I once thought that world federal government was needed to prevent a nuclear holocaust and the destruction of civilization as we know it. The prevention of nuclear holocaust is no longer the reason for world government. That threat has all but disappeared and has been replaced by the threatened puncturing of the ozone layer, the greenhouse effect, and other irreversible deteriorations of the environment that can be effectively countered only by enforceable legal regulation of human activities on a worldwide basis.

Finally, I come to the world that lies outside my ivory tower. Detached from the world of action, I have been able to carry on my philosophical pursuits even in this inhospitable and intellectually deprived twentieth century. I must confess that I have always found dealing with ideas more pleasurable than trying to solve problems that involve dealing with people. I must also confess that in dealing with human problems, whether political, economic, or educational, I have always persisted in taking the long-range view. Nothing worth accomplishing in the realm of action can be achieved by quick fixes and superficial remedies. I, therefore, have little interest in the ebb and flow of current events—the reports that fill daily newspapers, weekly news magazines, and news programs on radio or television.

In the realm of action, outside the world of detached thought, I have been engaged for many years in the radical reform of the thoroughly undemocratic, as well as ineffectively conducted, school system in the United States. The difficulties I have encountered are not in the sphere of what is thought to be the relevant educational ideas. I think that the Paideia program, which my associates and I have developed, contains the needed ideas about teaching and learning and about the obstacles to be overcome in delivering the same quality of education to all children in the first twelve years of school. All the difficulties that have been encountered arise from the recalcitrance to change and the desire for quick fixes on the part of the human beings that must be dealt with in accomplishing a nationwide educational reform, one that may take fifty years or more into the next century to achieve.

Nowhere in the contemporary world is there a truly democratic school system in which equal educational opportunity genuinely exists and in which teaching is conducted as a cooperative art that respects the activity of the learner's own mind as the primary cause of all genuine learning. This is not surprising in view of the extraordinary recency of democracy and socialism. But now that these two institutions have at last come into being, my hopes increase for the radical reform of schools all over the world.

These reforms could not have been initiated without the advent of constitutional democracy and democratic socialism. Being involved in their initiation has been for me personally the greatest opportunity afforded by this century. Political and economic democracy will never be able to reach their full maturity without the accomplishment of these educational reforms. They are necessary to prepare all human beings for the intelligent discharge of their duties as citizens, for a beneficent use of their opportunities as owners of capital, and for the philosophical pursuit of truth, which may become, as it should become, everybody's business.

CHAPTER 9

A PHILOSOPHER'S RELIGIOUS FAITH

My interest in theology antedated by many years my interest in religion. In my view of the matter, I had no religious upbringing. My parents may have thought otherwise.

In my pre-adolescent years, I was taken by my mother and my maternal grandmother to religious services in a Reform synagogue on Saturday mornings, but without any effect on my mind or soul. The innoculation did not take, or the patient was too intransigent. The dose may have been too slight.

My father was born in Bavaria and came to the United States in his late teens. He was brought up in an Orthodox Jewish household and the ritualistic habits of his youth persisted. My mother and my grandmother who lived with us catered to his dietary scruples and he, in turn, tolerated the rest of the family's transgressions of or deviations from them. If I thought about his Orthodoxy at all, I regarded it as an anomaly, a vestige of the old country which he could not shake off, but totally out of place and meaningless in the world in which we were living.

My father's Orthodoxy did not prevent us as a family from celebrating Christmas as well as Hanukkah, and Easter as well as Passover. The difference between secular and religious holidays did not mean anything to me, though I am sure that I enjoyed what went on at Christmas and Easter better than I did at Hanukkah and Passover. Of course, we observed the Jewish holy days on Rosh Hashanah and Yom Kippur, but only my father fasted on the latter day. For me, they were two days that I did not go to school.

I went to high school when I was twelve and a half years old and I was at that stage of my schooling when the time came for me to go through the Jewish rite of passage known as Bar Mitzvah. I remember quarreling with the rabbi about the speech that I was to give to the congregation on that occasion, but the points in contention were philosophical, not religious. I do not recall the rabbi's ever asking me whether I believed in God. I simply had to memorize enough Hebrew to appear to read, while reciting, a passage from the Old Testament. It was an act of filial, not religious, piety on my part. I was simply an obedient boy, complying with my parent's wishes. My parents may have taken it more seriously than my joining a fraternity or my becoming a Boy Scout, but it had no more spiritual content for me than that.

In my adolescent years, and especially when I was in college, I gave up my ambition to become a journalist, cherishing the hope of becoming a philosopher instead. I ceased to have anything to do with the Jewish religion. My mother no longer expected me to go to synagogue with her on Saturday mornings. My father never mentioned my irreligiosity. For all intents and purposes, I was a pagan and a somewhat rebellious one at that.

It was through my study of philosophy, not through religious observances and rituals, that I became interested in God—as an object of thought, not as an object of love and worship. It was the God of Aristotle and of Spinoza, not the God of Judaism and Christianity. When I graduated from college at twenty and started to conduct great books seminars with Mark Van Doren, I first came into contact with the Treatise on God in the *Summa Theologica* of Thomas Aquinas.

The intellectual austerity, integrity, precision, and brilliance of that book, incomparably different from all the philosophical books that I had read up to that time, and much more exciting to me, put the study of theology highest among all of my philosophical interests.

What for Aquinas were his articles of Christian faith, I was willing to take as postulates or assumptions that called upon him or anyone else to engage in philosophical thought for the sake of discovering their implications or consequences. What for Aquinas was philosophy serving as the handmaiden of theology in the process of faith seeking understanding was for me just a philosophical exercise, as exacting in its demands on the intellect and as rigorous as higher mathematics.

2

In the next twenty or thirty years, I read all the treatises in Part One of the *Summa Theologica* and many of the later parts, dealing with moral theology, but not all of the *Summa*. I also read St. Augustine's *Confessions* again and again, as well as his *City of God*, his *Enchiridion*, and his essay on *Christian Doctrine*. I became acquainted with the thought of St. Anselm, as well as with the doctrines of the great Jewish theologian Maimonides (whom Aquinas referred to as *the* rabbi) and with Aquinas' criticisms of the errors of Averroës (the Arabic philosopher whom Aquinas referred to as *the* commentator for his contributions to the study of Aristotelian philosophy).

Since at this time I had no religious faith, my preoccupation with theology was entirely philosophical, and I did not yet fully understand the relation of the three domains of theology: sacred, natural, and philosophical theology.

All, or almost all, of the theologians in the Middle Ages (whether of Jewish, Christian, or Islamic religious faith) were sacred or dogmatic theologians. Their religious faith, or the dogmas of their religions, provided them with the unquestionable principles of their theology. I learned from Aquinas that their faith was a gift from God. They had faith by the grace of God, not by a voluntary act on their part, an exercise of what William James called "the will to believe."

On the other hand, the three branches of theoretical philosophy according to Aristotle were physics, mathematics, and metaphysics; and in Book Lambda of his *Metaphysics,* we find Aristotle's theology—his teaching about God, the prime mover or first cause of an eternal (or, more precisely, an everlasting) cosmos or universe.

This is not sacred or dogmatic theology, but purely philosophical theology. From the point of view of the mediaeval Jewish and

Christian disciples of Aristotle, he was a pagan theologian. That did not prevent them from borrowing arguments from him when they tried to prove the existence of God, even though Aristotle's conception of God differed so radically from the God in whom they believed that, while acknowledging his pagan attempts, they should have pointed out his serious errors.

There is a third domain in which theological thinking occurs. In addition to sacred or dogmatic and philosophical or pagan theology, there is something usually miscalled "natural theology," which is apologetics. A mediaeval example of Christian apologetics is to be found in a work of Thomas Aquinas entitled *Summa Contra Gentiles,* addressed to the Jews and Moors in Spain. It is written as if it were philosophical theology, but that it is not because it was written by a Christian, not by a pagan. There are theses and arguments in the doctrine it attempts to teach that no pagan, but only a person of Christian faith, could have affirmed and developed.

The first principles of Christian apologetics are principles of reason, not dogmas of religion. However, as the history of such natural theology reveals, it is for the most part the work of individuals who are not pagans, but persons of religious faith, by virtue of which they assert about God and about man's relation to God propositions that cannot be on purely rational grounds.

Such Christian apologetics, which is neither dogmatically sacred theology nor philosophically pagan theology, became in modern times, beginning with the *Meditations* of Descartes, the work of philosophers who were also Christians or of Christian divines who also tried to be philosophers. A prime example of such work is the late eighteenth-century treatise by an Anglican priest, William Paley, entitled *A View of the Evidence of Christianity* and a later work entitled *Natural Theology.*

These works were required reading for entrance to Cambridge University until the end of the nineteenth century. The Gifford Lectures in the twentieth century at the University of Edinburgh produced books in natural theology by scientists and philosophers who were also Christians. In my judgment, few if any of these books, and many more like them, are sound as works in philosophical theology, because they are not written by pagans.

I did not fully understand the philosophical deficiencies of what in modern times was called "natural theology" until fairly late in my life when I finally wrote the book I had been preparing to write for many years—*How to Think About God* (1980). The subtitle of that book was "A Guide for the 20th-Century Pagan," and on its title page, the word "pagan" was defined as "one who does not worship the God of Christians, Jews, or Muslims; irreligious persons." Furthermore, Chapter 3 informed the book's readers that the book was not only written for pagans, but also written by a pagan.

As what follows will show, it is much easier to be a philosopher without religion than to be a philosopher after acquiring religious faith. It is much easier to have blind faith, but that is not an option open to a philosopher. If he has religious faith, he then has the obligation to think about the dogmas of his religion.

I suspect that most of the individuals who have religious faith are content with blind faith. They feel no obligation to understand what they believe. They may even wish not to have their beliefs disturbed by thought. But if the God in whom they believe created them with intellectual and rational powers, that imposes upon them the duty to try to understand the creed of their religion. Not to do so is to verge on superstition.

3

Stories that I have told earlier in this book anticipate what remains to be told in this chapter. In Chapter 8, Section 3, I reported how I came to join the American Catholic Philosophical Association in 1932; and in Chapter 2, Section 5, I reported the steps that led me to deliver my address on "God and the Professors" at the opening session of the First Conference on Science, Philosophy and Religion, sponsored by Rabbi Louis Finkelstein of the Jewish Theological Seminary of America in New York City.[1]

Without becoming a Roman Catholic, I had become a Thomist in philosophy as a result of my intensive study of the *Summa*

1. Other relevant anticipations will be found in *Philosopher at Large,* Chapter 14, and especially pp. 314–317.

Theologica of Thomas Aquinas. For the give and take of philosophical discussion, I found fellow Thomists in the American Catholic Philosophical Association a more receptive audience for the books and essays that I was then disposed to write than were my colleagues at the University of Chicago, or the professors of philosophy at other secular universities.

The Dominican House of Studies in Washington, D.C. published a magazine called *The Thomist*. After delivering a paper on the demonstration of democracy at the annual meeting of the American Catholic Philosophical Association in 1939, Father Walter Farrell and I co-authored a book-length series of essays entitled "The Theory of Democracy," which was published in *The Thomist* in successive issues from 1941 to 1943. *The Thomist* also published my long essay on "The Problem of Species" (which elicited a storm of adverse criticism from my fellow Thomists) and the essay I contributed to the special issue of *The Thomist* in 1943, celebrating the sixtieth birthday of my friend Jacques Maritain. That essay, entitled "The Demonstration of God's Existence," attempted to show why the five ways of proving God's existence presented by Aquinas in Part One, Question 2, Article 2 did not succeed. That elicited an even greater storm of protest from the Thomists.

During these years and also in the following decade, I was a frequent guest at the Dominican House of Studies in Washington, D.C., and also at the Benedictine Abbey in Collegeville, Minnesota, where I gave lectures at Saint John's University, run by the Benedictine monks. I also gave lectures at the University of Notre Dame and became a close friend of Father John Cavanaugh, its President then, and later of Father Theodore Hesburgh, his successor.

I am sure that many of my Roman Catholic friends wondered why I did not become a Roman Catholic, but with the one exception of Father Robert Slavin of the Dominican House of Studies, none of them ever broached that question explicitly in conversation with me.

There were moments in the late 1930s and throughout the 1940s that I put that question to myself. As I look back at the answers that I then gave myself, I think the reasons I gave were superficial. They cloaked my disinclination to become religious. I simply did not wish to exercise a will to believe; and from what I understood about faith as a supernatural, theological virtue, which was a gift of divine grace, my will was not moved by faith.[2]

When Clare Boothe Luce, who had herself then recently become a convert to Roman Catholicism, made a strenuous effort to convert me, I explained to her the difference between dead and living faith—faith without hope and charity, and faith that is enriched by the other two theological virtues, hope and charity. I told Clare that simply being able to understand Thomist theology was what Aquinas called dead faith. It was not enough to carry one into a Christian religious life.[3]

I should add here that my first wife, Helen, was born an Episcopalian. My Jewish father and mother were reconciled to that mixed marriage. The two sons that Helen and I adopted, Mark and Michael, were baptized and confirmed in the Episcopal Church, and I attended religious services with them at the Church of the Redeemer, in the neighborhood of the University of Chicago, also attended by T. S. Eliot when he was a visiting lecturer there. Father Francis Lickfield, the rector, and I became good friends, but, as I recall, he never tried to convert me.

My second wife, Caroline, was also born an Episcopalian, and our two sons, Douglas and Philip, were baptized and confirmed in the Episcopal Church. As a family, we became members of the parish community of Saint Chrysostom's Church in Chicago, of which Father Robert Howell was the rector; and, as in the earlier case of Father Lickfield at the Church of the Redeemer, Bob Howell became a friend, but he never raised any question about my becoming a baptized Christian.

There is one other coincidence that I should mention. Father Howell had a close friend in Chicago, Father William Casady, who was the rector of Grace Episcopal Church downtown in the Chicago loop. I had complained to Caroline that many of the sermons

2. See ibid.

3. See ibid.

we had heard together in the churches that we attended together in San Francisco and in London were not, in my judgment, sufficiently theological in their exegesis of the gospel text appointed in the liturgy of the day.

On the occasion of a party for me, to which Caroline had invited Father Howell and Father Casady, she mentioned my complaint about sermons. Father Casady responded at once by inviting me to deliver a sermon at his church. He followed that up with a letter asking me to deliver a sermon on Mother's Day, May 11, 1980.

I did so, avoiding the text that was appointed for that day in the church calendar. I tried to explain the relation between the Mosaic decalogue and Christ's two precepts of charity, from which, Jesus said, "hang all the law and the prophets." The title of my sermon was "The Old Law and the New " and, since it was delivered on Mother's Day, I gave special attention to the commandment about honoring thy father and thy mother "that the days of thy life may be long in the land the Lord thy God giveth thee."

Since then, I have delivered about twelve sermons in Grace Episcopal Church in Chicago and in Christ Episcopal Church in Aspen, and in one or two other Episcopal churches elsewhere. About half of these sermons were delivered before I became an Episcopalian, and half after my conversion to Christianity, not from Judaism, but from being an irreligious person.

Caroline, who has listened to all the sermons I have given, thinks that they are not good pastoral homilies. They are not exhortative at all, but entirely explicative and exegetical—philosophical disquisitions about biblical texts and points in Christian doctrine.

All the facts I have just mentioned are in the background of my conversion to Christianity in 1984. Before I try to explain that event, there are two preambles to it, both philosophical, that I must report. One is the address I gave at the opening conference on Science, Philosophy and Religion in 1940, entitled "God and the Professors." The other is my continuous effort, from 1943 to 1978, to improve the philosophical arguments for the existence of God—revision after revision of a lecture on that subject, all of them having their seed in my dissatisfaction with Aquinas' five ways of proving God's existence.

My writing *How to Think About God* in 1979 was the culmination of all those efforts from 1943 on. It was also a crucial step in my becoming a religious Christian. When I wrote *Philosopher at Large* in 1974–1975, I did not foresee the book I was to write in 1979; for in the closing sentence of Chapter 14,[4] I wrote:

> Whether or not I shall ever be able to resolve the difficulties I have encountered in all earliest attempts to construct a valid proof of God's existence, the best judgment I can reach about the matter would, in my opinion, be a fitting close . . . to my philosophical career.

It turned out to be much more than that, as I will relate after I have dealt with the two preambles that I mentioned above, which preceded *How to Think About God.*

4

Though I had become a person of Christian faith when I wrote *Truth in Religion* in 1990, I tried to write that book as a work in philosophy, not as a work of Christian apologetics. If I did not wholly succeed in this endeavor, my 1940 address, "God and the Professors," was a philosophical statement about religion at a time when I was not a person of Christian faith.

The excerpt from that address, which I have placed in the Notes at the end of this chapter, immediately followed the excerpted portion of the address appended to Chapter 2. That excerpt stated eight propositions about philosophy in relation to science that should be affirmed; or if not affirmed, then the denials should be rationally defended. The conference should not consist of professorial papers on loosely related topics, but rather of issues joined and disputed. The propositions set forth, which I affirmed, would most probably be denied by others and thus become the focus of debate. I meant this to be the case of the eight propositions I presented with respect to religion, as well as with respect to the propositions I stated about philosophy.

My essay on the philosophy of religion in 1991 reaffirmed, in a somewhat different manner, the eight propositions enumerated

4. See ibid., p. 317.

forty-nine years earlier in 1940. But it went further. The subtitle of *Truth in Religion* was "The Plurality of Religions and the Unity of Truth." The unity of truth required that any religion that claimed truth—factual, not poetical, truth—for its beliefs had to be consistent and compatible with whatever truths were known at the time, with certitude or probability, in history, science, and philosophy.

Among the plurality of religions that claimed truth for their beliefs, those that were in conflict with one another in such claims could not all be true; as, for example, theistic religions that are monotheistic and those that are polytheistic, or religions that are theistic and religions that are nontheistic. Therefore, with regard to truth in religion, we are confronted with the question: Which of the recognized world religions has the best claim to being true, or which among them has a better claim than others?

In the concluding chapter of *Truth in Religion,* I enumerated the considerations that individuals should have in mind when trying to answer this question for themselves. If the religions of Far Eastern origins do not claim to be supernatural knowledge, based on divine revelation, then they are theoretical or moral philosophies masquerading as religions. Even as counterfeit religions, if they are polytheistic or nontheistic, then their philosophical doctrines come into conflict with the truths of philosophical theology, and must be rejected. That leaves the three monotheistic and revealed religions of Western origin: Judaism, Christianity, and Islam. These conflict with one another in their truth claims. If one has a better claim to being true, the others may partially share in that truth. Each is compatible with the truths affirmed in philosophical theology, but all three may not be equally compatible with the established truths of empirical science and history.

I thought of four other considerations that must be taken into account in deciding which of these three religions might have a better claim to being factually true.[5] I enumerated them as follows:

> One involves the matter of proselytizing: Should not a religion that claims logical and factual truth for its orthodoxy engage in missionary efforts to convert others to its beliefs?

5. See Adler, *Truth in Religion,* 1990, p. 109.

> Another criterion is the differing eschatology of these three religions—their views about the ultimate destiny of the individual human being or of mankind as a whole, their views about immortality, and about life after death, about divine rewards and punishments, and about salvation.
>
> Still another is the difference in their views concerning the immanence as well as the transcendence of the supreme being.
>
> A fourth criterion of the greatest importance is the extent to which God's self-revelation involves mysteries—mysteries, not miracles. Mysteries are articles of religious faith that exceed our natural human powers of knowing and understanding. They may be intelligible in themselves, but they are not completely intelligible to us.

Since at the time I wrote *Truth in Religion,* I was a believing Christian, I felt that my own religious faith might be ill-concealed in the enumeration of those four considerations, which certainly favored Christianity over Judaism and Islam. Was I writing as a philosopher or as a Christian apologist defending the truth claims of his own religion? With this in mind, I concluded the book with the following paragraph.

> As a philosopher concerned with truth in religion, I would like to hear leading twentieth-century theologians speaking as apologists for Judaism, Christianity, and Islam engage in a disputation. The question at issue would be which of these three religions had a greater claim to truth. It being conceded that each has a claim to some measure of truth, which of the three can rightly claim more truth than the other two?[6]

In 1979, when I wrote *How to Think About God,* I was not yet a Christian. I wrote that book as a pagan for pagans. As I said earlier, the argument therein for God's existence was, for me, the satisfactory culmination of fifty years of dissatisfaction with the arguments adapted by Aquinas from Aristotle in his statement of the first three ways of proving God's existence.

In that fifty years, I had written lecture after lecture trying to do

6. Ibid., pp. 109–110.

better as a pagan philosophical theologian. In that fifty years, I had finally learned how to turn St. Anselm's so-called ontological argument from being an invalid argument for God's existence into an illuminating way of coming to understand what God is like and unlike. In that period, I learned from Thomas Aquinas and from Etienne Gilson of the Sorbonne, his disciple, the crucial premise in the proof of God's existence—not to be found in the *Summa*'s Treatise on God, but in later treatises in the First Part of the *Summa* especially the Treatise on Creation and the Treatise on the Divine Government. Hence I would say that my *one* argument that concludes with affirming God's existence beyond a reasonable doubt (not with certitude beyond the shadow of a doubt), is Thomistic even though it does not appear in his *Summa Theologica* in the words of the formulation that I gave it.

This is not the place to summarize the analysis and reasoning in *How to Think About God* (which has recently been republished in a handsome paperback edition). But I might here call attention to a number of points that I regard as original contributions on my part. One was explaining that any sound argument for God's existence as the exnihilating cause of the existence of the cosmos must assume that the cosmos always existed, and did not have a beginning, as the first verse in *Genesis* proclaims. That is a matter of faith, not of reason, and so on the contrary assumption, which does not beg the question, God exnihilates the cosmos by preserving it in existence, or preventing it from ceasing to be.

Another point was that God as cause of the existence of the cosmos is not to be thought of as the first efficient cause in a chain of causes (and certainly not as the prime mover) but as the *only* cause of being, acting *directly* on the cosmos as a whole that is radically contingent (or capable of not being as a whole). The superficially contingent things, which are component parts of the cosmos, never totally cease to be, but merely undergo transformation when they perish, as animals do when they die.[7]

7. The point I have just made indicates the signifcant difference between Aristotle's pagan, philosophical theology, written in total ignorance of the Old and New Testament, and the pagan, philosophical theology of those who try to prove the existence of a God that, in the light of Sacred Scriptures, is seen as the creator of this radically contingent cosmos.

The most important points of originality appeared in the Epilogue of the book. Reading the *Pensées* of Pascal, I had been impressed by his statement that the God of the philosophers was not the God of Abraham, Isaac, and Jacob, or of Moses and Jesus. But Pascal merely said that and did not explain why that was so, in what respects the God of the philosophers was deficient, and how that conception of God was related to the God believed in by faithful Jews and Christians.

The sound argument for God's existence that I claimed to have formulated did not conclude with *belief in God,* but only in a philosophical affirmation of God's existence. The divinity thus affirmed to exist closely resembled the God believed in by faithful Jews and Christians in all the negative traits of a supreme being—immateriality, eternity (which means "nontemporality"), infinity, uncaused. It also includes certain positive traits, such as ontological perfections as omnipotence, omnipresence, and omniscience, and even such analogically understood perfections as living, knowing, willing, and God's freedom in His act of creation.

But there is one perfection that the philosophical conception of God does not include and that cannot be established by purely philosophical reasoning. That is the goodness of God, not his ontological perfection; but His benevolent love of His creatures, His providential government of and care for them, His being a gracious God who is both just and merciful, who answers our prayers and forgives our sins.

I, therefore, concluded by saying that the soundest rational argument for God's existence could carry us only to the edge of the chasm that separated the philosophical affirmation of God's existence from the religious belief in God. What is usually called "a leap of faith" is needed to carry anyone across the chasm. But the leap of faith is usually misunderstood as being a progress from

---

Aristotle's God is the *primary* cause of motion in a universe that he conceived as eternal or everlasting, whereas the God of the Old and New Testament is the *only* cause of being of a cosmos that would totally cease to be without that causation at every instant of its existence.

This does not mean that modern pagan philosophical theology proves the existence of the God believed in by persons of Jewish, Christian, or Islamic faith. Such faith attributes to God many properties that exceed the power of rational proof; but starting from the radical contingency of the cosmos, philosophical theology affirms the indispensable existence of its exnihilating creative cause.

having insufficient reasons for affirming God's existence to a state of greater certitude in that affirmation. That is not the case. The leap of faith consists in going from the conclusion of a merely philosophical theology to a religious belief in a God that has revealed Himself as a loving, just, and merciful creator of the cosmos, a God to be loved, worshiped, and prayed to.

The God of the philosophers is not a God to be loved, worshiped, or prayed to. A God who is not concerned with human destiny by being law-giving and grace-giving is the God of philosophical and irreligious deists, not the self-revealing God of religious theists.

I think I have said enough about *How to Think About God* (published in 1980) to explain how that was the penultimate step in my progress from being a philosophical theologian to being a religious believer in God. What remains to be told are the events in 1984 that attended my leap of faith.

5

In March of 1984, after a trip to Mexico in February, I fell ill, probably from a virus that I had picked up there. The illness was protracted. I was in the hospital for five weeks and, after leaving the hospital, was in bed at home for several months or more. Though I underwent all the diagnostic tests and procedures that the physicians could think of, the illness was never adequately diagnosed; and the cure, when it finally came, involved numerous antibiotics and two blood transfusions that brought my red corpuscle blood count back to normal.

During this long stay in the hospital, I suffered a mild depression, and often when Caroline visited me I would, unaccountably, burst into tears. Father Howell, the Rector of Saint Chrysostom's Church, also visited me, and once when, at my bedside, he prayed for my recovery, I choked up and wept. The only prayer that I knew word for word, was the *Pater Noster*. On that day and in the days after it, I found myself repeating the Lord's Prayer, again and again, and meaning every word of it. Quite suddenly, when I was awake one night, a light dawned on me, and I realized what had happened without my recognizing it clearly when first it happened.

I had been seriously praying to God. But had I not said at the end of *How to Think About God,* that no one who understood the God of the philosophers as well as I thought I did, would worship that God or pray to him. Only if, by the gift of grace, one made the leap of faith across the chasm to the God of religious Jews and Christians, would one engage in worship and prayer, believing in a morally good, loving, just, and merciful God.

Here after many years of affirming God's existence and trying to give adequate reasons for that affirmation, I found myself believing in God and praying to Him. I rang for the night nurse and asked for paper and pen, and with great difficulty—for I was at that time not very mobile in bed—I managed to sit up and scrawl a letter to Father Howell. The letter which, the next day, Caroline transcribed for me, and then typed out before sending it to Father Howell, was dated April 1, 1984.

In it, I told Father Howell of the conflicts and difficulties in my life and thought that had been obstacles to my becoming a Christian. I told him that when, at my bedside, he prayed for me, I wept, and was convulsed. With no audible voice accessible to me, I was saying voicelessly to myself "Dear God, yes, I do believe, not just in the God my reason so stoutly affirms, but the God to whom Father Howell is now praying, and on whose grace and love I now joyfully rely."

I went on by saying that "Caroline, I know, will receive this news with as much joy as you. She and I have talked about how our Christian marriage would end up. It has been a good marriage, but would not have been fulfilled without the step I am now prepared to take." I ended the letter by asking Father Howell to pay me a visit after I returned home.

He did and, on April 21, I was baptized a Christian by Father Howell in the presence of Caroline. A year later, at Father Howell's request, I took the pulpit at Saint Chrysostom's Church and gave an account of conversion to the congregation, of which I had been a nonbelieving member for many years.

In that brief address, I reminded them that two years earlier, I had given three Lenten talks about the substance of my book, *How to Think About God,* which had just been published. I reminded them especially about what I had to say concerning the leap of faith—that no one in his right senses would pray to the God affirmed in philosophical theology, but only to a God believed in and worshiped for His love and care, His grace and providence. I told the congregation of Father Howell's visit to me in the hospital and how at last I had been moved to prayer, which I recognized as an act of faith on my part, a living faith with hope and charity to complete it. I said that I still had residual difficulties—things that I still do not understand, and may never fully understand. But these, I said, do not matter. I ended by quoting the passage from *Mark* 9:23–24, in which Jesus says to the father whose child is ill: " 'All things are possible to him who believes; to which the father replies: "O Lord, I do believe, help thou my unbelief.' "

As I look back now upon the years of my life since then, I think I have not been as good a Christian as I promised myself I would be. To whatever degree I possessed moral virtue before I became a Christian, it was not augmented, certainly not to an heroic degree. I may probably be no worse a Christian than the many who confess their sins in church on Sunday, for having done things they ought not to have done and failing to do things they ought to have done, repenting having sinned and asking for forgiveness.

If I have not been a sinless Christian, I have at least been a thoughtful one. I have pondered the mysteries that in the concluding pages of *Truth in Religion,* I said were one of the things to be considered in deciding where greater truth was to be found among the three monotheistic religions of Western origin.

For both Judaism and Islam the God believed in is entirely transcendent—outside the cosmos as its creator and governor. Only for Christianity is God both transcendent and immanent—at once the eternal creator of the cosmos and the earthly redeemer of mankind, as well as its indwelling spirit, omnipresent as well as omnipotent. This is, of course, the mystery of the Trinity—the one God, of which there are three persons or aspects, the one God who is both in heaven and on earth.

When dogmatic theologians conceive themselves as engaged in the process of faith seeking understanding, they acknowledge an insuperable limit to that process. The limit consists in the mysteries of faith, which, however intelligible they may be in themselves, will never be fully intelligible to us on earth.

In the concluding section of this chapter, I will briefly report the thinking I have done, since I became a Christian, about the mysteries of Christian faith.

6

Inseparable from the mystery of the Trinity is the mystery of the incarnation of the second person in Jesus Christ, one person with two natures, divine and human, and the mystery of Christ's passion on the cross, His resurrection, and ascent into Heaven.

This complex mystery requires us to try—albeit unsuccessfully—to understand heaven as a purely spiritual place, totally distinct from this vast physical cosmos, as well as in eternity and totally timeless.

The Nicene Creed contains words that refer to all the elements in the complex mystery. Its most important words are those that declare the Son to be of *one substance* with the Father, words that apply to the Holy Spirit as well. All three persons of the Trinity are "one substance," which is to say that they are existentially one.

In the physical cosmos anything that is existentally one entity or substance cannot be in two places at the same time. But God is a purely spiritual being, not in physical time or space, and so it can be said of God that He is existentially both transcendent and immanent. This is, of course, unimaginable (for nothing spiritual is imaginable), but it is not unthinkable.

We must be forever cautious to remember that the word "spiritual" has *only a negative meaning* for us: *not*-physical, *not*-material, *not*-corporeal. We must forever remember that we have no positive meaning for the words "spirit" and "spiritual." That is why Maimonides insisted that all the properties we attribute to God are negative, and why Aquinas went beyond that (adding such positive properties as living, knowing, and willing) by explaining that, when used of God and His creatures, these words are used analogically. God lives, knows, and wills, but *not* in the sense in which creatures like us live, know, and will.

In short, we fail miserably in our attempt to understand God if we ever allow ourselves to employ our imagination. The realm of spirits and the spiritual is utterly beyond the power of our imagination, which is rooted in our sense experience of the physical, material, and corporeal world. That is why the fundamentalist literal reading of the words in Sacred Scriptures or in the Nicene Creed—many of which have sensible, physical connotations—is such a disastrous mistake. It makes a mockery of the Christian faith and its mysteries.

7

I kept thinking about the mysteries at the heart of my Christian faith. My mind kept returning to the word "heaven," which too many Christians, I feared, imagined as a place somewhere out there or up there in physical space, from which the second person of the Trinity descended and to which He ascended after His resurrection.

I remembered, of course, St. Augustine's interpretation of the word "heaven" in the first sentence of *Genesis*. That word used there referred to God's creation of spiritual creatures, the angels, as the word "earth" referred to all of God's physical creatures, not to the planet earth. Several verses later in the first chapter of *Genesis,* the physical earth and heaven—that is, this planet and the skies above it—are mentioned as being created in the order of the six days. St. Augustine's interpretation of the word "heaven" in the first verse avoids a contradiction with the reference to the physical skies and seas in the later verse, which the fundamentalists, reading *Genesis* literally, do not observe.

The trouble with the word "heaven" is that that one word has both an eschatological meaning in Christian theology and a physical meaning in ancient astronomy and modern cosmology. In the centuries before Christ, Aristotle used the word in his book, the title of which in English is "Of the Heavens."[8] In earlier centuries, the Old Testament, unknown to Aristotle, referred not only in *Genesis,* but in many of its later books, to heaven as the abode of God.

I arranged a conference at Christ Episcopal Church in Aspen to be held in August of 1991. At that conference, I called attention to

8. In Greek the title is π ερτ οὐράνου; in Latin, it is *De Caelo*.

the fact that the Egyptian, Chaldean, Greek, and Alexandrian astronomy of antiquity knew a universe no larger than the visible solar system and the visible stars, visible to the naked eye. The Ptolemaic astronomy of the Hellenistic era had the same limited scope. That was the very small known physical world at the time of St. Augustine and at the time when the Nicene Creed was formulated. The known cosmos did not increase in size in the thirteenth century when Thomas Aquinas wrote his *Summa Theologica*; nor did it change in size when the astronomy of Galileo, Copernicus, Kepler, and Newton was substituted for that of Ptolemy. The telescopes of Galileo and Tycho Brahe made little difference because the observational power of their primitive instruments was so slight.

Under these circumstances it was almost impossible to prevent most Christians from imagining heaven as if it were a physical place up there beyond the visible sun, moon, and stars. So, too, the words "came down from heaven" and "ascended up to heaven" were imagined as physical directions. Even the phrase "resurrection of the body" led most Christians at that time to imagine heaven as a place where the physical bodies as well as the souls of the blessed would live together in eternal life after their earthly death. Whether any Christian theologians during these centuries totally escaped making such grave errors, I do not know. Their writings are not explicitly clear on these points.

Unfortunately as I found out at my Aspen conference in 1991, there are still many persons of Christian faith who hang on to these ancient and mediaeval superstitions about heaven. They appear to be disappointed when told that they are not going to rejoin their departed loved ones in a bodily reunion in an afterlife in the world to come. This is true even of those who have been informed by twentieth-century cosmology about the millions of galaxies beyond the one constellation in which our tiny solar system exists. They have been informed about the recession of the furthest galaxies known to us; and those acquainted with Albert Einstein may even remember his statement that the universe is finite but unbounded.

For there to be factual, as distinguished from poetical, truth in Christian theology in the twentieth century, it must be consistent and compatible with what we now know about the physical universe in terms of twentieth-century cosmology. We cannot allow our imaginations to give physical meaning to such words as "up there," "out there," or even "beyond" the physical cosmos. As a purely spiritual realm is simply *other than* the realm of physical, material, corporeal things.

It should always have been so understood though the error in thinking otherwise of heaven may have been more excusable when Christians in antiquity and the Middle Ages were misled by imagining heaven as if it were a place in the physical universe.[9]

If heaven as well as hell are purely spiritual places, then our understanding of them must turn on our relation to God, whose kingdom is in heaven. Heaven is the place where those who love God are in the presence of God and where they enjoy heavenly rest in the beatific vision or contemplation of God. Hell is the place where those who do not love God deprive themselves of God's love, and of the knowledge of God through the beatific vision. The damned in hell do not suffer bodily fires or tortures. Their punishment is a pain of loss, not of sense.

I concluded the Christ Episcopal Church conference in 1991 by asking why we should not expect progress in Christian theology in the centuries to come. If we abide by Augustine's second precept for interpreting Sacred Scriptures, we should look forward to changes and improvements in Christian theology that are in accord with progress in our scientific knowledge.

I will not live long enough to see the unforeseeable changes and improvements that are bound to occur; but on one point about the

9. It may be asked why Holy Scripture is filled with metaphorical—metaphorical not analogical—language that gives many of its narrative passages the aspect of myth rather than factual historical truth. Does not such metaphorical language impel readers of Scripture to use their imagination rather than their intellect?

The answer given by Thomas Aquinas to these questions is very much to the point. He wrote: "It is befitting [for] Holy Writ to put forward divine and spiritual truths under the likenesses of material things. For God provides for everything according to the capacity of its nature. Now it is natural to man to attain to intellectual truths through sensible things, because all our knowledge originates from sense. Hence in Holy Writ spiritual truths are fittingly taught under the metaphors of [sensible] material things."

In this respect, Aquinas goes on to say, Holy Writ is like poetry, but it differs from poetry in that Sacred Scripture "makes use of metaphors as both necessary and useful" for the learning of divine and spiritual truths. (Thomas Aquinas, *Summa Theologica,* Pt. I, Q. 1, Art. 9, Response and Reply to Obj. 1).

future, I may be excusably blind. I do not foresee future progress in our scientific knowledge that will require any advances in philosophical theology. I feel secure in my rational affirmation of God's existence and of my understanding of the chasm between that philosophical conclusion and belief in God. I thank God for the leap of faith that enabled me to cross that chasm.

NOTE TO CHAPTER 9

Excerpt from "God and the Professors"* (Paper Presented at the First Conference on Science, Philosophy and Religion, New York City, September 10, 1940)

With respect to religion, the following propositions must be affirmed. He who denies any one of them denies religion, in any sense which makes it distinct in character from science and philosophy. (1) Religion involves knowledge of God and of man's destiny, knowledge which is not naturally acquired in the sense in which both science and philosophy are natural knowledge. (2) Religious faith, on which sacred theology rests, is itself a supernatural act of the human intellect, and is thus a Divine gift. (3) Because God is its cause, faith is more certain than knowledge resulting from the purely natural action of the human faculties. (4) What is known by faith about God's nature and man's destiny is knowledge which exceeds the power of the human intellect to attain without God's revelation of Himself and His Providence. (5) Sacred theology is independent of philosophy, in that its principles are truths of faith, whereas philosophical principles are truths of reason, but this does not mean that theology can be speculatively developed without reason serving faith. (6) There can be no conflict between philosophical and theological truths, although theologians may correct the errors of philosophers who try to answer questions beyond the competence of natural reason, just as philoso-

*Adler, "God and the Professors," *Science, Philosophy and Religion: A Symposium* (Conference on Science, Philosophy and Religion in Their Relation to the Democratic Way of Life, Inc., September 9–11, 1940). New York, 1941, Chapter VII, pp. 130–134.

phers can correct the errors of theologians who violate the autonomy of reason. (7) Sacred theology is superior to philosophy, both theoretically and practically: theoretically, because it is more perfect knowledge of God and His creatures; practically, because moral philosophy is insufficient to direct man to God as his last end. (8) Just as there are no systems of philosophy, but only philosophical knowledge less or more adequately possessed by different men, so there is only one true religion, less or more adequately embodied in the existing diversity of creeds.

These eight propositions, like those concerning philosophy, are far from exhaustive. They are intended simply as a device to bring professional positivism—or shall I call it "negativism?"—out into the open. Those who claim to respect the distinct place of religion in modern culture, but refuse to grant that religion rests upon supernatural knowledge, or that it is superior to both philosophy and science, either know not what they say or are guilty of profound hypocrisy. For unless religion involves supernatural knowledge, it has no separate status whatsoever; and if it rests upon supernatural knowledge, it must be accorded the supreme place in the cultural hierarchy.

Religion cannot be regarded as just another aspect of culture, one among many human occupations, of indifferent importance along with science and art, history and philosophy. Religion is either the supreme human discipline, because it is God's discipline of man, and as such dominates our culture, or it has no place at all. The mere toleration of religion, which implies indifference to or denial of its claims, produces a secularized culture as much as militant atheism or Nazi nihilism.

Philosophers who think that all the significant questions men ask are either answerable by reason or not at all, are naturalists in a sense analogous to the positivism of scientists who think that science alone is valid knowledge, and that science is enough for the conduct of life. If the professors are positivists, they are certainly naturalists. They dishonor themselves as well as religion by tolerating it when, all equivocations overcome, they really think that faith is superstition, just as they really think philosophy is opinion. The kind of positivism and naturalism which is revealed in all their works and all their teaching, is at the root of modern secularized culture. . . .

The central problem of mediaeval culture was the relation of faith and reason, religion and philosophy, supernatural and natural knowledge. The so-called mediaeval synthesis, the cultural harmony and unity of the mediaeval world, depended on the solution of that problem. It was not solved by conferences, although in the middle ages something much better than conferences of this sort took place: patient, honest, forthright, hard-thinking discussions.

Centuries of earnest disputation, despised by modern professors as logic-chopping and wordy dialectic, prepared the way, because in every case the disputants were seeking to agree about the truth, not to maintain their individuality by holding to a difference of opinion. When, after such preparation, the time was ripe, two men solved the problem by sheer intellectual mastery of every relevant truth: Moses Maimonides solved it for the Jewish community, and St. Thomas Aquinas for the Christian world. That later Jews and Christians did not sustain the solution, or even repudiated it, was part of the cultural tragedy which the modern era went through at its birth.

The central problem of modern culture is more complicated, and much more difficult, than the mediaeval, because in our times science has become a distinct and important enterprise, both theoretically and practically. The modern synthesis, the harmony and unity of modern culture, will be achieved only when all the goodness of science can be praised without sacrificing any of the goodness in philosophy and religion, only when the truths of philosophy and religion can be integrally retained without losing any of the genuine advances in knowledge or production that science has contributed.

The modern synthesis must necessarily include the mediaeval solution, but it can do so only by carrying the mediaeval principles to a higher level of comprehension. In order that every cultural good shall be preserved to the fullness of its own unique value, each must be recognized precisely for what it is, and according to its distinctive character it must be ordered to the others. Since in the world of values, there is no order without hierarchy, science, philosophy and religion can never be harmonized so long as they are all asked to lie down together, but only when each is called upon to perform its proper function, whether that be to serve or to rule.

The time is obviously not yet ripe for a modern solution. There are not enough scientists who understand the truths of philosophy and religion, nor enough philosophers and men of faith who are at home in the domain of science. Much work by representatives of all three disciplines is required to prepare the way for the modern analogue of Maimonides or Aquinas, perhaps even centuries of patient discussion and incisive disputation.

This Conference might have been an occasion for such work. That it was called at all indicates a vague realization of the task to be undertaken. But if I am right about the professorial mind—and I look to the actual proceedings of this Conference for confirmation—there will be no discussion of fundamental issues, nor even a formulation of them. The members of this Conference are not co-operatively seeking to agree about the truth, through the painful ordeal of intellectual debate. Each is content to express his own opinions, and to indulge everyone else in the opportunity for similar self-expression.

CHAPTER 10

THE BLESSINGS OF GOOD FORTUNE

Early in life I learned a lesson from Aristotle. Whether or not we succeed in having lived a good life is not entirely a matter of free choice and moral virtue. Virtue is certainly a necessary condition; it may even be the most important factor; but by itself it is not sufficient. The other necessary, but also insufficient, condition is having good fortune.

Fortune, good or bad, plays a part in everyone's life. The accidents of fortune are the things that happen to you. When good luck happens, you may aid and abet it by seizing the opportunities it affords, but its happening to you is beyond your control. The only things entirely within your own power are the things you freely choose to do, and even some of these require attendant good fortune for them to be fully achieved. You may take care of your health by virtuous conduct on your part, but your achievement of a healthy body may also require a healthy environment, which may or may not be your good fortune to enjoy.[1]

In a book in which I have recited the free choices I made to devote myself to teaching and learning, to writing books and editing them, and above all to the vocation of philosophy, it seems fitting that at its close I should briefly recount the incidents of good fortune with which I have been blessed.

1. In my youth, I went through serious influenza and poliomyelitis epidemics unharmed. Through diligent care by my parents I escaped being ill but that was still a blessing of good fortune.

2

With the exception of one's mate, one does not choose one's family—parents, siblings, offspring, and in-laws. In these respects, I experienced good fortune, but not entirely. My parents came from good stock, as evidenced by their longevity and my own. I am grateful to them not only for the genes they bestowed on me, but also for their wise and benevolent treatment of me as a child, a schoolboy, and a college student.

My mother was a schoolteacher, disposed to encourage study on my part. My father's German upbringing led him to demand excellence in that performance. Anything less than an A-A-A report card from school was severely frowned upon. In addition, I had the good luck of being their firstborn child, as my sister, Carolyn, will testify about the less-privileged status of being the second child.

Though marriage falls within the range of free choice, it is also partly attended by unforseeable consequences that are in the realm of chance. I was less fortunate in my first marriage than in my second. At my eightieth birthday party, I proposed, with regard to marriage, the maxim that if you don't succeed at first, try again. I did, and it has worked wonderfully well. I think I summed this up at Caroline's fiftieth birthday party, when I toasted her as "my best friend and severest critic."

It has been said that the smile on Adam's face in the Garden of Eden betrays his enjoyment of the fact that he had no mother-in-law. In spite of the fact that Eleanor Pring, Caroline's mother, was my mother-in-law, I still smile about my association with her and with Caroline's two sisters, Polly and Margaret. The family I married into by choice has been, by good luck, as good for me as the family of my birth.

Having two adopted sons in my first marriage with Helen was clearly a matter of choice. My second marriage with Caroline gave birth to two children, both boys, also matters of choice. But how Mark and Michael, the first two, and Douglas and Philip, the second two, have turned out has not been entirely within my control, or within Helen's or Caroline's.

I found the job of being a father taxing and difficult. I am quick to confess that I sometimes shirked my duties, did not devote enough of my time and energy to being a parent, and, in addition, was probably not temperamentally inclined to do better. Much that happened in the course of their upbringing may have been my fault, which I regret and for which I have tried to make amends, differently in each of the four cases. The four boys have matured at different rates of speed and under different circumstances, but the good fortune that I can now report is that they have finally developed into good human beings, enjoyable to be with, as well as good citizens. Only the first two, Mark and Michael, are now married and have children—my grandchildren—to whom they are good parents. I hope I live long enough to see the other two, Douglas and Philip, married and with anticipated offspring.

3

After one's family, comes one's friends. Here, too, I have been extremely fortunate. In a sense, of course, one chooses one's friends, but acquaintance with the individuals with whom one later elects to develop a friendship is a happenstance.

Two individuals whom I became acquainted with accidentally because they happened to be students of mine in my early years of teaching at Columbia University, Clifton Fadiman and Jacques Barzun, have developed into lifelong friends, and have also become the friends of my wife, Caroline. I cannot recount all the ways in which friendship with them has influenced my life and my work; I am grateful that they have grown old along with me and are still alive.

The third friend of my early years, no longer alive, was Robert Hutchins, but as long as he lived, he and I were close friends. But my good fortune in meeting Bob in 1927 when he was acting Dean of the Yale School, was both so accidental and so consequential, that I must repeat here the story about it that I told in *Philosopher at Large.*[2]

2. *Philosopher at Large,* pp. 107–111.

In 1925–1926, I wrote my first book, *Dialectic,* published in 1927. In it, while describing the process of argument and disputation, I dropped a footnote which said that this process is exemplified in the Anglo-American law of evidence. C. K. Ogden was editor of the series in which that book was published, and while visiting Hutchins at the Yale School early in 1927, Ogden was carrying the page proofs of one thirty-two-page unit from my book. It just happened to include the page in which I had placed that footnote about the Anglo-American law of evidence. While talking to Hutchins about other matters, Ogden mentioned me in a complimentary fashion and gave Hutchins the thirty-two-page unit of page proof he had been carrying in his pocket. So far, everything that happened was *pure chance.*

At that time, Hutchins was not only Acting Dean, but was also Professor of the Law of Evidence. The footnote caught his attention and, in June, he wrote me a letter, mentioning the footnote which he thought signified that I had a lively interest in the law of evidence. He invited me to come up to New Haven sometime that summer to discuss with him problems in the laws of evidence on which he was currently working.

Now free choice came into play. Up to that point, I knew just enough about the law of evidence to make that footnote I had written substantially correct, but nothing more. I must have thought at the time that the invitation from Hutchins opened up an academic opportunity of which I should take advantage. So I wrote to Hutchins accepting his invitation and setting the time for my visit to New Haven in early August.

I then spent the intervening time in July studying the law of evidence, by taking out of the law library J. H. Wigmore's five-volume classic textbook on the subject. Since the brief opening pages of each chapter contained Wigmore's explanation of the law on that subject, followed by pages of discussion of cases in the federal and the forty-eight state jurisdictions, I could read through Wigmore's five volumes, skipping all the pages dealing with cases.

As it turned out, when I met with Bob Hutchins in August, I appeared to him to have a firm grasp of the underlying principles of the law of evidence, and we hit it off in general. Shortly after my visit, I received a letter from him inviting me to leave Columbia and join him in New Haven to work with him on some essays he was planning to write about the psychological and philosophical aspects of certain rules of evidence, especially the hearsay rule.

I turned his invitation down, for no other reason, so far as I can remember, other than my unwillingness to change my residence from Manhattan Island, where I had been born and reared, to what, in comparison, was the sleepy little village of New Haven. My refusal to move to New Haven did not divert Hutchins from his aim to get me involved in work on the law of evidence.

He came down to New York to persuade Young B. Smith, then Dean of the Columbia Law School, to have me work with Jerome Michael, his Professor of the Procedural Law of Pleading and Evidence. I did so, while still remaining an instructor in psychology. We co-authored a book, entitled *The Nature of Judicial Proof: An Inquiry into the Logical, Legal, and Empirical Aspects of the Law of Evidence,* published in 1931.

Not only did that result in my friendship with Jerome Michael as long as he lived, and with whom I wrote another book, *Crime, Law and Social Science,* published in 1933, but it also led to a whole series of fortuitous consequences that represented a train of good fortune at work in the making of my life.

First of all, when Hutchins in 1929 became, at the age of thirty, President of the University of Chicago, he invited me to join him there as an associate professor in three areas—in the philosophy and psychology departments and in the law school. My salary as a Columbia instructor, $2,400 a year, was to be increased to $6,000. Quite apart from that advantage, I had the good sense to perceive greater academic opportunities for me at Chicago than I would have had had if I had remained at Columbia. Since I was not yet disillusioned about the "joys" of academic life, I went to Chicago, not only to teach in the philosophy and psychology departments and in the law school, but primarily to conduct a great books seminar for entering freshman in the college, with Bob Hutchins as my co-moderator. That was an opportunity I could not turn down, and my taking it has had many consequences, all fortunate for me.

William Benton had been a classmate of Bob Hutchins at Yale. After he retired from the advertising firm of Benton and Bowles, Hutchins brought Benton to the University of Chicago, appointing him Vice-President in charge of Public Relations. Through my close association with Bob, I naturally came in contact with Bill Benton. This developed into a friendship that had many fortunate consequences for me, principally among which, after Benton became CEO of Enclyclopaedia Britannica, Inc., was my becoming Bob's Associate Editor of the first edition of *Great Books of the Western World,* my producing the *Syntopicon* that went with that set, my eventually succeeding Bob Hutchins as Chairman of the Britannica's Board of Editors, and my becoming Editor in Chief of the second edition of *Great Books of the Western World.*

That is not all the good fortune that derived from my friendship with Bob Hutchins. He departed in 1951 from the University of Chicago to become Vice-President of the Ford Foundation. By that time I had become completely fed up with academic life, and, as a result of my creating the *Syntopicon,* I wished to spend my philosophical energies on producing the Summa Dialectica, a project I had conceived in 1927 when I wrote *Dialectic.* I could not do that as a Professor of Law, which I had then become at the University of Chicago.

In 1952, through Bob's good auspices, I received a large grant from the Fund for the Advancement of Education, established by the Ford Foundation to establish the Institute for Philosophical Research, of which I have been the President since 1952. The Institute produced the two volumes of *The Idea of Freedom,* after eight years of research and writing. It later produced dialectical treatments of the ideas of justice, happiness, love, progress, beauty, and religion and, after operating in San Francisco from 1952 to 1963, it was moved to Chicago by Bill Benton when he wanted me there to work editorially for Encyclopaedia Britannica, while at the same time directing the work of the Institute for Philosophical Research.

As I have said earlier in this book, if I had remained at the University of Chicago after Bob Hutchins left it, I could never have done the philosophical work that has been the joy of my last forty years. Bob's enabling me to leave the University of Chicago and all the distractions and intrigues of academic life, and his enabling me to establish the Institute for Philosophical Research as the ivory tower in which the kind of philosophical work I wished to do could be accomplished, was certainly the greatest stroke of good fortune in my professional life.

I am still not finished with Bob Hutchins as my guardian angel. It was through his friendship with Walter and Elizabeth Paepcke that I also became their friends, and it was through them (as I have related earlier) that I became involved in the Aspen Institute after Walter established it in 1950. Meyer Kestnbaum, CEO of Hart Schaffner and Marx, another friend of Hutchins and mine, brought the Institute for Philosophical Research to the attention of Arthur Houghton, Jr., at a conference held at the Corning Glass Works that Arthur attended. I subsequently met Arthur at a conference in New York, which was sponsored by the Institute for Philosophical Research while it was working on the idea of freedom. That led to Arthur Houghton's becoming a substantial contributor to the budget of the Institute after the Ford Foundation grant expired; and, more important than that, Caroline and I developed a close friendship with Arthur, with whom we traveled extensively abroad.

There is still one further consequence of my friendship with Bob Hutchins. He introduced me to Henry Luce, the co-founder of *Time* magazine, and to his wife Clare, both of whom, as I have related, came to Aspen in August of 1950. We became friends and Caroline's and my friendship with Clare continued many years after Henry's death.[3]

I do not know this for a fact, but I think Clare had something to do with the cover story in *Time* about me and the *Syntopicon,* written by Henry Grunwald, who was then Senior Editor under Otto Fuerbringer as Managing Editor. In any case, I have enjoyed my friendship with Henry Grunwald in the subsequent years when he became Managing Editor of *Time* and then Editor-in-Chief of Time Inc.; and, after retiring from that position, became U.S. Am-

3. Once, when I dined with the Luces in Chicago, Harry asked me why, before the election in 1948, I predicted that Truman would win it. *Time* had predicted that Dewey would win. I told them that *Time* also reported that the audiences before which Truman spoke were getting larger and larger, while Dewey's audiences were shrinking. That was enough to persuade me that Truman would probably win.

bassador to Austria. Caroline and I visited him and his wife Louise in Vienna and spent an enjoyable weekend at the Ambassador's residence there.

Mentioning my involvement in the Aspen Institute as a fortuitous consequence of the great good fortune of my friendship with Bob Hutchins, I must also mention one other fortunate happenstance. Larry Aldrich, a famous dress designer, came to Aspen to participate in one of my seminars there early in the 1970s. Since then, Caroline and I have become close friends with Larry and his wife Wynn. We have traveled with them on many pleasant excursions here and abroad. Larry, having retired from the dress business, established the Aldrich Museum of Contemporary Art, in Ridgefield, Connecticut. His knowledge and expertise in the field of the visual arts has enriched my life; Wynn's knowledge of cuisines and gourmet skill in cooking, which my wife Caroline shared, sent them abroad together to cooking schools in Paris and Bologna.

4

I hope I have now made clear how one stroke of great good fortune—in this case, my friendship with Bob Hutchins—led to a train of consequences, all of them fortunate happenings. There are still others that I have not so far mentioned, friendships that have been fortunate for me, but not connected with Bob Hutchins.

One was the influence on my life of my friend Arthur Rubin, a friendship that began in the library of the Psychology Department at Columbia when I was still an undergraduate student in the college. This continued until his death. He saw me through the ordeal of my divorce from Helen and later celebrated my marriage to Caroline. He was extremely helpful to me in the rearing of our children.

One thing that I should not forget to mention was the inspiration I got from Arthur for the production of the Summa Dialectica at the time I talked to C. K. Ogden about the idea for my first book.

That, by the way, was another lucky happenstance. I met Ogden at a tea party given by Gardner Murphy, an associate of mine in the Psychology Department. Ogden mentioned a book he was editing by Boris Bogslavsky, to be entitled *The Art of Controversy.* It was that title, I think, which prompted me to outline another approach to the clarification and resolution of philosophical conflicts. Whatever I said caught and held Ogden's attention. He then and there invited me to submit a draft of the book I had outlined. That was in November. I wrote the book over the Christmas recess and during the January examination period, and delivered it to Ogden on the first of February.

Another of my lifelong friendships began when I taught a course in the Laboratory School of the University of Chicago. Philip Rosenthal was a student in that class. After that chance encounter, we met again many years later when we were both guests of Mortimer and Janet Fleishhacker on a cruise of the Greek islands. He helped me through many difficulties in my last years in San Francisco, difficulties both personal and professional. Since then, Philip has spent many summer weeks with Caroline and me in Aspen where, auditing my seminars, he has renewed our relationship as student and teacher.

A third has been the friendship that Caroline and I developed with Andrew and Shawn Block in Chicago, resulting from the fact that their children and ours were pupils in the elementary grades at Francis W. Parker School. Shawn and Caroline were thrown together by their interest in the affairs of the school. Out of that blossomed the warm friendship that has enriched our subsequent years in Chicago.

Glancing over the pages of *Philosopher at Large* to jog my memory of blessings that have befallen me, I found one of great importance to my life as a whole, one so important that I should not overlook it here. It is the fact that, with very few exceptions, all the work I have done in my life has consisted of activities that I consider leisuring rather than toiling; in other words, activities that one would engage in if one did not need monetary compensation for doing so, as opposed to the kind of drudgery that no one would undertake without being compensated for it. Let me quote the paragraph from *Philosopher at Large* that eloquently describes this fortunate circumstance.

> Looking back on my life since I left home, I count myself unusually fortunate that, during more than fifty years of earning a living, almost all the work I have elected to do has consisted of tasks that I would gladly have taken on even if I had had an independent income. If leisure work, as opposed to drudgery, comprises all those activities in which one would engage for reasons of intrinsic reward and without need of extrinsic compensation, then most of my paid employments have been largely leisure pursuits. . . . In between the extremes of subsistence work that is drudgery and leisure work for which one is paid, there lies a spectrum of occupations in which both aspects of work are found in varying degrees of admixture. My good fortune has been that I have had the opportunity to choose the occupations of my life so that they would be predominantly filled with leisure [pursuits].[4]

Last but not least was my good fortune to have been invited to teach a great books seminar with Mark Van Doren beginning in October 1923, after I had just completed my two-year stint of reading and discussing the great books with John Erskine in my junior and senior year in college at Columbia University.

Suppose that that had never happened. Suppose that after being graduated from college, I went to law school or into business. I might never had gone back to reading the great books again, under the illusion that I had mastered them in my first reading of them. After all, had I not graduated with honors? For all intents and purposes, was not my superior literacy confirmed by the high grades I received?

In my first two years of reading the same books that I had read as a student with Erskine, but now reading them again in order to collaborate with Mark Van Doren to discuss them with our students, my eyes were opened to the fact that I had not understood them very well, if at all, on my first reading. In the next five or six years, that discovery was repeated again and again, as I learned more each time I reread the same books I had read before.

Now at the end of my life, still rereading the great books that I started reading seventy years ago, I can summarize this whole process by repeating two insights mentioned before in this book:

4. Ibid., p. 327.

(1) the great books are the books that are inexhaustibly rereadable for both intellectual pleasure and profit: (2) understanding the ideas to be found in the great books develops slowly in the course of one's whole life, bearing its best fruits in one's mature years after fifty or sixty.

This does not complete my recollection of the wonderful seven years I spent co-moderating great books seminars with Mark Van Doren. I became close friends with Mark and his wife Dorothy, quite apart from our academic association as teachers. I gazed upon their two sons, Charles and John, when they were still in their cradles at the hospital in which they were born. Both Charles and John have been my friends ever since they have grown to manhood. Both have been my associates at the Institute for Philosophical Research, in editorial work for Encyclopaedia Britannica, Inc., and in the Paideia school reform project.

I cannot recall all the details of that friendship with the Van Dorens while I was still living in New York and teaching at Columbia, and when I went on many visits to New York after I moved to Chicago. But bright in my memory is Scott Buchanan, whom I met at Columbia, whose first book *Possibility* was published by C. K. Ogden along with my first book *Dialectic,* and who later, after coming to the University of Chicago to work with Hutchins and me, became Dean of St. John's College, and innovator of the New Program there.

He and I were closely associated in our friendship with the Van Dorens. All of us spent our summers in Cornwall, Connecticut, where the Van Dorens had a house on one side of the valley, and where Scott and Miriam Buchanan had another house on the other side, which Helen, my first wife, and I shared.

I recently found in my files two items that help to complete the picture of those years. They paint a portrait of me that is flattering to an embarrassing degree. I hope I can be forgiven the immodesty of quoting them here. I do so because I cannot myself remember the details of my behavior in the ambience of my relationship to the Van Dorens and the Buchanans.

The first item is an excerpt from the Foreward written by Dorothy Van Doren to a collection of her husband Mark's letters. It follows:

Another friend with whom my husband corresponded was Mortimer Adler. Mark knew Adler slightly as a student, but shortly after Adler graduated, they shared a section of the General Honors course, the forerunner of the humanities series. Adler was lively, enormously energetic, a great talker, and incomparably intelligent. They had a great time together, and my husband felt that he had to work his hardest to keep up with this volatile, yet deadly serious student. In his *Autobiography,* Mark writes, "he would talk so fast that his tongue, as I told him, fell over itself." Soon they began to see each other away from the university, and as with so many of Mark's friends, the wives were included. After the General Honors class, on Wednesday evenings as I remember, I would meet the two men at the Adler apartment and Helen Adler would make muffins for us. I particularly remember the four flights of stairs I had to climb, as our son Charles was born that winter. My husband has always said that he learned everything he knew about philosophy from Adler and Buchanan, and a great deal from Adler about poetry, which Adler denies. At any rate, the friendship flourished for more than forty years.[5]

The second item is an excerpt from a letter written by Mark Van Doren to his son John in 1946.

I have been thinking over one part of your letter, the part about wise men, and have collected this thought about Mortimer [Adler]. He may not be wise, but he makes other men wise; he is almost the necessary condition for wisdom in others. They resist him, correct him, soften him, relax him, interpret him, and in the process feel superior to him; but there he is all the time, furiously thinking and speaking, and fanatically faithful to the truth—and that is precious too. He has made Scott wiser—by reaction—than he was, and so I think with each of his friends. He is an angelic dope, and as such they worship him. They couldn't do what he does even if they tried. Their wisdom has a negative feel when he's around, as God's does, maybe, when he contemplates the sons of men. He is greater than they, but only they could make him know it. This, I'm sure, is one reason he loves them. Or put it this way, Mortimer alone among

5. Dorothy Van Doren, "Foreword," to *The Selected Letters of Mark Van Doren,* edited, with an Introduction, by George Hendrick, Baton Rouge and London, Louisiana State University Press, 1987, p. 4. Reprinted by permission of the author.

> the men we know is irreplaceable. The rest are more or less wise, but whatever he is, he is absolutely. . . .[6]

As I now reread these two extracts, I can only say that I think William Wordsworth was wrong in that line of his about the Child being father of the Man; though I share the sentiment expressed in the two lines that follow:

> And I could wish my days to be
> Bound each to each by natural piety.

6. Mark Van Doren to John Van Doren, January 25, 1946, *The Selected Letters of Mark Van Doren,* edited by George Hendrick, Baton Rouge and London, Louisana State University Press, 1987. pp. 178–179. Reprinted by permission.

EPILOGUE

Chapter 14 of *Philosopher at Large*—the chapter dealing with my philosophical career—concludes with the following paragraph:

> In the years ahead, if by good fortune they should turn out to be sufficient for the purpose, I would like to complete the picture by writing a book dealing with some of the most difficult, and most central, of philosophical problems—the problems of metaphysics, questions about being and becoming, about the modes of being, about existence and nonexistence, and about the existence of God. Whether or not I shall ever be able to resolve the difficulties I have encountered in all earlier attempts to construct a valid proof of God's existence, the best judgment I can reach about the matter would, in my opinion, be a fitting close not only to that book, which remains to be written, but also to my philosophical career.

That was written more than fifteen years ago when I was approaching the age of seventy-five. I have written many books since then, including *How to Think About God,* in which I presented my mature effort to prove the existence of God. But I have not yet written the book that deals with the most central and most difficult of philosophical problems—the problems of metaphysics.

Now at the age of ninety, it is difficult to make plans for the future without saying *Deo volente* in every sentence. Nevertheless, I have discussed with my publisher the titles and outlines of three books that I hope I will live long enough to write, God willing.

One, to be published in 1993, is a book entitled *Philosophy: Its Four Dimensions*, in a major part of which I would like to consider the questions about being and becoming, about the modes of being, and about existence and nonexistence.

A second book, to be published in 1994, is one entitled *Art, the Arts, and the Great Ideas*, in which I hope to deal with all the manifestations of art, both useful and fine, and both liberal and servile, not just the visual arts of painting, etching, and sculpture.

Finally, in 1995, I would like to do a useful summing up of all the philosophical insights and clarifications that I have accumulated in my long life, by doing for the twenty-first century what Voltaire did for the Enlightenment in the eighteenth century.

Since philosophical discourse should be expressed in the language of ordinary speech, avoiding all technical jargon, the words of everyday speech must be used with great precision.

In the eighteenth century, Voltaire wrote *A Philosophical Dictionary,* expressing a wide range of philosophical insights by expounding the meaning of ordinary words in the alphabetical order of a *lexicon*. Borrowing that title and method from Voltaire, I would like to do the same for a vocabulary that is rich in philosophical significance, with the hope that it will help to clarify the thought of the next century.

Beyond that, I have made no plans for the future that remains.

BIBLIOGRAPHY OF MORTIMER J. ADLER

Compiled by Otto A. Bird, Sue Montgomery, and Marlys G. Allen

Books

1927

Dialectic, London, Kegan Paul, Trench Trubner & Co., Ltd., and New York, Harcourt, Brace and Company, Inc., 1927.

1929

Music Appreciation: An Experimental Approach to Its Measurement, New York, *Archives of Psychology,* No. 110, 1929 (Ph.D. dissertation).

1931

(with Jerome Michael) *The Nature of Judicial Proof: An Inquiry into the Logical, Legal, and Empirical Aspects of the Law of Evidence,* New York, Columbia University Law School, 1931.

1932

(with Maude Phelps Hutchins) *Diagrammatics,* New York, Random House, Inc., 1935.

1933

(with Jerome Michael) *Crime, Law and Social Science,* London, Kegan Paul, Trench Trubner & Co., Ltd., and New York, Harcourt, Brace and Company, 1933; reprinted with Introduction by Gilbert Geis, Montclair, N.J., Patterson Smith, 1971.

1937

Art and Prudence: A Study in Practical Philosophy, New York and Toronto, Longmans, Green and Co., 1937; Chapters 1–5; 12, reprinted with Introduction by Samuel Hazo as *Poetry and Politics,* Pittsburgh, Pa., Duquesne University Press, 1965.

What Man Has Made of Man: A Study of the Consequences of Platonism and Positivism in Psychology (based on the lectures given at the Institute for Psychoanalysis in Chicago, 1937), Introduction by Dr. Franz Alexander, New York and Toronto, Longmans, Green and Co., 1937, reprinted New York, Frederick Ungar Publishing Co., 1957; as *The Consequences of Platonism and Positivism*, New Brunswick, N.J., Transaction Publishers, Rutgers University, 1993.

1938

Saint Thomas and the Gentiles (The Aquinas Lecture), Milwaukee, Wis., Marquette University Press, 1938.

1940

Problems for Thomists: The Problem of Species, New York, Sheed & Ward, 1940.

The Philosophy and Science of Man: A Collection of Texts as a Foundation for Ethics and Politics, The University of Chicago Bookstore, 1940 (mimeograph).

How to Read a Book: The Art of Getting a Liberal Education, New York, Simon and Schuster, Inc., 1940.

1941

A Dialectic of Morals, Towards the Foundations of Political Philosophy, Notre Dame, Ind., University of Notre Dame Press, 1941, reprinted New York, Frederick Ungar Publishing Co., 1958.

1944

How to Think About War and Peace, New York, Simon and Schuster, Inc., 1944.

1954

Research on Freedom, 2 vols., San Francisco, Institute for Philosophical Research, 1954.

1958

(with Milton Mayer) *The Revolution in Education,* Introduction by Clarence Faust, Chicago, The University of Chicago Press, 1958.

(with Louis O. Kelso) *The Capitalist Manifesto,* New York, Random House, Inc., 1958, reprinted Westport, Conn., Greenwood Press, Publishers, 1975.

The Idea of Freedom: A Dialectical Examination of the Conceptions of Freedom, Volume 1, Garden City, N.Y., Doubleday & Company, Inc., 1958, reprinted Westport, Conn., Greenwood Press, Publishers, 1973.

1961

(with Louis O. Kelso) *The New Capitalists: A Proposal to Free Economic Growth from the Slavery of Savings,* New York, Random House, Inc., 1961, reprinted Westport, Conn., Greenwood Press, Publishers, 1975.

The Idea of Freedom: A Dialectical Examination of the Controversies about Freedom, Volume II, Garden City, N.Y., Doubleday & Company, Inc., 1961, reprinted Westport, Conn., Greenwood Press, Publishers, 1973.

Great Ideas from the Great Books (based on Questions and Answers from Syndicated Column), Introduction by William Benton, New York, Washington Square Press, 1961; Pocket Books, 1976.

1965

The Conditions of Philosophy: Its Checkered Past, Its Present Disorder, and Its Future Promise (based on the Encyclopaedia Britannica Lectures delivered at the University of Chicago, 1964). New York, Atheneum Publishers, 1965; New York, Delta Books, Dell Publishing Co., 1967.

1966

How to Read a Book: A Guide to Reading the Great Books, Special Edition, New York, Simon and Schuster, Inc., 1966.

1967

The Difference of Man and the Difference It Makes (based on the Encyclopaedia Britannica Lectures delivered at the University of Chicago, 1966), Introduction by Theodore T. Puck, New York, Holt, Rinehart and Winston, Inc., 1967.

1970

The Time of Our Lives: The Ethics of Common Sense (based on the Encyclopaedia Britannica Lectures delivered at the University of Chicago, 1969), New York, Holt, Rinehart and Winston, Inc., 1970.

1971

The Common Sense of Politics (based on the Encyclopaedia Britannica Lectures delivered at the University of Chicago, 1970), New York, Holt, Rinehart and Winston, Inc., 1971.

1972

(with Charles Van Doren) *How to Read a Book: The Classic Guide to Intelligent Reading,* Revised and Updated Edition, New York, Simon and Schuster, Inc., 1972; Touchstone Books, 1972.

1975

(with William Gorman) *The American Testament,* New York, Praeger Publishers, Inc., 1975.

1976

Some Questions About Language: A Theory of Human Discourse and Its Objects, La Salle, Ill., Open Court Publishing Co., 1976; First Paperback Edition, 1991.

1977

Philosopher at Large: An Intellectual Autobiography, New York, Macmillan Publishing Company, 1977; Collier Books, 1992.

Reforming Education: The Schooling of a People and Their Education Beyond Schooling, Edited by Geraldine Van Doren, Boulder, Colo., Westview Press, 1977.

1978

Aristotle for Everybody: Difficult Thought Made Easy, New York, Macmillan Publishing Company, 1978; Bantam Books, 1980; Collier Books, 1991.

1980

How to Think About God: A Guide for the 20th-Century Pagan, New York, Macmillan Publishing Company, 1980; Bantam Books, 1982, 1988; Collier Books, 1991.

1981

Six Great Ideas, New York, Macmillan Publishing Company, 1981; Collier Books, 1984.

1982

The Angels and Us, New York, Macmillan Publishing Company, 1982; Collier Books, 1988.

(On Behalf of the Paideia Group) *The Paideia Proposal: An Educational Manifesto,* New York, Collier Books, Macmillan Publishing Company, 1982.

1983

How to Speak/How to Listen, New York, Macmillan Publishing Company, 1983; Collier Books, 1985.

(On Behalf of the Paideia Group) *Paideia Problems and Possibilities: A Consideration of Questions Raised by* The Paideia Proposal, New York, Collier Books, Macmillan Publishing Company, 1983.

1984

A Vision of the Future: Twelve Ideas for a Better Life and a Better Society, New York, Macmillan Publishing Company, 1984.

(with Members of the Paideia Group) *The Paideia Program: An Educational Syllabus,* New York, Collier Books, Macmillan Publishing Company, 1984.

1985

Ten Philosophical Mistakes, New York, Macmillan Publishing Company, 1985; Collier Books, 1987.

1986

A Guidebook to Learning: For a Lifelong Pursuit of Wisdom, New York, Macmillan Publishing Company, 1986.

1987

We Hold These Truths: Understanding the Ideas and Ideals of the Constitution, Foreword by Harry A. Blackmun, with Annotated Appendices by Wayne Moquin, New York, Macmillan Publishing Company, 1987; Collier Books, 1988.

1988

Reforming Education: The Opening of the American Mind, Edited by Geraldine Van Doren, New York, Macmillan Publishing Company, 1988; Collier Books, 1990.

1990

Intellect: Mind Over Matter, New York, Macmillan Publishing Company, 1990.

Truth in Religion: The Plurality of Religions and the Unity of Truth, New York, Macmillan Publishing Company, 1990, Collier Books, 1992.

1991

Haves Without Have-Nots: Essays for the 21st Century on Democracy and Socialism, New York, Macmillan Publishing Company, 1991.

Desires, Right & Wrong: The Ethics of Enough, New York, Macmillan Publishing Company, 1991.

1992

The Great Ideas: A Lexicon of Western Thought, New York, Macmillan Publishing Company, 1992.

A Second Look in the Rearview Mirror, New York, Macmillan Publishing Company, 1992.

Articles

1927

"The Human Equation in Dialectic," *Psyche,* 28 (April 1927), 68–82.

"Spengler, The Spenglerites, and Spenglerism," *Psyche,* 29 (July 1927), 73–84.

1931

"Legal Certainty," in "Law and the Modern Mind: A Symposium," *Columbia Law Review,* XXXI (January 1931), 91–108.

1933

"A Determination of Useful Observables," in "A Symposium on the Observability of Social Phenomena with Respect to Statistical Analysis," *Sociologus,* 9 (March 1933), 38–44.

1934

(with Jerome Michael) "The Trial of an Issue of Fact," *Columbia Law Review,* XXXIV (November–December 1934), 1–115.

"Art and Aesthetics," *Comment,* The University of Chicago Literary and Critical Quarterly, 2 (Winter 1934), 1–2.

1935

"Creation and Imitation: An Analysis of *Poiesis,*" *Proceedings of the American Catholic Philosophical Association,* December 1935, 153–174.

1937

"Tradition and Communication," *Proceedings of the American Catholic Philosophical Association,* December 1937, 101–131.

1938

"Reading," *The University of Chicago Magazine,* June 1938, 10–13.

1939

"A Christian Educator," *Orates Fratres,* XIII (January 22, 1939), Saint John's Abbey, Collegeville, Minn., Liturgical Press, 123–129, reprinted as an Afterword in *Liberal Education: Essays on the Philosophy of Higher Learning by Father Virgil Michel,* selected and edited by Robert L. Spaeth Collegeville, Minn., Office of Academic Affairs, Saint John's University, 1981, 67–72.

"Parties and the Common Good," *The Review of Politics,* 1 (January 1939), 51–83.

"The Crisis in Contemporary Education," *The Social Frontier,* V (February 1939), 140–145.

"Are the Schools Doing Their Job?" *Town Meeting,* Columbia University Press, 4 (March 6, 1939), 11–16.

"Education and Democracy," *The Commonweal,* XXIX (March 17, 1939), 581–583.

"Can Catholic Education Be Criticized?" *The Commonweal,* XXIX (April 14, 1939), 680–683.

"Hierarchy," *Saint Mary's Chimes,* XLVIII (June 1939), 111–116, reprinted *Catholic Digest,* 4 (October 1940), 39–43.

"Tradition and Novelty in Education," *Better Schools,* 1 (June 1939), 104; 108.

"Liberalism and Liberal Education," *The Educational Record,* July 1939, 422–436.

"Lesson in Criticism," *The Commonweal,* XXX (October 13, 1939), 548–551.

"The Demonstration of Democracy," *Proceedings of the American Catholic Philosophical Association,* December 1939, 1–44.

1940

"The Great Books: 1," *The University of Chicago Magazine,* February 1940, 10–11; 26–28.

"The Great Books: 2," *The University of Chicago Magazine,* March 1940, 8–10; 25–26.

"Education in Contemporary America," *Better Schools,* 2 (March–April 1940), 76–80.

"Docility and Authority," *The Commonweal,* XXXI (April 5, 1940), 504–507.

"Docility and History," *The Commonweal,* XXXII (April 26, 1940), 4–8.

"To the College Graduate—June, 1940," *The Commonweal,* XXXII (June 28, 1940), 201–203.

"How to Mark a Book," *The Saturday Review of Literature,* July 6, 1940, 11–12, reprinted *The Paideia Bulletin,* IV (September–October 1988), Chicago, Institute for Philosophical Research, 2–3.

"The Use and Abuse of Dictionaries," *Good Housekeeping,* September 1940, 160–161.

"How to Answer Questions," *Good Housekeeping,* October 1940, 73; 201–202.

"This Pre-War Generation," *Harper's Magazine,* October 1940, 524–534.

"God and the Professors" (A paper given at the First Conference on Science, Philosophy and Religion, September 1940), *Our Sunday Visitor,* A Weekly Catholic National Newspaper, December 1, 1940; *Science, Philosophy and Religion: A Symposium,* New York, Science, Philosophy and Religion in Their Relation to the Democratic Way of Life, Inc., 1941, 120–138.

"Before You Read a Book," *Good Housekeeping,* December 1940, 32–33.

"How To Keep Awake While Reading," *Good Housekeeping,* June 1940, 62.

1941

"Invitation to the Pain of Learning," *The Journal of Educational Sociology,* 14 (February 1941), 358–363.

"What Is Basic About English?" (An address at a general session of the National

Council of Teachers of English, November 1940), *College English,* 2 (April 1941), 653–675 (outline).
"The Demonstrability of Democracy: A Reply to Dr. [Charles] O'Neil," *The New Scholasticism,* XV (April 1941), 162–168.
"Solution of the Problem of Species," *The Thomist,* III (April 1941), 279–379.
(with Walter Farrell, O.P.) "The Theory of Democracy," *The Thomist,* III (July 1941), 397–449.
"Are There Absolute and Universal Principles on Which Education Should Be Founded?" (A debate in which Adler takes Pro view and Paul A. Schilpp takes Con), *Educational Trends,* Northwestern University, IX (July–August 1941), 11–18. [Adler's portion]
"The Order of Learning." *The Moraga Quarterly,* Autumn 1941, 3–25.
"The Chicago School," *Harper's Magazine,* September 1941, 377–388.
"Progressive Education? No!" *The Rotarian,* September 1941, 29–30; 56–57.
(with Walter Farrell, O.P.) "The Theory of Democracy—Part II," *The Thomist,* III (October 1941), 588–652.
"How to Read a Dictionary," *The Saturday Review of Literature,* December 13, 1941, 3–4; 18–20.
"A Question About Law," *Essays in Thomism,* edited by R. E. Brennan, New York, Sheed & Ward, 1941, 207–236.
"Introduction" to *Thomistic Psychology,* by R. E. Brennan, New York, Macmillan, Inc., 1941, vii–xiv.

1942

(with Walter Farrell, O.P.) "The Theory of Democracy—Part III, *The Thomist,* IV (January 1942), 121–181.
"What Every Schoolboy Doesn't Know," *Pulse,* March 1942, 7–9; 32, excerpted and adapted *Coronet,* January 1944, 87–91.
(with Walter Farrell, O.P.) "The Theory of Democracy—Part III (Continued)," *The Thomist,* IV (April 1942), 286–354.
(with Walter Farrell, O.P.) "The Theory of Democracy—Part IV," *The Thomist,* IV (July 1942), 446–522.
(with Walter Farrell, O.P.) "The Theory of Democracy—Part IV (Continued)" *The Thomist,* IV (October 1942), 692–761.
"In Defense of the Philosophy of Education," *Philosophies of Education,* Forty-first Yearbook, Part I, 1942, 197–249.

1943

"The Demonstration of God's Existence," *The Thomist,* V (January 1943), 188–218.
(with Walter Farrell, O.P.) "The Theory of Democracy—Part IV (Continued)," *The Thomist,* VI (April 1943), 49–118.
(with Walter Farrell, O.P.) "The Theory of Democracy—Part IV (Continued)," *The Thomist,* VI (July 1943), 251–277.
(with Walter Farrell, O.P.) "The Theory of Democracy—Part V," *The Thomist,* VI (October 1943), 367–407.

1944

"Thinking Straight on War and Peace," *Vogue,* January 15, 1944, 61–62.
"The Fetish of Internationalism," *Common Sense,* XIII (January 1944), 15–19.
(with Walter Farrell, O.P.) "The Theory of Democracy—Part V (Continued)," *The Thomist,* VII (January 1944), 80–131.
"Can Adults Think?" *Ladies Home Journal,* April 1944, 24; 188.
"How to Talk Sense in Company," *Esquire,* June 1944, 59; 171–176.

"War and the Rule of Law," *War and the Law,* edited by Ernst W. Puttkammer, Chicago, The University of Chicago Press, 1944, 178–198.

1945

"Liberal Education—Theory and Practice," *The University of Chicago Magazine,* 37 (March 1945), 10–11, reprinted *Vassar Alumnae Magazine,* November 15, 1945.

"The State of the Nation's Higher Education—Two Views of Benjamin Fine's New Book [*Democratic Education: A Report on the Colleges*]," *Saturday Review,* December 29, 1945, 7–8; 31 (Adler's view).

"The Future of Democracy," *Proceedings of the American Catholic Philosophical Association,* 1945, 3–24.

1947

"The Philosopher," *The Works of the Mind,* edited by Robert B. Heywood, Chicago and London, The University of Chicago Press, 1947, 215–246.

"The Doctrine of Natural Law in Philosophy," *Natural Law Institute Proceedings,* 1947, University of Notre Dame, 1 (1949), 65–84.

1951

"The Next Twenty-five Years in Philosophy," *The New Scholasticism,* XXV (January 1951), 81–110.

"Labor, Leisure, and Liberal Education," *The Journal of General Education,* VI (October 1951), 35–45.

1952

"Adult Education," *Journal of Higher Education,* XXIII (February 1952), 59–68.

(with Jerome Michael) "Real Proof: I," *Vanderbilt Law Review,* 5 (April 1952), 344–384.

"Doctor and Disciple," *Journal of Higher Education,* XXIII (April 1952), 173–180.

"The Hierarchy of Essences," *The Review of Metaphysics,* VI (September 1952), 3–30.

(with Philip F. Mulhern, O.P.) "Footnote to *The Theory of Democracy,*" in *From an Abundant Spring,* The Walter Farrell Memorial Volume of *The Thomist,* edited by The Staff, New York, P. J. Kenedy & Sons, 1952, 137–151.

1953

"Jerome Michael," *Columbia Law Review,* 53 (March 1953), 310–311.

1956

"Controversy in the Life and Teaching of Philosophy," *Proceedings of the American Catholic Philosophical Association,* 1956, 3–22.

1957

"The Questions Science Cannot Answer," *Bulletin of the Atomic Scientists,* XIII (April 1957), 120–125.

1958

"Freedom: A Study of the Development of the Concept in the English and American Traditions of Philosophy," *The Review of Metaphysics,* XI (March 1958), 380–410.

"What is an Idea?" *Saturday Review,* November 22, 1958, 13; 40–41.

"Leisure and Retirement," *Eagle,* November 1958, 12–13.

"Hard Reading Made Easy," *Mayfair* (Montreal), November 1958, condensed *Reader's Digest,* December 1958, 81–83.

1959

"The Professor or the Dialogue?" *The Owl,* Santa Clara University, 1959, 10–19.

1963

"Challenges of Philosophies in Communication," *Journalism Quarterly,* University of Washington, June 14, 1962, Special Summer Supplement 1963, 449–459.

"How to Read a Book Superficially," *Playboy,* December 1963, 115; 122; 196; 199.

"Never Say 'Retire,' " *The Journal of the American Society of Chartered Life Underwriters,* XVII (Winter 1963), 5–14.

1964

"The Future of Democracy: A Swan Song," *Humanistic Education and Western Civilization: Essays for Robert M. Hutchins,* edited by Arthur A. Cohen, New York, Holt, Rinehart and Winston, Inc., 1964, 30–43.

1966

"The Great Books of 2066," *Playboy,* January 1966, 137; 224–226; 228.

"Contributions of the West," *The Barat Review,* 1 (June 1966), 91–97.

"God and Modern Man," *The Critic,* XXV (October–November 1966), 18–23.

1967

"Intentionality and Immateriality," *The New Scholasticism,* XLI (Summer 1967), 312–344.

"The Immateriality of Conceptual Thought," *The New Scholasticism,* XLI (Autumn 1967), 489–497.

1968

"Sense Cognition: Aristotle vs. Aquinas," *The New Scholasticism,* XLII (Autumn 1968), 578–591.

1974

"Little Errors in the Beginning," *The Thomist,* XXXVIII (January 1974), 27–48.

"The Equivocal Use of the Word 'Analogical,' " *The New Scholasticism,* XLVIII (Winter 1974), 4–18.

"The Joy of Learning," *KNOW,* I (1974), Chicago, Encyclopaedia Britannica, Inc., 18–21.

1975

"The Confusion on the Animalists," *The Great Ideas Today 1975,* Chicago, Encyclopaedia Britannica, Inc., 1975, 73–89.

1976

"Education and the Pursuit of Happiness," Commencement Address, University of Denver, May 29, 1976 (pamphlet).

"Declaration v. Manifesto," *The Center Magazine,* IX (September–October 1976), Center for the Study of Democratic Institutions, 38–48.

"Teaching and Learning," *From Parnassus: Essays in Honor of Jacques Barzun,* edited by Dora B. Weiner and William R. Keylor, New York, Harper & Row, Publishers, 1976, 57–65.

"The Schooling of a People," *The Americans: 1976,* Critical Choices for Americans, Volume II, edited by Irving Kristol and Paul H. Weaver, Lexington, Mass., D. C. Heath and Company, 1976, 131–149.

"The Bodyguards of Truth" (The Aquinas Medal Acceptance Speech), *Proceedings of the American Catholic Philosophical Association,* 1976, 125–133.

1977

"The Great Books (Contd.): Adler's List," *Time,* March 7, 1977, 65–66.

"Which Are the Classics?" *The Center Magazine,* X (May–June 1977), Center for the Study of Democratic Institutions, 49–51.

"The 'Chicago Fight,' " *The Center Magazine,* X (September–October 1977), Center for the Study of Democratic Institutions, 50–60.

"Reflections on the Law School in the '30's" (Speech given at the 45th Anniversary Dinner of the University of Chicago Law School, Class of 1932, *The Law Alumni Journal,* 3 (Fall 1977), 37–40.

1978

"Books, Television, and Learning" (An address given at a seminar co-sponsored by the Center for the Book and the U.S. Office of Education at the Library of Congress, April 26, 1978), *Television, the Book, and the Classroom,* edited by John Y. Cole, Washington, D.C. Library of Congress, 1978, 15–27.

"World Peace in Truth," *The Center Magazine,* XI (March–April 1978), Center for the Study of Democratic Institutions, 56–64, reprinted in *Leonardo,* 13, Oxford, England, Pergamon Press, 1980, 317–322.

"The Disappearance of Culture" (My Turn), *Newsweek,* August 21, 1978, 15.

"Children Must Be Taught How to Learn," *Long Island Newsday,* September 17, 1978.

"What *Is* a Great Book?" *Reader's Digest,* November 1978, 94–96, condensed from *How to Read a Book.*

"Aristotle's Conception of Practical Truth and the Consequences of that Conception," *Paideia,* Special Aristotle Issue, MCMXLXXVIII, George C. Simmons, ed., State University College at Buffalo and State University College at Brockport, 158–166.

1979

"Aristotle on Virtue and Happiness" (A presentation given at Spring Hill Center in Wayzata, Minnesota, January 13, 1979), Dialogue Series, Spring Hill Center, 1979, 1–12.

"Education in a Democracy," *American Educator,* 3 (Spring 1979), 6–9.

"Success Means Never Feeling Tired," *Reader's Digest,* March 1979, 141–143.

"Everybody's Business" (A lecture given at the University of Kansas at Lawrence, March 23, 1978), *The Integration of Knowledge: Discourses on Education,* edited by Dennis B. Quinn, The Integration Humanities Program, University of Kansas at Lawrence, 1979, 21–41 (outline), reprinted *Philosophy for Education* (A *Festschrift* dedicated to Robert Maynard Hutchins), edited by Seymour Fox, The Van Leer Jerusalem Foundation, Israel, 1983, 1–15 (prose).

"Has Philosophy Lost Contact With People?" *Long Island Newsday,* November 18, 1979.

1981

(with Wayne F. Moquin) "Hans Küng: Does God Exist?" *The Great Ideas Today 1981,* Chicago, Encyclopaedia Britannica, Inc., 188–203.

1982

"A Great Teacher Tells—Step by Step—How to Teach Great Ideas," *The American School Board Journal,* 169 (January 1982), 30–32.

"The Essential Elements for a New Educational System," *The Institute Newsletter,* 1 (February–March 1982), The Dallas Institute of Humanities & Culture, 6–8.

"A Reminiscence . . ." (Speech given at 80th Birthday Celebration, April 2, 1982), The Aspen Institute, 1990 (pamphlet).

"The Paideia Proposal: Rediscovering the Essence of Education," *American School Board Journal,* 169 (July 1982), 17–20, reprinted "A Revolution in Education," *American Educator,* 6 (Winter 1982), 20–24.

"The Paideia Proposal," *The Rotarian,* September 1982, 32–35.

"Minds and Brains: Angels, Humans, and Brutes" (The 1982 Harvey Cushing Oration delivered at the annual meeting of the American Association of Neurological Surgeons, Honolulu, April 26, 1982), *Journal of Neurosurgery,* 57 (September 1982), 309–315, reprinted *The Great Ideas Today 1982,* Chicago, Encyclopaedia Britannica, Inc., 2–14.

"Philosophy in Our Time" (Review of *Philosophical Explanations* by Robert Nozick and *After Virtue* by Alasdair MacIntyre), *The Great Ideas Today 1982,* Chicago, Encyclopaedia Britannica, Inc., 238–255.

1983

"Revising American Education," *The Commonwealth,* LXXVII (December 19, 1983), The Commonwealth of [San Francisco] California, 380–381, 384.

"The Reform of Public Schools" (Opening remarks at a dialogue at the Center on *The Paideia Proposal*/Discussion), *The Center Magazine,* XVI (September–October 1983), Center for the Study of Democratic Institutions, 12–33.

(On Behalf of the Paideia Group) "The Paideia Response," *The Paideia Proposal: A Symposium, Harvard Educational Review,* 53 (November 1983), 407–411.

"Understanding the U.S.A.," *Journal of Teacher Education,* XXXIV (November–December 1983), 35–37.

1984

"Every Executive a Generalist First and a Specialist Second," *New Management,* 1, Graduate School of Business Administration, University of Southern California, 1984, 6–12.

1985

"Hard Reading Made Easy," *Evelyn Wood Reading Dynamics,* American Learning Corporation, 1985, 29–30 (adapted).

"The Paideia Proposal" (The Beall-Russell Lectures in the Humanities), Baylor University, Waco, Texas, November 7, 1985, 5–28.

"Narrative Grading," *The Paideia Bulletin,* I (December 1985), Chicago, Institute for Philosophical Research, 1, 4.

1986

"Minimal vs. Maximal Reforms," *The Paideia Bulletin,* II (March–April 1986, Chicago, Institute for Philosophical Research, 1, 5.

"The Wednesday Revolution," *The Paideia Bulletin,* II (May–June 1986), Chicago, Institute for Philosophical Research, 2.

"Teaching as a Cooperative Art," *Basic Education,* 30 (June 1986), 13–14.

"The Latest Educational Mania—Critical Thinking," *The Paideia Bulletin,* II (September–October 1986), Chicago, Institute for Philosophical Research, 2, 6.

" 'Critical Thinking' Programs: Why They Won't Work," *Education Week,* VI (September 17, 1986), 28, condensed *The Education Digest,* LII (March 1987), 9–11.

"Schooling *Is* Not Education," *The New York Times,* December 2, 1986.

"The Idea of Dialectic," *The Great Ideas Today 1986,* Chicago, Encyclopaedia Britannica, Inc., 1986, 154–177.

"Two Approaches to the Authors of the Great Books," *The Great Ideas Today 1986,* Chicago, Encyclopaedia Britannica, Inc., 1986, 178–183, excerpted *The Paideia Bulletin,* III (January–February 1987), Chicago, Institute for Philosophical Research, 1987, 2.

1987

"The Three Columns Revisited with Special Attention to the Conduct of Seminars," *The Paideia Bulletin,* Special Edition (May 1987), Chicago, Institute for Philosophical Research, 1–6.

"35 Years of the *Great Books*," *KNOW*, XXIV (Summer 1987), Chicago, Encyclopaedia Britannica, Inc., 2–5.

"Column One—The Stumbling Block," *The Paideia Bulletin*, III (September–October 1987), Chicago, Institute for Philosophical Research, 1987, 2.

1988

"Learning Disputes," *Los Angeles Times*, January 10, 1988, 1, 6.

"Further Reflections on Column Two," *The Paideia Bulletin*, IV (January–February 1988), Chicago, Institute for Philosophical Research, 1988, 2, 6.

"We Hold These Truths," *The Commonwealth*, LXXXII (March 7, 1988), The Commonwealth Club of [San Francisco] California, 108–111.

"Sexism, Racism, and the Recommended Readings for Paideia Seminars," *The Paideia Bulletin*, IV (November–December 1988), Chicago, Institute for Philosophical Research, 1988, 1.

"Ethics: Fourth Century B.C. and Twentieth Century A.D.," *The Great Ideas Today 1988*, Chicago, Encyclopaedia Britannica, Inc., 274–287.

"A Commentary on Aristotle's *Nicomachean Ethics*," *The Great Ideas Today 1988*, Chicago, Encyclopaedia Britannica, Inc., 290–311.

1989

"The Intrinsic and Extrinsic Obstacles to Good Schooling for All," *The Paideia Bulletin*, V (May–June 1989), Chicago, Institute for Philosophical Research, 1–2.

"Six Great Ideas and the Twenty-First Century," *Proceedings of the CIOS XXI World Management Congress* (September 21–23, 1989), North American Management Council, 1990, 4–5.

"The Editorial Conscience," *KNOW*, XXVI (Fall 1989), Chicago, Encyclopaedia Britannica, Inc., 2–6.

"On Growing Old with Pleasure and Profit," *1989 Medical and Health Annual*, Chicago, Encyclopaedia Britannica, Inc., 6–13.

"The State of Philosophy in the Modern World," *Whatsoever Things Are True: Essays on the Occasion of the Diamond Jubilee of Saint Joseph's College, 1986–1987*, edited with Introduction by P. Wallace Platt, Edmonton, Alberta, Canada, 1989, 5–18 (taken from a lecture given in the Humanities Centre, University of Alberta, November 1985).

1990

"No Watered-Down Seminars," *The Paideia Bulletin*, VI (January–February 1990), Chicago, Institute for Philosophical Research, 1,6.

"The Great Books, the Great Ideas, and a Lifetime of Learning" (The Lowell Lecture sponsored jointly by the Lowell Institute of Boston and Harvard Extension School), Harvard University, April 11, 1990, 5–11 (pamphlet).

"A Realistic Appraisal of Paideia's Future: The Good News and the Bad News," *The Paideia Bulletin*, VII (September–October 1990), Chicago, Institute for Philosophical Research, 3–4, 6.

"Britannica's Commitment: *The Great Books of the Western World* Second Edition," *KNOW*, XXVII (Winter 1990), Chicago, Encyclopaedia Britannica, Inc., 2–6.

"Concerning God, Modern Man and Religion," *The Aspen Institute Quarterly*, 2 (Winter 1990), 99–120.

"A Philosopher Looks Back and Forward," *Living Philosophies: The Reflections of Some Eminent Men and Women of Our Time*, edited by Clifton Fadiman, New York, Doubleday, 1990, 271–277.

1991

"The End of the Conflict Between Capitalism and Communism" (An address given before the Los Angeles World Affairs Council, April 23, 1991), *World*

Affairs Journal: A Compendium, 3, 1, Los Angeles World Affairs Council, 1991, 218–227.
"The Transcultural and the Multicultural," *The Great Ideas Today 1991,* Chicago, Encyclopaedia Britannica, Inc., 1991, 227–240, reprinted *The Aspen Institute Quarterly,* 3 (Autumn 1991), 98–116.

1992

"This [Joseph] Campbell Person," *National Review,* February 17, 1992, 48–50.
"Six Amendments to the Constitution: A Commentary," *Law and Philosophy, The Practice of Theory: Essays in Honor of George Anastaplo* (2 vols.), edited by John A. Murley, Robert L. Stone, and William L. Braithwaite, Athens, Ohio University Press, 1992 (Adler's portion, Vol. II, 747–750).
"Natural Theology, Chance, and God," *The Great Ideas Today 1992,* Chicago, Encyclopaedia Britannica, Inc., 1992.

Edited Works

Jacques Maritain: *Scholasticism and Politics,* New York, Macmillan Publishing Company, 1940.
Great Books of the Western World (52 vols.), Chicago, Encyclopaedia Britannica, Inc., 1952; 2nd Edition (60 vols.), 1990.
The Great Ideas, A Syntopicon of Great Books of the Western World (2 vols.), Chicago, Encyclopaedia Britannica, Inc., 1952; 2nd Edition, 1990.
(with Robert M. Hutchins) *The Great Ideas Today,* Chicago, Encyclopaedia Britannica, Inc., 1961–1977; 1978– .
(with Robert M. Hutchins) *Gateway to the Great Books* (10 vols.), Chicago, Encyclopaedia Britannica, Inc., 1963; 1990.
The Annals of America (21 vols.), Chicago, Encyclopaedia Britannica, Inc., 1968– .
Propaedia: Outline of Knowledge and Guide to the Britannica, The New Encyclopaedia Britannica (30 vols.), 15th Edition, Chicago, Encyclopaedia Britannica, Inc., 1974.
(with Charles Van Doren) *Great Treasury of Western Thought,* New York, R. R. Bowker Company, 1977.

INDEX